SURFACE

UNLOCKING THE GIFT OF HIGH SENSITIVITY

MEG BUCHER

To my family …

You are living proof God blesses us more than we can ever ask for or imagine.

TABLE OF CONTENTS

SURFACE

UNLOCKING THE GIFT OF HIGH SENSITIVITY

THE SUDDEN GASP FOR AIR

Knowing Something was Missing.

"Drowning tends to be a quiet, silent act." MedicineNet.com

Soft waves of cool freshwater enveloped me as I swam underneath its blanket, combing for nothing in particular but the thrill of being able to see life from a fish's point of view. When my childhood head wasn't stuck between the pages of a riveting story, it was donning a mask and snorkel. Summer days were spent cutting a path through the early morning glass and dropping anchor in our favorite spot. I felt more refreshed from the aqua water than ten showers could accomplish.

I live by the water.
Every day, I drive by the water.
My running routes take me alongside the water.
I can't imagine life apart from the water.

Dry land feels akin to drowning. Discovering my high sensitivity helped me to better understand my connection to the water, and God's hand on the totality of my life. He is the God of my memories, able to go back and reframe old moments infused with new wisdom. In this book, we will unlock the gift of high sensitivity. HSP can reveal important aspects of who we are, and help us to better understand how to love the people in our lives.

Water is refreshing, and beautiful to behold, but it can also be deadly. The great lake changes daily. Especially when it's stuck between freezing and thawing, like an indecisive teenager. Water is too big for us to handle on our own. We're still discovering depths of the oceans. We can easily find ourselves gasping for air.

Jesus is Living Water. He is the key to understanding all that flows through us, around us, and spiritually resides in us. God is purposeful. He doesn't throw us into life at a coincidental time and place. Contrary to the popular misquoting of "God will not give you more than you can handle ..." (1 Corinthians 10:12-14), He pushes, stretches, and grows us in ways that cause us to depend on Him. More accurately, to hang on for dear life.

Jeremiah 33:3 says, "Call to me and I will answer you and tell you great and unreachable things you do not know." (NIV) The meaning of the word 'call' means more than just to yell out. It also entails reciting, reading, proclaiming, and crying out. (Brown) When we are drowning, our calling isn't cordial, it comes from the depths of desperation. There is great power in worshipping God when we gasp for air. We can trust the Holy Spirit will translate what we cannot put into words.

Jeremiah had a hard message to deliver to God's people. More is known about the struggles of Jeremiah than any other prophet. His name means "The Lord throws," an accurate picture of the messy society he was hurled into with warnings from God. But his name also means "The Lord exalts," and "The Lord establishes." (NIV)

God will always answer, but most likely not in a booming voice from above. When we seek God, we will find Him …and who we are in Him. Isaiah 48:6 says, *"You have heard these things; look at them all. Will you not admit them? From now on I will tell you of new things, of hidden things unknown to you." NIV*

How do we understand the hidden things God is speaking of? The answer is Jesus. Romans 16:25-26 says, *"Now to him who is able to establish you in accordance with my gospel, the message I proclaim about Jesus Christ, in keeping with the revelation of the mystery hidden for long ages past, but now revealed and made known through the prophetic writings by the command of the eternal God, so that all the Gentiles might come to the obedience that comes from faith." NIV*

Paul received the gospel straight from the Source. Jesus revealed the hidden things. He saves us in our drowning. When we accept Christ as our Savior, Light pierces the darkness. We are yanked out of the water and set on dry land. Paul realized not all will understand this "mystery."

The Gospel will eventually reach every ear, but not all will hear. To *hear* it means to perceive it by the ear, know what it concerns, and have the spiritual capacity to understand. It's an emphatic interest in understanding the Gospel. When we truly hear the Word, it permeates our hearts and conscious minds.

This is the process of surfacing. In order to yield and submit to God in obedience to His word, we must prepare our hearts to hear it. We have to accept it on our own terms. God isn't forcing the alarm to go off. He's not pressing us to our last breath nor holding us down in the depths. We must stop thrashing about and trust in His rescue.

I had no idea I was a highly sensitive person. I think there are a lot of people who probably don't know they are highly sensitive people. It's a gift to be unpacked gently in layers, reframing one memory at a time.

I always felt like I heard more than everyone else, and it was overwhelming. Writing has always been my escape from all of the noise. I covered every space of my notebooks in doodles, mind whirring while I tried to process everything around me. Photography connects what I hear to what I see. I think in poetry. I'm high energy and love people, but am easily affected by careless words. Distance running probably saved me from adolescence. Team *and* individual sport …it's no wonder I thrived there.

Highly sensitive people tend to know something is wrong with the people around them before they do. My love of people has me wanting to be friends with everyone, but I need serious downtime, maybe even days of solitude to recharge. Comments like, "Too sensitive," or "Toughen up," have been aimed at me my entire life. (Solo)

I was overwhelmed.

I was drowning.

I was a highly sensitive person, *"a normal, healthy trait- and it comes with a distinct evolutionary advantage." (Solo)*

Being different hardly ever feels like an advantage.

THE REACH

"You have the ability to see things others don't, and that makes you especially vulnerable." (Solo)

I love the water. I'm not always so sure I want to be plucked out of it. I don't always see the warning signs of my proverbial drowning. Temptation is like that. It's tailored to our weaknesses and appears to ease the aches we struggle with. We buy into the ease of it all, and suddenly find ourselves struggling to breathe. It's not easy to find self-confidence when the world and a lot of the people in it are critical of who we are. (Ward)

"It usually starts at an early age. You're teased for being a cry baby, criticized for being too sensitive, pressured into toughening up and judged for being too picky. Add to that daunting list the urges of your friends, family, and teachers to be more like everyone else, for your own good, and it's no wonder a highly sensitive person's self-esteem starts to resemble Swiss cheese." (Ward)

Thankfully, my parents encouraged my writing and photography. They were proud of me and encouraged me to pursue those gifts. My distance running coaches made some of the biggest marks on my life. No one knew I was a Highly Sensitive Person. If ships follow navigational lights to keep from running ashore, my parents, coaches, and mentors were mine.

"My people have committed two sins: They have forsaken me, the spring of living water, and they have dug their own cisterns, broken cisterns that cannot hold water." Jeremiah 2:13 NIV

We do need water, Living Water. Our desire for the water isn't completely wrong, but the purity of the source is everything. Cisterns, in ancient culture, stored food and grain or rainwater. Rainwater was important to sustain the life of the crop during the dry season. These cisterns dug into the ground were susceptible to subtle cracks, through which the water would leak out. Jeremiah used this metaphor to describe the way God's people …and we …neglect to fill our lives with the source of all life, and instead try to depend on cracked cisterns. (NIV Cultural)

This is what happens when we jump into the water trying to pursue happiness aligned to the world's standards. Sometimes, when life happens to us or people hurt us, we run from God. We end up drowning if we try to jump into, run to, cry out for justice, or anything else other than God. He alone is Living Water. The temptation that threatens to deceive and accuse us is meant to destroy us. The ocean is remarkably serene on a calm day, but can ravage life and property during a hurricane. That's the lure. Jesus says, ***"The thief comes only to steal and kill and destroy; I have come that they may have life, and have it to the full." (John 10:10 NIV)***

Full. Abundant. (Thayer) When we fight, we end up thrashing … gasping for air. Christ is the Peace in our lives, filling every leaking crack, so we can stop struggling and float while He fixes us. In the middle of the storm, He plucks us to the surface, and calls us "His."

When you jump into a pool and dive to the bottom, there's pressure because of the weight of the water. Swimming to the surface, the pressure begins to release until we break through the surface and suck in a breath of fresh air.

Getting stuck under the water can be deadly. Drowning is a very real epidemic. It's the third most common cause of accidental death worldwide, encompassing 7% of all injury related deaths. 350, 000 die every year from drowning. This doesn't even include those who drown in floods and boating accidents. The treatment and outcome is the same whether a person drowns in the water or on dry land. (MedicineNet)

I've never experienced a literal drowning, but I've struggled and panicked through quite a few figurative drownings in my life. It's described as a panicked experience, recognized by the following observations, via MedicineNet.com:

- feeble and ineffective attempt to swim
- bobbing in an uncoordinated way
- head drops underwater
- attempt to roll on their back, but not always successful
- repeated attempt to keep head above water

If we're lucky enough to discern these signs, the drowning victim can be rushed into treatment with high hopes of recovery. Sadly, though, the first sign is often a body found floating and lifeless. (MedicineNet)

The key to the treatment of drowning? Prevention:

- learn how to swim
- swim with a buddy
- don't swim alone
- never leave infants alone
- supervise children when near water
- fence in pools and have locked gates kids cannot access

- water flotation devices should always be used during activities on the water.

If the worst happens, can we recover from drowning?
It depends on whether we are still able to breathe on our own, how cold and clean the water was, and how long we were immersed.

I thought I needed to be on and around the water, but really I just needed …Water. Living Water. He flows through me. I thought I could never live anywhere landlocked and separated from the water …turns out I just can't live without Him.

The Book of Consolation is a section of the Book of Jeremiah (Chs. 30-33) that focuses on Israel's restoration. (Asbury) Hope in the midst of hardship, consequences, and a fallen world gave Jeremiah's people hope. His words give us hope today, as we feel pressure from others, apply our own, and succumb to the those of this world. We're not so different from God's people in Jeremiah's day. As Christians, we are thrown into a world catapulting towards darkness at a rapid rate. It's one thing to feel like we're drowning in a season of suffering …but sometimes the darkness of the world can feel more pressing than we can bear. The tragedy, loss, and unfair circumstances. It can leave us gasping for air. But God has purposefully created each one of us to love the people in our lives and of this world well. As part of His great plan, we can begin to unlock the reality of who we are in Him. This process of sanctification is like walking through life immersed in our favorite Instagram filter. It's not just a highlight real. It's who God really is.

In the middle of a drowning, something stirred me to seek counseling from a professional Christian counselor. "I think you might have this," she said as she handed me some papers. "Take a look and let me know what you think."

Highly Sensitive Person.

A part of me cringed. I'd been labeled "too sensitive" all my life when it inconvenienced others, but told I was wise for the same bouts of intuition when it helped people. I read on and researched after I left that day, and through tears felt chains falling off.

HSP isn't having something wrong …it's having something right. It's a gift. A genetic trait with a built in evolutionary advantage. The challenges in self-esteem and confidence I battled all my life suddenly fell off of me. I couldn't stop learning about who I was, and I started thinking of my daughters. Praise God, for answering my prayer to be the mother they need me to be. Knowing they are HSP kids is crucial. Had I missed this, surely they would have suffered misunderstanding. And then, I started to think about you.

20% of the world today are HSP people. Do you know ten people? Two of them have the HSP trait. Relationally, this knowledge can help us love and understand ourselves and the people in our lives. Sheer knowledge can give way to fast-forwarded compassion. In fact, if we aimed to love ourselves and others as if we were all blessed with this trait, perhaps some undue suffering would end.

THE REALIZATION

In my research of Highly Sensitive People, I discovered downtime in nature and by the water are common and helpful ways to recharge. So is restful meditation. For me, quiet time with God and walking or running along the water with Him give my life balance. (Aron) This particular article of research concluded with a poem about longing for God. I was craving God for reasons I didn't even realize.

I still love the water, but my perspective has shifted. Realization doesn't come in lightbulb filled conversation bubbles over our heads. We were made to work, and work hard for the glory of God. He had been preparing my heart for many years, and pulled me out of other drowning experiences.

The discipline of getting up each morning and reading God's Word didn't start easy for me, but I started. I have sought Him for answers to everything. There are always more questions, and He is always revealing more. I began to take the research of Highly Sensitive People straight to God. Surely, my Creator was behind the brushstrokes of this discovery, and I wanted Him to show me everything.

I rescued my sister from drowning twice when we were little kids. I don't remember much about it, but still have the unicorn earrings my parents got me as a reward for pulling her out of there …twice. Why did she do it again? I have often wondered. Lots of possibilities, I'm sure. Little kids are curious.

I do this with Jesus. I jump in over my head repetitively. Every time, He plucks me out of the water, and resets my feet. This time, it was a huge revelation …a huge growth spurt in faith …and a crucial piece to understanding that little girl who wished to swim with the fish.

Not only am I a Highly Sensitive Person, but an extroverted highly sensitive person. It makes me a 30% of a 20% of the HSP population. High sensitivity can feel like drowning. We live in a world where 80% don't and won't understand and or be able to empathize with what's "going on" with us. Before I was equipped with this knowledge …life kind of felt like drowning on dry land at times …lots of times, if I'm being really honest. Now I know why.

John 7:37-38 says, *"If anyone is thirsty, let him come to me and drink. Whoever believes in me, as the Scripture has said, streams of living water will flow from within him."* We're always thirsty. Our bodies need water to function everyday. But so do our souls. I was thirsty to know more about why I was drowning in this gift of a genetic personality trait. A thirst quenched only by Living Water, Himself.

THE ABILITY TO REMEMBER

When God has truly reached down and broken a chain in our lives, we see both joy and pain in a new Light. The fresh perspective I have for water reminds me of it's many forms and functions. Water is not confined to a shape or single image. Neither is Jesus Christ, the power His name carries …nor the weight of His hand upon our lives to set us free.

Romans 12:2 says "Do not conform any longer to the pattern of this world, but be transformed by the renewing of your mind. Then you will be able to test and approve what God's will is- His good, pleasing, and perfect will." YOUR mind. YOUR WILL. God has created each one of us, HSP or not, with specificity and care … intense purpose and direction …and immense uniqueness. Understanding who we are allows us to have a greater appreciation with the commonality we all share …humanity.

Let this be a call to splash the water on our faces and open our eyes to the people around us. Look at everyone through the cool Instagram filter. Whether we realize why people are the way they are or not, we're commanded to love one another.

There are introverted and extroverted Highly Sensitive people. Dr. Elaine Aron has identified four characteristics all HSP's have, regardless: depth of processing, over stimulation, emotional responsiveness & empathy, and sensitive to subtleties. (Aron) *"The other 80% of the population, who are not highly sensitive," Aron explains, "do not possess these four characteristics, nor the implications associated with them." (Aron)* Through the following chapters, we'll discover what those traits are, and how they flesh out in real life. Most importantly, we will unlock the gift of each trait, and High Sensitivity as a whole.

THE WAY WE RECALCULATE

My social media footprint tells of my obsession with the sunrise over water. I remember unwrapping my first skinny pink camera as a kid

…the kind we had to load film into and wait to be developed. I am still finding stacks of old pictures. How many developed pictures of the sun rising and setting over the water does one person need?

Each one of those photographs records a conversation with my Creator. I once blogged, "I look to the sky, and He meets me there." Jesus is the Light of the World and the Living Water. Anyone who's witnessed the combination of the two knows it never looks the same way twice. Who is that creative? Yet, God promises He crafted us with even more care. In His image. Fearfully and wonderfully made. Is it any wonder we're still discovering who we are? *Ephesians 2:10 says, "For we are God's handiwork, created in Christ Jesus to do good works, which God prepared in advance for us to do." NIV*

If we allow the way of the world to run our gifts, they become bricks, pinning us underwater. God reveals who He made us to be. Without Him, we will never find contentment and peace at the surface.

"Call to me and I will answer you and tell you great and unsearchable things you do not know." Jeremiah 33:3 NIV

My calling out to God has always been ugly. It takes a figurative drowning for my stubborn knees to hit the ground. I have witnessed Him turn my disease into my miracle. My sensitivity has become fuel for my other gifts. I've learned to trade my expectations for His restoration. My boundaries have became God-guided and Christ-installed. In my reflection, I now see His smile. His light in my own eyes. My hard heart is being softened and slowly sanctified to reflect His. I didn't always see, and I have far yet to go. I didn't understand the thrashing and gasping going on in my heart, and there is still endless curves of learning to navigate. But praise God for the people He's placed in my life to teach and remind me I am never alone. Nor are you. If you have experienced any of the following, you, too, could be highly sensitive: (Solo)

- Being sensitive has become a joke, even with family and close friends.
- Picked on for being too sensitive or "weak."
- Feeling like something is wrong.
- Confidence issues.
- Problems dealing with criticism.
- Experience overwhelm, crashes or panic.
- Feelings of profound loneliness.
- Inability to ask for help.
- Anxiety.

Dr. Aron has developed a wonderful test to gauge the accuracy of our own self-identification as highly sensitive people: *https://hsperson.com/test/highly-sensitive-test/* If the results reveal high sensitivity, talk to a counselor alongside this book. Neither I, nor this book, are to take the place of a professional diagnosis and/or treatment plan. Most importantly, start and keep the conversation going with Christ. God is the Author of humanity, and our hearts. He has the power to reveal understanding in ways we cannot fathom. His love for us is real, palpable, and life-changing.

THE PROCESS OF RECLAIMING

There are many ways we can recover from undetected high-sensitivity, including but not limited to: (Solo)

- *Get to know and accept yourself.*
- *Accept that your feelings, needs, and wants matter as much as anyone else's.*
- *Start to express your needs.*
- *Practice self-soothing.*

Humanity is made to crave closeness with our Creator. He is the One who knows our hearts from beginning to end, comforts us with a peace that surpasses all understanding and loves us with unmatched compassion. I can feel His love ooze out of the first piercing piece of the sun slicing open a pink morning sky.

Jesus is a personal Savior. God's people couldn't lift themselves out from under the destructive hand of their oppressors, nor their own disobedience, rebellion, and sin. We cannot surface to breath and live the life God has called us to without Jesus. Sometimes He grabs our hand before we drown. Other times, He unties the bricks and lets us swim to the surface.

Without Jesus' death on the cross, we wouldn't be able to fully recognize who He created us to be, or live the life He has purposed for us. We can come close. We can even see the light getting closer, but without the work on the cross, we don't have enough breath in our lungs to reach down, untie the bricks, and swim freely to the surface. When we're drowning, it's hard to give up control, let go, stop struggling, and trust it's going to be OK …but that's the submission required to follow Christ. The relinquishing of complete control. Entering into a relationship with Jesus, to follow His lead. Not become a puppet, or free from the consequences of our own bad decisions, laziness, and sin. But to travel through it all with Him. Not only can we surface, I believe we can figuratively walk on water. Meaning, to do the seemingly impossible. With our eyes fixed on Him, we can live radically.

"'Lord, if it's you,' Peter replied, 'tell me to come to you on the water.'" Of course, Jesus replied, "Come," and Peter did the impossible with his eyes fixed on Christ. (*Matthew 14:22-33*) We will do the same, until we let our gaze drift from Jesus. It will happen. We will forget, take control, or stop seeking Him. And we'll fall, make mistakes, screw things up BAD. It's not OK, but we'l always be forgiven …never loved less.

Through Christ's death on the cross we can confess, repent, and be restored to better than we were when we took our eyes off of our

Savior. The sinking moments can feel like drowning. But listen to Jesus' love for Peter:

"Then Peter got down out of the boat, walked on the water and came toward Jesus. But when he saw the wind he was afraid and, beginning to sink, cried out, 'Lord, save me!' Immediately Jesus reached out his hand and caught him. 'You of little faith,' he said, 'why did you doubt?'" Matthew 14: 29b-31 NIV

We all fall short, look away, and begin to sink like Peter. (Romans 3:23) We all doubt, though we believe. (Romans 7:15-20) Jesus' love and sacrificial death has nothing to do with what we deserve or could ever earn. He loves us. He died out of love for us. He *immediately* reached out His hand. There isn't even a comma after 'Immediately!' He intentionally loves us beyond our comprehension. John 3:16 says, *"For God so loved the world that he gave his one and only Son, that whoever believes in him shall not perish but have eternal life." NIV*

"Whoever."

"Immediately."

Nothing to earn. No mold to fill. Just to believe, work with what He gives us, and honor Him with all we are. To follow Christ isn't rigid religious rules. I'm sorry on behalf of anyone who told you otherwise. Christianity is about being moldable, growing in wisdom, and seeking Peace and Love to *become* peace and love on this earth until we go home to Him for an eternity of it.

THE RESTORATION

The depth of water is deceiving. Signs by the shore warn us not to dive into deceptively deep-looking shallow water. Adversely, when we jump in fully expecting the ground to meet our feet but slip under the water, it shocks us. We have to suddenly adjust the momentum we had prepared to push back off the bottom. Instead, we scramble to tread back to the surface.

As I stood at the top of a giant sand dune last summer, I stared out in awe of what I didn't even know existed. I had grown up around and on a Great Lake, gone down to bask in the salty sea air, but had never experienced the expansive blue fresh water of Lake Michigan. I was unexpectedly blown away.

Discovering high sensitivity is like looking out over that big blue lake, with new landscape to discover as far as my eyes can see or my mind can fathom.

If you have ever felt misunderstood, unappreciated, lost, hopeless, confused, or alone ...this book is for you. If you just want to know how to love the people in your life better - this book is for you. If you wonder what God has to do with this, and why Jesus is Living Water -this book is for you. I'll share what I've learned so far about high sensitivity, why it's a gift, why *you're* a gift, how you can r come alongside the other people in your life with empathy and understanding. I'll tell you all about Jesus, and how I almost drowned before He reached down, grabbed onto my hand, and pulled me to the surface.

I have prayed for you, reader. I love you already. Let's do this.

Father,

Praise You for High Sensitivity! Thank you for Dr. Aron and all of the other researchers and writers whose passion have led to comfort for so many HSP people feeling ...and being told ...there is something wrong with the way they are made. Thank you for providing a way for this revelation in humanity.

Father, thank You that we are created fearfully and wonderfully. Thank you for Jesus' sacrifice, which fills in all of the gaps and

cracks of this fallen world and the sin that so easily entangles us.
Help us to throw it off during this journey together, seeking what you
have to say about who we are. Amplify Your voice above all others,
and allow us to see ourselves the way that You see us ...as dearly
loved, and importantly purposed. Our uniqueness is an
extraordinary gift. Let all we do and who we are honor You as we
were created to. Bless all who have high sensitivity and are unaware
and/or oppressed for it.

Praise for all those who know it's part of what makes them special.
Prayers of blessings and direction to all those who are about to
unlock a revelation from You, Father ...and for chains that are about
to fall off. Quiet our struggling and slow our gasping for air.
Replace it with the reminder of Peace that is ours if we choose it.
Jesus, thank you for dying for us, walking with us, and loving us.
May we walk through these pages together equipped and inspired by
Your endless love.

In Jesus' Name,
Amen.

CHAPTER 1

SURFACE
UNLOCKING THE GIFT OF HIGH SENSITIVITY

SUNKEN.
Waking up to Life Below the Surface.

Muffled but familiar, voices wafted down my snorkel and reverberated off the water. A sanctuary of sorts, I loved to be under the water. Though I wouldn't understand why for decades, I needed to muffle the world so I could cope with it. I experienced the soft clarity of swimming underwater vividly. No one from my Northern Ohio hometown believed how clear the water was in the middle of the lake, so I would bring water bottles full of it back as proof.

"You got that from the sink," skeptical classmates retorted, "be honest."

Some things are just meant to be between God and us, unproved and undiscovered. Pockets of time paused so we can align our breathing with His. Everything underwater swishes and sways as the waves push it onto the shore. The pressure of the Great Lake took the weight off of my life.

Growing up, the question of my place in the world and worthiness of it echoed all around. Under the surface of the water, only the swishing and gurgling of the water was magnified. God communicates through His creation. We all have pinnacle moments that highlight our memories. Snorkeling under the safety net of the soft and clear Canadian water, God weaved growth and comfort into my heart. I didn't realize how near He was then. Searching …my hand grazing softly over the sandy bottom looking for nothing in particular and everything all at once. Just floating …reaching … listening …being …and breathing.

God's voice is always crystal clear. Whether we get quiet enough to listen effects how accurately and fully we hear Him. His presence never diminishes and His peace is always present. We often come up for air before He's done speaking, unable to float …search …reach …listen …be …and breathe.

Growing up puts us on the spin cycle. All of the sudden there's less time to cruise the bottom of the lake. In my lack to slow down and breathe with God, the world sucked me straight down to the bottom. I worked hard and fought to reach the surface, when in reality I needed more time looking up at the Light through the filter of the last layer of water. I broke through the surface unprepared, and thus failed to keep myself afloat on my own power. Out too far and in too deep …I ran out of energy to tread water, and began to sink below the surface. I couldn't breathe, let alone align my breath with God's.

I wasn't drowning in the cold, clear, Canadian fresh water …but in lies, doubts, fears, and failures. The reality of life made it harder to get back in the water to recover. My high sensitivity made death, change and loss much harder to process than the other 80% of the world's population. When disappointment, confusion, loss, failure, hurt, divorce, disloyalty, and unexpected change started to stack up in my life, I started to drown.

It was like being underwater without my snorkel and mask. A completely different experience. I couldn't breathe or see. Even if I tried to open up my eyes, everything was blurry. Eventually, I came to the end of myself. I ran out of breath. Only because of the traumatic touch of suicide on my life as a child, did I not choose that path, myself. I can look back and feel Jesus holding me together in those moments. He knew something about me I didn't. And it wasn't meant to kill me or destroy me. It was meant to give me life to the full.

But my life verse isn't John 10:10, *"The thief comes only to steal and kill and destroy; I came that they may have life, and have it abundantly."* My life verse is, *"Be joyful always." 1 Thessalonians 5:16*. It took me forty years to discover my high sensitivity. Along the way, I can name people who I know prayed for me. I am a product of prayer. Faith in Christ compels us to pray forward, and in His great compassion for us He reveals some of those answered prayers.

"How did this happen?"

Those are the questions I would ask myself every time I found myself far from who I felt like I was.

"Am I crazy?"

I asked myself that a lot. Now, I know it's because I am a Highly Sensitive Person. But for forty years, I really just masked my worry of why I picked up on everything by channeling it into laughter. Everyone knew my laugh. Everyone knows my laugh. If you know me, you know I laugh a lot. Sometimes inappropriately, because laughter has been my coping mechanism all along. "Be joyful always," meant to smile, laugh and stop worrying. I doodled it everywhere growing up, alongside daisies and smiley faces, and eventually AU Eagles. I only began to realize what 1 Thessalonians 5:16 joy really was when I started to gasp for air.

What doodles match feelings of utter failure and despair? The kind of mistakes I judged others for making, I made. The failures no one foresaw in my future became a permanent part of my past. But alongside, God placed people in my life to grow my faith. Seeds of faith planted in my childhood continued to be watered in high school and college. They pulled me to the surface over and over again, but I never paused long enough to recalibrate my breathing. Back down I would go …but the seeds were growing. I officially gave my life to Christ in college …and thank God. Because after that, I almost drowned to death.

Where *Does* our Hope Come From?

How do we hold on to hope in sunken situations? Jeremiah knew a thing or two about encouraging others in the midst of drowning. God's people were IN TROUBLE. They were about to be punished for running from God in every possible way. Jeremiah was hand picked by God to deliver their consequential message. Lucky dude. It's no wonder he's known as the "weeping prophet!" I'd cry, too! People DO NOT want to hear what they DON'T want to hear. Most of us would rather drown than stop and take advice that could spin us back into alignment on a dime. Self-reliance reigns true in our world. We learn it early and are immersed in it constantly. It speaks volumes of Jeremiah's faith that he lived out the mission God purposed for Him.

"How awful that day will be! It will be a time of trouble for Jacob, but he will be saved out of it." Jeremiah 30:7 NIV

Can you imagine Jeremiah's inner monologue? 'God, seriously? That's what you want me to tell them you said?' This verse refers to a day in Jeremiah's foreseeable future, but also refers to another day to come in the Messianic age (Mt 24:21, Rev 16:18, NIV Study). The Messianic Age began when Jesus Christ came to earth, and will end when He returns again, *"characterized by righteousness, justice and peace, by the outpouring of the Holy Spirit and by the restoration and renewal of God's people and of creation." (Dictionary of Bible Themes)* This verse is significant for God's people, who have been looking towards the coming of the Messiah.

God's words through Jeremiah seem to bring only grim news, but "saved out of it," literally means to be saved in battle. God is referring to a victory past the state of their current and oncoming suffering. A final victory, delivering them from moral trouble, too! (Brown)

"'In that day, declares the Lord Almighty, 'I will break the yoke off their necks and will tear off there bonds; no longer will foreigners enslave them." Jeremiah 30:8 NIV

Yokes were symbols of submissive oppression. Oxen wore yokes to steered them in the way the farmer wanted them to go. The root of the Hebrew word for yoke means to act severely, to make a fool of someone. It's to be severely dealt with. (Brown.) That's much more than the simple steering of the farmer. For an oxen to resist and turn the other way would take a lot of effort. Rebellion, even. Hmmm. Much like God's people. Much like us. The root of *yoke* also speaks of gleaning. God's people would be saved by the Messiah, but it would be dependent upon their own submission. (NIV Study) It was going to take *gleaning,* which means to gather and grow slowly. The learning curve would be enormously steep.

The literal Hebrew translation of bonds is "break their chains." (NIV Study) In the literal sense, their ties to foreign nations. A do-it-again promise from God just as He freed His people from slavery in Egypt. We sometimes fail to identify what holds us in chains, keeping us from living the full and free lives Jesus came, suffered, and died for us to live. God preemptively promises chains will fall off when we follow Christ.

"So do not be afraid, Jacob my servant; do not be dismayed, Israel,' declares the Lord. 'I will surely save you out of a distant place, your descendants from the land of their exile. Jacob will again have peace and security, and no one will make him afraid."
Jeremiah 30:10 NIV

Jacob means "heel holder," in reference to his grabbing at the heal of his twin brother, Esau, at birth. He ended up swindling him out of his inheritance, too. Jacob was the son of Isaac, grandson of Abraham, and father of the twelve patriarchs of the tribes of Israel. (Brown) When Jeremiah refers to Jacob, he's referring to God's people. "Save" is a deliverance from danger, either from personal enemies or sickness. (Mounce) God assured the people He would come to their rescue no matter what tragedy befell them. We cannot outrun the reach of God's compassionate hand. He is sovereign over all.

God assured restoration to His people long before they suffered. We benefit from this same assurance. Waves of suffering crash over us in this life. Some things happen on accord of our own choices. Other hurts happen because of the world we live in and the imperfect people we co-exist with. God's presence is constant, regardless of our circumstances. Whether we feel or hear Him, His sovereign hand reigns over all creation. What I thought would drown me pushed me to break through the surface, into a revitalizing breath of new life.

The Covenant of Hope

"I am with you and will save you, declares the Lord. 'Though I will completely destroy all the nations among which I scatter you, I will not completely destroy you. I will discipline you but only in due measure; I will not let you go entirely unpunished." Jeremiah 30:11 NIV

God doesn't cause bad things to happen to us. We live in a fallen world, where suffering is inevitable. God is good. In His goodness, He allows us to make bad choices even though, like all good fathers, He wants us to choose Him every time. But He knows we won't. We never could.

God's people in Jeremiah's day lived according to the Old Testament Covenant. One they could never live up to. They literally could not, because of the fallen state of humanity thanks to Adam and Even and the deceptive serpent. God had a plan of restoration in place from the beginning.

The New Covenant is Jesus. We live in New Testament times, under the New Covenant. We, through salvation in Jesus Christ, enjoy an open line of communication with God through His Word and prayer, in addition to His creation. His Holy Spirit resides within believers, and we are sealed and saved as His for all eternity. But in Jeremiah's day, the Bible as the book we know it today didn't exist. They had the Old Testament, and prophets like Jeremiah to proclaim the Truth, guide and explain to God's people His love for them.

God's Love is woven throughout the entirety of Scripture. Jesus is woven throughout the entirety of Scripture. Jesus life, death and resurrection is the full expression of God's love for us. When we accept it and follow Him, we are sealed for eternity. In Genesis, after the infamous fruit was taken, eaten and digested, God said:

"So the Lord God said to the serpent, "Because you have done this, 'Cursed are you above all livestock and all wild animals! You will crawl on your belly and you will eat dust all the days of you life. And I will put enmity between you and the woman, and between your offspring and hers; and he will crush your head, and you will strike his heel." Genesis 3:14-15 NIV

The serpent is the devil, and the one who crushed his head is Jesus.

"The days are coming,' declares the Lord, 'when I will make a new covenant with people of Israel and with the people of Judah." Jeremiah 31:31 NIV

Jesus came. He is the New Covenant.

"In the beginning was the Word, and the Word was with God, and the Word was God. He was with God in the beginning. Through him all things were made; without him nothing was made that has been made. In him was life, and that life was the light of all mankind. The light shines in the darkness, and the darkness has not overcome it." John 1:1-5 NIV

John knew Jesus was the Creator, Himself, walking the earth in alignment with the text of Genesis, and the words of restoration Jeremiah prophesied to God's people before and in the midst of destruction over their inability to keep the Old Covenant. The old was gone …the new had come. And then …

"Father, forgive them, for they do not know what they are doing." Luke 23:34 NIV

They certainly did not know they were about to crucify the Son of God, but Jesus knew what they were doing and why it was necessary. The death we deserve for our sins had to be atoned for. Someone had to pay for it; to speak for us. Jesus chose to. As we study the destruction and terror Jeremiah speaks of throughout these chapters, we will also fast forward to the Light of Light …and scale back to see Him throughout all of Scripture. Jesus didn't just show up on the first page of the New Testament. Jesus is the Word of God, from cover to cover, beginning to end.

"I am the Alpha and Omega, the First and the Last, the Beginning and the End." Revelation 22:13 NIV

The Book of Revelation prophesies the next chapter of the story. When Jesus said, "It is finished," (John 19:30 NIV) He was talking about the divine work He came to do on earth. But *all* is not finished. We are here to spread His Love …what He did …who He is …the Gospel …until all have had the chance to hear. And then …He'll be back for us. This world isn't the end.

"God's discipline of his people brings about restoration, character, and godliness. God's discipline of unbelievers results in destruction, banishment and suffering. For God's people, mercy ultimately triumphs over judgement because God's justice has been satisfied through the one-time sacrifice of Jesus Christ, the Son of God." (NIV Quest)

There's a whole lot going on in the universe beyond what we can see, hear, or prove. There's a spirituality which we were born with, created to crave our Father in heaven and His presence. That's what makes Jesus' death such a big deal. It literally completes us. Without Christ, we cannot enter the presence of God, our Creator whom we naturally crave a relationship with. But in Christ, we not only look forward to an eternity in His presence, but a life filled with joy in the midst of …well ..the world and all it's tragedy and unfairness. In

Christ, we have a strength that is not our own, and a joy that cannot be snatched.

And by that will, we have been made holy though the sacrifice of the body of Jesus Christ once for all." Hebrews 10:10 NIV

Joy isn't the smiley faces and doodles and "don't worry ….be happy's" with eagles flying all around my notebooks. It's more. It's WAY more.

Knowledge is Powerful.

When I look back at what I've been through in my life, I know without a shadow of a doubt He was there for every moment. Jesus, my friend, knows my whole heart. Over time, He has revealed, restored, and miraculous healed me. Sometimes, healing has come through new knowledge. Discovering the psychology of a Highly Sensitive Person unlocked a part of me I didn't even realize had been trapped.

"'I will restore you to health and heal your wounds,' declares the Lord," Jeremiah 30: 17 NIV

The Lord would restore them from what labeled them outcasts, and unspeakable pain. Like moments of our lives all encompassed by monumental screw-ups, embarrassing mistakes and slips in our character, God promised, *"I will restore you to health and heal your wounds."* Only a declaration from the Lord could take His people from where they were to where He knew they would ultimately be. I can't believe the person He's molded *me* into, today. If I had remained in those slips of character and seasons of defeat, hopelessness would have drowned me. God cures the seemingly incurable, with unexplainable timing and an incredibly compassionate and forgiving heart of love.

"I will restore the fortunes of Jacob's tents and have compassion on his dwellings; the city will be rebuilt on her ruins, and the balance will stand in its proper place. From them will come songs of thanksgiving and the sound of rejoicing. I will add to their numbers, and they will not be decreased; I will bring them honor, and they will not be disdained. Their children will be as in days of old, and their community will be established before me; I will punish all who oppress them. Their leader will be one of their own; their ruler will arise from among them. I will bring him near and he will come close to me- for who is he who will devote himself to be close to me?' declares the Lord." Jeremiah 30: 18-32 NIV

Coming close to God would strike fear into the hearts of Jeremiah and the ancient people he was speaking to. *"Unauthorized approaches into God's presence were punishable by death."* (NIV Study) Restoration, compassion, reconstruction, restored balance, reestablishment, thanksgiving, rejoicing, honor, and establishment reflect a God who knows what we do not. Just as He encouraged these disobedient, idol worshipping people about to be destroyed and scattered, so He encourages and loves us in and through our seasons of suffering.

Restored fortunes would be rebuilt on ruins. Historically, this refers to the mounds of the debris left as a result of conflict or occupation. (NIV Study.) We don't have to be completely wiped out to come close to God. *"If we confess our sins, he is faithful and just and will forgive us our sins and purify us from all unrighteousness." (1 John 1:9 NIV)* The meaning of this verse is a substantial cornerstone to our faith in the New Covenant era we reside in. The NIV Study Bible Notes explain the gravity of God's faithfulness in this way:

1. *faithful and just indicates that God's response toward those who confess their sins will be in accordance with is nature and his gracious commitment to his people.*
2. *God is faithful to his promise to forgive*
3. *God provides the faithfulness that restores the communion with God that had been interrupted by sin.*

(emphasis by numbering, mine)

'Leader' refers to leaders after the exile, but ultimately points to Jesus. (NIV Study) Undeservedly, Jesus voluntarily died a horrific death so we would be restored, rebuilt, and re-established. We are taught to put up healthy boundaries when people consistently let us down and treat us badly. But God? He made it possible for us to come closer. Boundaries help us keep our thought life in check, but only in Christ can we can forgive, and wait on God to reconcile and restore. He, alone, can change hearts. One of the most earth shattering things I learned in my quest to be friends with everyone (as I talk about in my first book, *Friends with Everyone*) was the difference between forgiveness and reconciliation. God, in His sovereignty, reconciles and restores.

Childhood morals, standards and priorities serve as healthy boundaries. It is true what Proverbs says, ***"Train up a child in the way they should go, and when they are old they will not turn from it."*** I weaved in and out of the lane I was raised in A LOT, but ended up back on the path to righteousness because of all the people that prayed and pointed me to Jesus.

The Highly Sensitive Person.

"HSP's exhibit 'differential susceptibility,' suffering more in bad environments but doing especially well in good ones." (Aron) Growing up in the water fed my need for positivity. We pay more attention to positive stimuli in good environments. (Aron) It makes total sense, now, why I remember swimming under the water so vividly. My parents set good channel markers for me, with positive experiences, encouragement, godly love and guidance. They had no idea what kind of kid they were raising, and I had no idea what kind of kid I was.

My childhood actually fostered this genetic trait before I knew it was there, because growing up in a positive environment gave me more time to look at things deeper …which I love to do so naturally. They trusted Jesus and followed Him to the best of their ability, and because of that, so did I. Despite their shortcomings, and mine, faith was enough to be our lifeboat when we needed it.

"Such a childhood increases especially strongly their self-awareness, arousal, self-control, and calm, which are so important when responding to any emotion laden-situation." (Aron) I cannot imagine being more emotional than I was growing up. My dad tapping the doorframe back on after I'd slammed it off once again will forever be burned into my memory. He never condemned me. He simply reattached what was broken. They say our earthly fathers affect our view of God our Father. And wow. My dad nailed it. No pun intended. (OK, yes there totally was.)

Dr. Aron, Ph.D, is highly sensitive, herself. I hope I get to thank and hug her in person one day, for being the outlet of love God used to break through and help me discover my sensitivity. She said in a recent article, being highly sensitive without knowing it is like living under a burden. (Aron) I can testify, and am tearing up just writing this. It's ignited a newfound compassion in me for those who are misunderstood and not known or appreciated for who they are, and a mission to reach out and love as many as I can.

"If everyone is sensitive, we all notice the same details and it no longer gives anyone a special advantage." (Solo) I never looked at myself as a special advantage. But in my life, to those around me, God says I am. All of this time I spent encouraging others to face outward and see people, I needed to apply to my own heart.

Highly sensitive people notice more. All of that capacity to empathize with others left a gaping hole in my thoughts about myself. I remember not feeling good enough since I remember thinking anything about myself. But my parents were good. My faith is good. Not realizing who I was meant neglecting to care for myself in the way God designed me to. HSP's need downtime.

I can spend huge chunks of time away from everyone and feel recharged. But I love people, so when I am recharged I have to get out and be with people! That would make anyone feel a little insane and crazy, right? But knowing that now calms my whole, "not good enough" soundtrack and instead plays, "this is how I am it's totally normal."

I have two tween daughters. I spend a lot of time reassuring them "I know it's hard …weird …pick an adjective, right …but you're completely normal." I had rarely ever said that to myself in four decades of life on this earth. That will take a toll on a soul. Almost a lost cause …but we learned from Jeremiah that God heals the incurable and unimaginable. No one's fault, just the design of my soul in need of the Author's cliff notes.

Feeling too much or too deep (Ni) as a child was overwhelming. Thank goodness my parents encouraged my creativity. They enrolled me in dance, drawing lessons, piano, photography, creative writing, library programs …anything that stuck they encouraged wholeheartedly. They recognized my gifts and encouraged them. I loved Jesus from an early age, embraced Catholic school and was involved in Youth Renewal Team, where I got to write, create and talk about my faith.

When I found distance running in high school, I woke up at dawn voluntarily before school to get lost in my thoughts for an hour before the homeroom bell rang. I loved it. And it kept me alive when I went through adolescence and young adult hood …where every customized temptation came flying at me like all the other people growing up. But in my 30% of a 20% …I had a long road ahead of me. All of these roots would keep me alive.

When I read through categories of HSP people (Ni), I started to cry. I remember thinking, "oh, wow …this is a thing …this is ME …holy cow."

Yes, I hold onto negative feelings and emotions even when I am consciously trying to let go of them. I am extremely hard on myself, setting expectations so high I'm sometimes afraid to even try to achieve them. Rejection plagues me, even in little situations like wondering why the checkout clerk doesn't like me as much as the last customer. *Right?!*

Comparison has affected every area of my life: physical, relational, social, work, financial; but the social aspect …since I want to be friends with everyone …affects me the most. I can't stand not to be reconciled with someone I've forgiven or had a disagreement with. Other annoyances most people can easily let go of, I struggle to.

My husband's snoring is enough to make me lose my ever loving mind some nights. Even when it's not that loud! I feel deeply, so I hurt easily and it hurts more for me than it does for most. I vividly remember an argument via mail over an English Lit final with a college professor, because I had such a hard time accepting her criticism! I'm thankful for it to this day, and grateful she honored my communication at all. (I've grown to crave criticism, now, and love to grow from it …but that was a hard lesson for me to learn!) I fight a pretty rough battle with distorted thoughts, and struggle with awkwardness in groups where I don't feel free to be my whole self.

I startle easily, and I don't just dislike scary and suspenseful movies …they disturb me. I can't even watch a preview! It's a crazy sensitive reaction. I have to prepare ahead of time to be able to enjoy big events and crowded places, and I sleep a lot afterwards to recover. I don't like surprises. I don't watch the news, because the negativity seeps into my soul more than the majority, and for the same reasoning unfollow negative drama on social media. (I set up a lot of news alerts to hit my phone all day everyday, but I can simply put it down or swipe it away after reading a sentence or two and stay informed.)

Throughout my life, certain observations in my behavior have been overwhelming. We'll just call it feedback, which happens to fit the mold of an HSP person perfectly: (Azab)

- too analytical
- too sensitive
- too emotional
- not handling criticism well
- not handling stress well

A simple thing like transitioning (Aron) throughout the day is a challenge for me. For example, when I'm pushing out a book baby, I'm up at 4am. I take a couple of breaks to get my kids ready for school, pick them up and feed them dinner, and drop them back off to their activities. The rest of the time, I write. Only getting up to use the loo, warm up my coffee and make a smoothie. If I try to cram in coffee with friend, I can't enjoy it because of the looming task at hand.

On the contrary, if I schedule in coffee with a friend, I make sure to leave my schedule open. My good friends will testify, I'm notorious for two to three hour coffee dates!

Transitioning is challenging, and procrastination is a real struggle for me. The discipline to sit down and start extracting the work I've been doing in my head is something I've had to consciously develop over the years. I write like crazy for months on end, and then I don't work at all for a couple of weeks while I decompress.

HSP affects a lot, and knowing more about it helps me understand myself better. It helps me live the full life Jesus died for me to live. But what about the other people in our lives? This was a telling explanation of a relationship pattern that was baffling me:

"Ask anyone who is a highly sensitive person and they will tell you that at some point in their lives, they have been in a relationship with a narcissist. Most did not know it at the time, but increasingly, they began to feel taken advantage of, used and then wonder how to get out. They couldn't always put a name to it or even explain away what was happening. But it didn't feel good and the harder they tried, the worse it got." (Ward)

Highly Sensitive people are particularly vulnerable to toxic relationships. (Ward) Why? We have crazy intuition. How do we not see this coming? But this was a pattern in my life that far surpassed but most definitely encompassed my lack of boundaries.

What is a narcissist? That term seems to be a popular buzz word, lately. Their behavior is not always noticeable at first, but they are very good at getting what they want through charm, deception, passive-aggression, control tactics and manipulation. (Ward) These people tend to be pre-occupied with achievement of any and all categories, even beauty, and have a complete lack of empathy for others, including their own family and friends. (Ward) Bottom line? They take advantage. And on a personal note, I think adults grow into full blow narcissism without realizing who they are, either.

Highly Sensitive people, more than others, need a positive environment to thrive. (Solo) Only Christ has the power to save us from toxicity. Putting our life in His hands protects us from ourselves, and from what the world would have us believe about things that make us amazing.

Being a minority in any aspect of life is hard. I cannot even imagine what it is like to be a racial minority, or many of the adversities that people suffer for around the world. I understand my experiences are not comparable, but my perspective compassion for people has grown as a result.

Counseling helped me break a cycle of covering up what I thought was broken, and uncover some lies for what they really were. I was disappointed in myself. For such strong faith, I sure did believe some hefty lies at the hands of others seeking to justify their behavior. "Overwhelming feelings that have been disassociated hold the undervalued self, often serving to dissuade us from approaching any experience that could repeat the trauma." (Aron)

It's easy to feel marginalized in a society of an"all inclusive and everyone's accepted" mantra. We may appear accepting on our social media highlight reel. Maybe we're checking off all the boxes we know to check off, and including all the people we know we're supposed to include. But we sure aren't doing a very good job loving each other despite differing opinions and …dare I say it …feelings.

What happens when Highly Sensitive People don't grow up in positive environments? There is mounting research stating many otherwise healthy families raise their children with emotional neglect, which is a failure to value or respond to emotions. (Solo) I didn't feel this growing up, but I walked through it as I became an adult. Suddenly my support system wasn't emotionally available for me anymore. Not like I was used to. I surrounded myself with as many friends as I could, and looking back I can see the void I was trying to fill. I missed my family, but in a way I didn't understand, because I didn't know who I was.

They weren't in my everyday life anymore. My younger brother and sister entered high school, and life got busy. I remember feeling extremely alone, but silly for it. My grandma and I were extremely close. I cried every time she sent me a card or a note in the mail. Looking back, I can clearly see how I ended up in an emotional tornado. I missed my people.

Since I put too much pressure on my friendships to be my support system, many unraveled. My expectations were too high, and I had no idea at the time it was due to the fact I noticed so much more than 80% of the other people around me. Had I known, I would like to think I would have been a little more empathetic towards myself, and my friends.

Everyone knew me by my laugh, and I doubt many knew I suffered through many lonely moments. Laughter made me feel better, and back then I didn't even realize the full scope of why.

I matured super late in life. Puberty hit me dead last. Jokes and snickers are something most kids deal with in one way or another sometime in their growing up experience. But they hit me to the core, doing extensive damage I didn't outgrow until I had my own kids. Though the remarks hurt, I laughed along or acted like I didn't hear what was said. In hindsight, I wish I would have just broken down and cried in front of everyone …instead of burying it. I was drowning, and it left some scars of unnecessary guilt, self-anger, low self-confidence, and a sense of being deeply flawed. (Solo)

"Emotions are, in many ways, an HSPs' first language. And an emotionally neglectful family basically doesn't speak that language. While the parents certainly have emotions of their own, they avoid expressing them outwardly or acknowledging the emotions of others. It's like they completely divorce themselves from the most important part of their HSP child's inner life." (Solo)

Can I just say, I am so sorry if this is you, and you grew up highly sensitive without the ability to be sensitive. I started to drown as soon as I walked out of my house and stepped into the world on my own. My family didn't realize it then, but they did speak my language. They had raised me well. I was as surrounded with as much love as any college student could ever be. The most amazing college, individual attention, amazing teammates and roommates, sorority sisters and friends around every corner I turned. This was no one's fault. My drowning was caused by something I didn't know. How could I fully accept myself if I didn't know who I was?

Coming up for air …

I heard my name muffled above the surface of the water, but I wasn't ready to surface yet. It was so peaceful under the waves, the gentle sound of them lapping the boat hull as it bobbed at anchor close to shore. The sun was making shadows dance on the bottom, and little mini waves of sand were stacked up in neat rows all the way up to shore. When I heard the muffling again, sure it was my name this time, I surfaced for air.

Breaking through the surface, all of the noises began to play at once. The music from the boats, the surface sound of the waves, loud laughter and engines whirring as inflatable dingy's zipped around the cove.

I always felt more exposed out of the water. Never fully comfortable in my own skin. I got out, squeezed a lemon into my hair, grabbed my book and headed to the bow to get lost in another story.

"'The days are coming,' declares the Lord, 'when I will raise up for David a righteous Branch, a King who will reign wisely and do what is just and right in the land.'" Jeremiah 23:5 NIV

This King, this righteous Branch, is Jesus. Being a Highly Sensitive Person, I need the refuge of the Water. The lesson all along was to realize who I was and learn to take refuge and recharge.

The Living Water, Jesus Christ, is my Refuge. He has taken me by the hand and walked me through every ugly crying separation from who I wasn't to dive into who I am …in Him. He saved my life. And He'll do it again. I'm certain of it. He goes before me, loves me in spite of my failures and celebrates victories with me. The image of hugging Him when I get to heaven brings instant tears to my eyes.

John 15:5 says, *"I am the vine; you are the branches. If you remain in me and I in you, you will bear much fruit; apart from me you can do nothing." NIV*

When the water turns dangerous, and I begin to drown, I hear the muffled sound of my name. This time, I want to surface but I can't. I'm trying to, but for some reason the top of the water is getting farther away and I can't feel the bottom to push up. I hear my name, this time, clear as day between my ears.

"Meg ...Let go and let me. Just hold on."

Discovering I have the genetic trait of High Sensitivity isn't the first time Jesus has yanked me out of the water.1 Peter 1:23-25 says:
 "For you have been born again, not of perishable seed, but of imperishable, through the living and enduring word of God. For, 'All people are like grass, and all their glory is like the flowers of the field; the grass withers and the flowers fall, but the word of the Lord endures forever.' And this is the word that was preached to you." NIV

The NIV Study Bible notes state new birth comes about through the direct action of the Holy Spirit, but the word of God also plays an important role, for it presents the gospel to sinners and calls on them to repent and believe in Christ. The seed is the doubtless Word of God, which is imperishable, living and enduring. (NIV Study)

People think being a Christian is all about following a bunch of rules. It's really about learning who we really are from the one who Created us, realizing how loved we are, and loving the people He places in our lives well. Being a Christian is about Love, accepting ourselves for who He made us to be, and honoring Him with everything He's gifted us to work hard at. When we surface, we are to reach for others who are drowning.

"Therefore, rid yourselves of all magic and all deceit, hypocrisy, envy, and slander of every kind. Like newborn babies, crave pure spiritual milk, so that by it you may grow up in your salvation, now that you have tested that the Lord is good." 1 Peter 2:1-3 NIV

The good we do in life is fruit produced from our attachment to the Vine. As we grow closer to Him, through time in God's Word and prayer, we change. Growth comes through conviction, confession, and repentance …resulting in a restored version of people we were always purposed to be.

Let's Pray,

Father, thank You for meeting us in this journey. For all those finding out they are Highly Sensitive People, I praise You! Bless every person that knows a little bit more about themselves than they did before. Every child of God is crafted in love, Father. Bless every person who has ever felt misunderstood to feel loved today. May the Peace of Christ be in every heart seeking answers to "why" questions, and reach to grab Christ's hand in drowning moments.

Father, thank you for the water, and for Living Water. Thank You for connecting the pieces of our lives together along strings of years and decades. In Your perfect time, the sun rises each day and our lives unfold. You are sovereign, You are Love, and You are AMAZING. Jesus, thank You for everything You sacrificed for us, and every reader of this prayer and person in this world. Your love is incredible and all-encompassing, personal and miraculous. Thank You for showing me who I am.

Bless our journey as we continue to unlock a little bit of the science behind High Sensitivity, and learn more about the Creator and

Savior behind it all. Send Your Spirit into our hearts to seek You more personally than ever before.
In Jesus' Name,
Amen.

CHAPTER 2

SURFACE
UNLOCKING THE GIFT OF HIGH SENSITIVITY

SATURATED.
Getting to the Bottom.

Swimming underneath the surface of the water takes strength. Our bodies instinctively want to float. Our lungs crave fresh air. Divers use weights, or ballast, to lesson the strain of buoyancy's natural pull to the surface. The added weight increases the enjoyment and efficiency of the experience.

Ballast is the technical term for temporary or permanent weight added for stability and steadiness. In the nautical world, it can provide a desired draft (depth); in aeronautics, it helps control altitude or center of gravity; it's also the gravel placed underneath railroad tracks for drainage and distribution. But for our everyday life, ballast gives us inner stability; the moral code by which we weigh our decisions and filter our emotions through.

Jesus' strength waters steadiness.

The tricky thing about sin and temptation is determining what is ballast, versus a brick intent on pinning us under the surface. We unintentionally carry burdens holding us down and back. The devil would like to confuse the difference between the two, so we get lost underwater in the muffled noise of what ails us. Once he has deceived, he isolates. Every voice muffled, but for the one convincing us we're terminally flawed. It can turn an underwater refuge into a unintentional hiding place.

Ballast is meant to steady us. My experience under the water restored and rejuvenated me. It allowed me to experience God in creation while He cut through loud noise threatening to derail me. There were also many times I ran to the water in panic, or sat confined to the edge of the shore. On dry land or in drowning moments, we question everything about who we are and what is happening.

We never feel ready to surface and face tragedy, loss, heartbreak, sickness, or failure. We want to remain submerged, where the sobs are muffled and the strain is light. When we're drowning, we want the life-ring, not the ballast. Christ knows which one will remedy each situation we swim through. For every person, and every situation, there is only one constant steadying us. Jesus.

When the weight of the world is too much for us, we can swap the heaviness of it all for His strength. When I recall "Be joyful always" in a sinking moment, it comes from the strength that surpasses all understanding. The Strength that took on the cross, let the nails pierce His sovereign skin, and wept blood-stained tears.

We sink because we try to hold on to all of the weight. We confuse duty with ballast. We listen to the wrong track, and amplify the wrong voice. Both may sound similar for a time. Submission is the process of transferring our trying into the hands of the Strong One. Some of our scarcity bricks have become burdens of security, falsely convincing us to hoard and hide.

The Bible says to lose it all is to gain everything.

Submit to be strong.

To set down what's weighing us down, we need to realize who we are, Whose we are, and *Who He is*. Jesus doesn't demand us to perform and achieve, His yoke is easy and His burden is light. He is our constant Ballast. He lets off weight when it's surface. He is the breath of life, and knows when we need a breath of fresh air. That's why running from Him feels like suffocating. Struggling in our own strength fails us every time. We will eventually come to the end of ourselves, in the process of learning who He …and we …are.

Instead of submitting to the suffocating cycle of shame, we can simply choose the other path. The narrow gate. The road less traveled. Not answers to why, but a journey to wisdom via Ballast and Living Water.

Who we are and Whose we are.

Highly Sensitive People speak a language of emotions, noticing so much more than the majority of the people placed around them. In my experience, counselors are angels, but the Great Counselor is the only one capable of setting the proper ballast in life. Adversely, the highly sensitive people in our lives can most assuredly guide us intuitively in many situations, but no one can replace the Counselor. He knows every thread of our being, heart, mind and soul. He goes before us and behind us, He is above us and below us. Creator of time, the Great I Am …there is no way to substitute the wisdom of His sovereignty and love.

I pray as we dig a little deeper into Jeremiah, and define more of what it means to be highly sensitive, we can see the Creator's hand at work. Human knowledge only uncovers a fraction of all He has made. Praying for Ballast, we can learn to find balance between what He has revealed and what still remains undiscovered.

Looking back, I can see how Christ hit the pause button on my life and immersed me in the water. In preparation for what only He knew lied ahead, I quieted my mind and let the sound of it swallow my fears. It was a conscious choice, to linger there longer. As I matured in my faith, the pieces started to lock together.

After childhood prayer books exhausted my attention, I pulled the King James Catholic Bible off the bookshelf in our basement. Every night, I read a little more of the book of Proverbs, and felt like an absolute rebel for underlining and folding down pages. The brevity of time I spent under the literal surface of the water made me thirsty for the Living Water.

I shared how I drifted out to deep and foreign waters when I went off to college, and how I didn't know then how much I would suffer without the core of people that spoke my emotional language. But teammate invited me to FCA, where I listened to everyone recite the verse of the week. I began to write Scriptures on my hand, Ballast setting the depths. But when tested in those formative years of my faith, I began to attach my own ballast. Stuck, I began to struggle, and started to drown. It wasn't a short-lived suffering. I continued to latch bricks onto my proverbial dive belt, pinning me under the surface for far too long with out a breath of fresh air.

God's steadiness to water the seeds I'd scribbled onto my arm eventually unstuck the strangling of my soul. High Sensitivity is ballast I'd blindly labeled as a brick. Jeremiah 32:40 says,"*I will make an everlasting covenant with them: I will never stop doing good to them, and I will inspire them to fear me, so that they will never turn away from me.*" (NIV)

Ballast is healthy dose of godly fear mixed with the weight of God's goodness. "I will never stop doing good to them …" He said in the verse above. Never. God means *never,* and is capable of upholding His promise. We are "never" capable of "always" upholding our promises. Especially, when we're in pain.

The new covenant is one of grace. Jeremiah prayed for God not to destroy what He had said He would destroy. He answered Jeremiah by instructing him to buy land, signifying an eventual restoration. Land that would be available and worthy of purchase.

God promised David, in what is known as The Davidic Covenant in 2 Samuel 7:8-16, *"your house and your kingdom will continue before me for all time, and your throne will be secure forever."* (v16 NIV) We could camp out on this passage for a long time, peeling back the promises of God to David and how they pointed to the covenant Jeremiah prophesied. Ultimately Jesus is the fulfillment of the New Covenant. Through the genetic line of King David, the Savior of the world was born on earth.

In last chapter's glimpse at Jeremiah, God was ensuring His people of Who He is, promising to come to their rescue and restore them even though they faced inevitable destruction. He mentions the new covenant, and then commands: ***"So you will be my people; and I will be your God."*** Jeremiah 30:22 NIV

Will be. Not *maybe.* Not *you'll have to earn it,* or *only until you screw up.* Will. Be.

People, in the verse above, refers also to countrymen; a nation, or compatriots in the original Hebrew language. Another word nestled into the bottom of the definition grabbed me: *kindred.*

Kindred is family.

Realize the weightiness of ballast. ***"You will be my people."***

Think about family for a moment. When I think about my family, I picture ballast. They are the people that speak my emotional language. I nearly drowned when I grew up and physically away from them. #life. #inevitible. #growingpains.

For a Highly Sensitive Person to transitionally shift away from stable and steady ballast, there has to be an underlying method of survival in place. Prayer prepared me. And reading, remembering, and watering the verses He planted as preparatory roots in my soul kicked in to keep me alive. God goes before us, highly sensitive or not, and provides all we need in every season of life. But the leap from one season to the next can shake, shatter and terrify.

Will be. Those are two very powerful words that describe how God prepares us daily for what we do not know lies in the future. We stand fully prepared and ready with all we need, but we have a very real enemy who aims to convince us bricks of consolation are the stuff of life. The easy way, the pain-free way. The only way we know the Truth is to read it, pray it, and live it. The result is not a pain or challenge free life, but the promise of Ballast and Steadiness throughout.

We don't call God our Heavenly Father because He is far off and out of reach. He is Abba, Father. Breath, Life, and Close. Family. I had a great family. Some of you reading this did not. Regardless of who was there for us or who failed us, He promises us we are never alone. He is all we need. Run to Jesus.

"I will be your God." There are many names of God throughout the Bible. My favorite name is Elohim, meaning God, our Creator. I utter this name in prayer when I am in awe of His creation, or need Him to stretch the minutes He created! *I will be your God* is extra significant to me when I look at that verse through the filter of Elohim, my Creator. I am His. I am created in His image. He knew me before He set the Old and the New Covenant in place. I am no coincidental by-product of the universe. I am, because He is.

This is what it means to be chosen. God's chosen family. He chose me to be a part of His family. He knew who I would be, despite the bricks I have tied onto my soul along the journey. The good Father He is, He loves His creation perfectly. In His image. His family. We often picture a far off God, but He is so close. *Yaweh* sounds like breathing. He *is* breath. That's incredible. Think of the power, awe and majesty we have been grafted into as family to the One True God.

I will be your God.

But tragically, we run the other way. Even when we've gripped His hand in desperation and watched Him pull us through ... we still run, fast and hard, to temporary comforts. It's tragic but true! Regardless, He proclaims, *I will be your God. And you will be my people. Jeremiah 31:1 says,* **"'At that time,' declares the Lord, 'I will be the God of all the families of Israel, and they will be my people.'"** NIV

All of the families of Israel is significant. The twelve tribes of Israel didn't always get along or agree, but He claimed them all. Zechariah 8:8 says, ***"I will bring them back to live in Jerusalem; they will be my people, and I will be faithful and righteous to them as their God."** (*NIV) The covenant relationship God has with His people is intimate (NIV Study). Restoration to covenant favor and blessing rests on the faithfulness (dependability) and righteousness of God. (NIV Study) It is here we see the blood of Jesus in the Old Testament.

The world is the world, and things happen to us at the hands of it, others, and even ourselves. But by the blood of Jesus, and the sacrifice He made, we are returned to God's favor. Jeremiah 7:22-23 says, ***"For when I brought your ancestors out of Egypt and spoke to them, I did not just give them commands about burnt offerings and sacrifices, but I gave them this command: Obey me, and I will be your God and you will be my people. Walk in obedience to all I command you, that it may go well with you."*** NIV

Here we go a little further back into the book of Jeremiah, to the beginning of God's message. And what do we see? Obedience. I do not like verses about obedience, because I am well aware of how painfully far I fall short of the word. Praise God I live under the blood-won covenant of Jesus Christ. The notes on this verse pushed me: "Sacrifices are valid only when accompanied by sincere repentance and joyful obedience." (NIV Study)

Our Relationship with Running

When I was younger, I trained for the mile and the 5K. My mantra was to train fast, so the race speed seemed manageable. The first time I attempted to train for a marathon with that mentality, I blew up my achilles and never made it to the starting line. What I thought was my victorious return to proclaim the miraculous healing of my diseased spine and triumphant return to the sport, simply wasn't.

What I thought was a life-ring to the surface became an unbalanced obsession with running again.

It took me three years to speak to the sport again. This time, I tried a half marathon. It took every note of discipline I had to run slow. It was TORTURE. I could not understand how I was going to be able to run farther, faster, when I never once ran a training run at that speed …until I crossed the finish line with my goal in hand and a huge smile on my face.

I learned something about distance running through a very painful and drawn out process, and also about rest, ballast, and God. Joyful sacrifice makes us better people, and more like Christ. It is the witness of Christ active in our hearts on display for others to become inspired by. My race was the result of miles of wisdom and growth logged along the last decade of my life.

Joyful sacrifice didn't look like me smiling as I crossed the finish. There were long training runs I could have walked faster. I rolled the ankle I destroyed in college along the way, and injury maintenance, ice and epsom salt soaks consumed time I wanted to spend on other tasks. I was consumed in hydrating, preparing and slowing down to get stronger.

Ballast.

Steadiness and stability usher in the joy that surpasses all understanding. It's not the easy road, rather the Christ-led road. That road entails a lot of hard work and humility, stepping far out of the comfort zone, and choosing to trust His agenda over our goals.

I used to put running first every day. Sneaking out into the darkness of morning, the sunrise over the lake was akin to the underwater refuge of my childhood. Without it, I became grumbly and cranky. After injury side-lined me, I had to learn how to "Be joyful always" without that morning run.

Now, I am free to simply enjoy the gift running has been to my life as ballast …not a brick compelling me to run, but a balance that allows me to enjoy it in between seasons of perpetual injury. I am who I am because of Whose I am. *You will be my people.* Will be. When we fight and scramble towards temptation and all it's deception, He doesn't shake His fatherly finger at us. When at long last the lesson is learned, He's simply still there. Knowing what He's always known, who we've always been to Him, and loving us all the same.

"Therefore, since we are surrounded by such a great cloud of witnesses, let us throw off everything that hinders and the sin that so easily entangles. And let us run with perseverance the race marked out for us, fixing our eyes on Jesus, the pioneer and perfecter of faith." Hebrews 12:1-2 NIV

Being a runner, I've always held this verse close, but never realized until I surfaced from my running obsession, how to embrace the slow pace and rest required to finish strong. *Jesus* is Ballast. He knows when we need to float up for air, and when we need a moment submerged to muffle the voices out of alignment with His. This experience has been repeated with many things in my life that I have put above Him. Idols, they are called. Idols are what got God's people into so much trouble as they piled on top of their disobedience.

Who Do We Idolize?

Idols are anything we place in importance and priority over God. "Fixing our eyes on Jesus," aligns our lives to avoid idol worship. Anything above Him is an idol, whether money, affluence, physical fitness …even people. God went to great lengths to discipline and destroy idols in the lives of His people. Jeremiah wept at the thought of what his people would endure as a result. But the promise of redemption and restoration were on the other side of discipline and consequences.

Will be.

In my life, and maybe in yours too, I've experienced a stripping of things I do and people I love more than Christ. He'll strip hobbies, health, family, friends, relationships … and control. He allows it all, and loves us too much to let us live half the life we were promised. (John 10:10)

Will be.

"So you will be my people; and I will be your God." Jeremiah 30:22 NIV

Life to the full.

"I have come that they may have life, and have it to the full." John 10:10 NIV

We have to let go to grow. Surrender the bricks to Jesus, our Ballast.

Distortion

Distorted thoughts are all-or-nothing, black-or-white. They focus on problems rather than solutions, generalizing catastrophic outcomes from one specific bad event. (The Powers …) In trying to make the people in my life feel better, I assigned everyone's emotions to myself. Highly Sensitive People are empathic to their surroundings, sensing what could make an environment more comfortable for others. (Aron) We pick up on other people's moods, which is really over-taxing. "In particular if you are a sensitive extrovert, you need to pay special attention to taking care of yourself because life is so rich and exciting. You are a special breed." (Aron)

Distorted thoughts and the HSP in me crashed and collided. Without knowing about my high sensitivity, distorted thoughts became weighty. Now, I can recognize those thoughts for what they are, align them with what is true, and peacefully move about my day.

Faith is a lot like this. The temptations we are deceived to latch onto as truth end up burning and blinding us. Rather than apologize we build the Fort Knox of justification. Our "enemies" on earth are not, yet feelings of judgement from others often preface any evidence to confirm it. (Ni)

We're all set at different levels of sensitivity. "Every living being needs to be sensitive to its environment, but as we know, about 25-35% are *highly* sensitive …41-47% are medium sensitive …and a low group of 20-35%." (Aron) This is why this book is so important for those with *and* without High Sensitivity. We all need to know HOW to coexist. We put the bumper stickers all over our cars and hashtag it to every whimsical post on peace, but we aren't seeing each other. Not for who we really are. We're missing this. Just look at the arguments as we scroll through our news feeds. Instead of seeing each other, we're slinging shame and entitlement. Pride is both the under and overestimation and of who we are. Either way, it's distorted.

Ballast, Perspective & Peace.

Anything worth doing takes some doing, and growing pains aren't called growing pains because they feel great. I'd rather be pulled through these lessons my whole life than drown from harboring hidden bricks. I want ballast in my life. Stability. Steadiness. "… individuals who took the time to notice all of the environmental cues before making a decision generally came out ahead- even with a high cost to doing so …Their sensitivity allowed them to make better and better decisions over time." (Solo) My genetic makeup leads me to be more sensitive to my environment, and more likely to learn lessons from it. (Solo)

To feel more is to experience more, and hopefully to increase in wisdom as a result. High sensitivity is like having more time under the water to process and steady ourselves. We notice things no one else does. Not just their existence, but the cause and effect of them. We learn more because we notice more than 80% of the people in the world.

High sensitivity allows me see my daughters in a new light. One is an extremely picky eater, one of the many quirks of being highly sensitive. My other daughter freaks out when her hands are dry. They are not being disdainful, just themselves. I am challenged as a mother, highly sensitive myself, to know who my daughters are and make a specific effort to feed compassion into those parts of them that even they don't yet understand. I don't want their self-esteem to start to resemble Swiss cheese. (Ward)

Downtime is important for HSP people. (Aron) Simply closing our eyes removes about 80 percent of the stimulation to our brains. (Aron) I close my eyes to worship. My church plays worship music LOUD every Sunday. I PAY to go to worship concerts to shut my eyes. Why? To focus. I don't always need to see on top of my other sensory perceptiveness. In fact, sometimes seeing distracts me. So I shut my eyes. Worship isn't about a show. It's personal. I don't want to look at anyone else. I want to feel God a little more than usual because He promises to be where we all are when we worship Him. I enjoy feeling Him extra close.

It helps HSP people to plan ahead. The process I use to pack my suitcase is thorough and extensive. I wake early to pack the car for day trips. I double check, pack a cooler of snacks, fill the gas tank to full and preview directions. I can't enjoy any of it if I'm not prepared.

My early morning run along the lake at sunrise now comes *after* my time with God. It helps me to prepare for the day with the One who has already counted it. HSP people are supposed to prepare in quiet if we can. (Aron) I need time to linger with God in the dark and quiet hours of morning. I journal my prayers, otherwise I lose focus and start making lists and reminders. I read right from the Bible, just me and God. I like to hear what He has to say to me before I plug in to a commentary or devotion to make sure my take on the text is accurate. I take notes. Sometimes pages. God tends to drop titles into my mind and lay verses on my heart to explore during those morning hours. That's how this book began. "Surface." is a title He dropped into my heart one morning.

Ballast. He knew when my first book,"Friends with Everyone," was ready to surface. But the moment I hit the button to release it into the world was terrifying. For an HSP person, the doubts and fears of a normal person are MAGNIFIED. I almost deleted the whole book that day. Years of work. Delete or publish. Transition feels like that for me. Like a big, dangerous leap. "May all your transitions be smooth and always towards something better. (And if something better is waiting for you, you can't get there until you make that transition.)" (Aron)

I will.

I clicked Publish. And I keep writing. Because it's our thing. It's His will. And I love it. And Him.

It's not always easy, even to do what we love. Being an HSP person brings that fact into hyper-clear focus for me. It's difficult for all of us. But if God is in it …who can stop us?

Going Forward.

"While Apollos was at Corinth, Paul took the road through the interior and arrived at Ephesus. There he found some disciples and asked them, 'Did you receive the Holy Spirit when you believed?' They answered, 'No we have not even heard that there is a Holy

Spirit.' So Paul asked, 'Then what baptism did you receive?'
'John's baptism,' they replied. Paul said, 'John's baptism was a
baptism of repentance. He told the people to believe in the one
coming after him, that is, in Jesus.' On hearing this, they were
baptized in the name of the Lord Jesus. When Paul placed his
hands on them, the Holy Spirit came on them, and they spoke in
tongues and prophesied. There were about twelve men in all."
Acts 19:1-7 NIV

Ephesus, leading commercial city of Asia Minor and capital of
provincial Asia and the warden of the temple of Artemis (Diana),
was Paul's third missionary journey. (NIV Study) In the beginning of
Acts 19, Paul is imparting the Holy Spirit on the twelve men he is
speaking to. (Mounce) Before this Paul explained the difference
between John's baptism of repentance (which recognized sin and
made way for forgiveness of it through Jesus) and the baptism of the
Holy Spirit. The verbiage Paul uses literally means to *put on* the
Holy Spirit, *to wear* the Spirit of God. Jesus tells us not to worry
about what we wear outwardly, but wearing the cloak of the Holy
Spirit inwardly is *EVERYTHING*.

Jesus alone can set us free from the sin weighing us down. His
ballast has no sin-weight to it. It's Holy Spirit restraint, and all of
other gifts mentioned in Galatians 5:22-23: *"But the fruit of the
Spirit is love, joy, peace, forbearance, kindness, goodness,
faithfulness, gentleness and self-control. Against such things there
is no law."* NIV

It's suggested that even Apollos might not have explained baptism to
these men well. Baptism is a literal washing of the soul. We're
getting wet on the outside to signify what's happened on the inside.
Our hearts didn't just go through the quick rinse cycle, but the
sanitize cycle. In the real-life world of laundry, "sanitize" is the
cycle we have to plan around because it takes so long. It's a work.
It's a miracle. The saving work of salvation.

The twelve men in Acts 19 spoke in tongues and prophesied. The Holy Spirit moves us to action. Not all speak in tongues and prophesy, but He stirs, kicking up the Living Water in us, and convicts us to propel ourselves out into the world for the love and honor of God. We're transformed inwardly, but our outward proclamation is important because of how we got there.

When we walk in pursuit of Christ, we begin to become the person we were created to be. Brick by brick, we shake off all that hinders us. It's a constant process called sanctification. The constant and lifelong process of the Holy Spirit convicting us to confess and repent so God can redeem and restore us. Each level up, we become a little bit more like Christ. Living a Christ-centered life looks different than living in and for the world. People *see* the change. Baptism is an important witness to that change.

God places people purposefully in our lives to witness the bricks falling off. To see the steadiness and stability of sustaining joy wash over and into every crack of our lives. We don't have to be Highly Sensitive to notice we're standing out in a world we used to fit right into.

We immerse ourselves in the water because we are saturated with the Spirit. It signifies where we stop and Jesus begins. He takes the wheel, as the famous song sings. Saturated means we are soaked to the bone, like being tossed overboard without warning, every thread of our clothing absorbed to the highest capacity with water. Like flush of color that returns in someone who has been rehydrated.

Overtime, every thread that has been soaked in the wisdom of God starts to revitalize our outward appearance. The saturation from within begins to hydrate the community God places us in. The Living Water moves in and through our lives to bead up and roll off on one another …and another …another.

Breaking through the surface when baptized causes many to cry tears of release. *"How did I get here?"* transforms into *"this is why and God is good."* Ballast. It's good water weight. Saturated, yet not weighing us down in the sense of stopping us or holding us back. It permeates all we do and touches all those exposed. Baptism is the outward witness of the Word of God alive and active in our lives.

The Secret to Survival

As I sit here writing, I just received one of those news alerts on my phone that scientists may have found a rare tortoise that hasn't' been seen in over one hundred years. Where has it been for the last century? Somehow surviving. Hidden away, but surviving.

Turtles are my favorite animal. I used to collect them as a child. They fascinated me because they could exist on land or in the water, and some in and on both. The longevity of their lives still amazes me, and I wondered what it would be like to cruise the ocean floor for CENTURIES.

The HSP person piece of me has been hidden away for a four decades. But in many ways, it hasn't been. I get to experience all of my memories in a new light. Every frame I replay has a different filter on it now. We truly get to a place of peace when we can make peace with our past. When I faced the totality of my human experience during all these trips around the sun, I began to gain the clarity I needed to heal, grow, and embrace who and Whose I am. Not the mistakes. Those are just things I did. Not the sickness and loss. Those were just things that happened to me. Not the accomplishments and highlight reel, those are just evidence of the goodness and faithfulness of God.

I learned how to embrace the entirety of who I am, in process. A highly sensitive person. An *extroverted* highly sensitive person. In some ways, I want to high-five that turtle coming out of one hundred years of hiding. I get that feeling. The turtle doesn't know he's been hiding, he's just been cruising around living his turtle life. Slowly, ever so slowly, cruising along the currents of life, I have stumbled upon something missing. There all along, but undiscovered. Like the great turtles of the world, I very much rode the currents and plodded along life until it was time to surface and be found.

"Their appearance is strange. They carry a roof-like structure on their back. They can be anywhere from one half to 1500 pounds. They are found in freshwater or in the sea, or on land. Undisturbed they can live 100 years. They are the only reptile with a shell. It is the turtle, of course. (Land dwellers are often called tortoises.)

Actually, the shell is part of the skeleton, being attached to the backbone. It is not a removable house. The turtle cannot leave its shell. Its shell does provide a hiding place when it is threatened. Even those who cannot pull themselves all the way into the shell find some protection from the shell.

Turtles are air breathers, but some can absorb oxygen from the water making them able to stay underwater for hours and even months during hibernation in temperate climates. Turtles have no teeth but they do have powerful jaws. They are omnivorous, meaning that they eat a variety of things dead and living, plant and animal.

Sea turtles, until recently, were rarely seen. They appear on land, returning to the beach of their birth, to mate, lay eggs and return again to the sea, sometimes traveling thousands of miles. The hatchlings must fend for themselves, digging out and making their way to the sea amidst many predators on land and in the sea. Only one or two out of up to two hundred hatchlings make it.

Land turtles (tortoises) can take five hours to walk one mile, but then again, there is no need to run. Tortoises are usually slow, quiet, and peaceful. They don't move fast, but they can plod.

The dictionary says that to plod is to walk slowly with a heavy tread, to work slowly, methodically, and thoroughly. Turtles plod. We live in an age of speed. To us faster is better. It is not so with God. God is not impressed with speed. Ecclesiastes 9:11 tells us that "the race is not to the swift." God looks for those who will walk with Him, those who will plod along, slowly, carefully, deliberately, loyally, faithfully. These are those who go from strength to strength (Psalm 84:7), from one degree of glory to another (2 Corinthians 3:18). They grow little by little (see Exodus 23:30 and Deuteronomy 7:22). Blades of grass grow quickly. They also die quickly. Giant oaks take years of sunshine and rain and winds and snows. Take time to plod along with God." (Children's Bible Min- Mister Steve gave me permission to quote his message on turtles in it's entirety.)

Do you see how God goes before us? Who knew my love of turtles meant more than I could ever imagine? I trust He will grow me at the pace fitting His perfect timing and plan for my life.

"I have seen something else under the sun:
The race is not to the swift or the battle to the strong, nor does food come to the wise or wealth to the brilliant or favor to the learned; but time and chance happen to them all." Ecclesiastes 9:11 NIV

Time and chance remind us success is uncertain and more evidence humans do not ultimately control events. (NIV STUDY) Time happens to us. We can't control time. Time is more than just the hour of the day. It's the experiences, fortunes, and occasions that bookmark our lives. High sensitivity doesn't mean I can interpret everything I notice better than 80% of the world's population. It just means I notice. I still have to filter all of those thoughts through the Truth of God's Word. Big task.

It's no wonder I need to turtle out sometimes and just ride the currents of life or plod along mindlessly. Under the water, brushing my hands against the sunken sand to muffle the sound of life around me. Sometimes ideas have to swim around in our minds for a while before it's time birth them. As a writer, I live this reality. We are not those kind of projects to God. God says, *I will*, and **He does**.

You are no accident, nor am I. Our God is a purposeful God, and He knows in this moment, on this page, on this particular day, you need to know how loved you are. The God of the universe sees you, loves you, and will steady you through the greatest storms if you will only let go and allow Him to. Eyes fixed on Jesus, He will make us newer and newer until we arrive on Heaven's doorstep for that hug.

If you've come this far on the journey, don't stop now. Keep unlocking what it means for you to discover high sensitivity in yourself, your children, or those you love and befriend. There is so much more to discover in the pages that follow.

Father,

Praise you for these pages, and Your purpose for them. Thank You for creating highly sensitive people. For reasons only You know, there's another level of intuitions that only a certain number of people have access to, genetically. I pray, Father, that every person, highly sensitive or not, knows how purposeful You created them. Father we know all too well the feeling of bricks keeping our heads underwater when we desperately want to breathe. The sin that so easily entangles us and drags us away from You threatens to drown and destroy us. Forgive us for our naiveté and ignorance. Stir our hearts with Living Water. Convict us and open our eyes to see bricks and welcome ballast. We hold your Peace in our hands along with our salvation. Remind us to grip it when we're tempted to unravel at the demands and pressures of this world.

Thank You for counselors who help us sort out the deep parts of our hearts. Bless and increase the number of counselors available to help hearts and minds here on earth, Father. Remove any fear from those thinking about seeking help beyond themselves and the people in their lives. Reassure the normality of keeping our mind, soul, and hearts healthy just as we would any other ailment or checkup. Empower us to be advocates for high sensitivity, and the research done to educate and enlighten so many who have never known they were born with this genetic trait. We pray those with these gifts will use them to honor God and love others well.

Bless and protect anyone feeling hopeless and overwhelmed today, Father. Bring Your peace, which surpasses all understanding, into any heart that does not know Jesus as their Savior. Our earthly knowledge and ability will only take us so far, Father, and then we need you to determine the ballast in our lives. Steady us and stabilize us, as we walk through a world littered with land mines of heartbreak and tragedy. Bless and send the research of high sensitivity around the world, to help, heal, and love people. Heal all those who have fallen prey to distorted thoughts and depression because they did not previously know who they were, Father. May they recognize the life-ring you are throwing to them and grab hold if it for dear life.

Jesus, I pray many will come to know You through this book, all I write, and the witness of my life. Let all I do be to honor You. Bless every word and motive in my heart to align with Your will. All the heartbreak and shattered pieces of life I share here are only a shred of what we all experience on this earth every day, Father. I pray for every suffering soul, today. Show me my place in this world, and the people You need me to help with the gifts You have given me. Remove the paralyzing fear of transition, and the lure of extended solitude. Bless my family, Father. May I be the mother my highly sensitive daughters need in this world. Let my life point them to You, the Living Water. May they find their refuge under the water, where the noises are muffled down so that Your voice can be amplified.

Let us be aware and compassionate towards each other. Bless our marriages and friendships to be enhanced by high sensitivity, not burdened. Bless us with a godly empathy and love, not just for highly sensitive people, but for all people. You love us all equally, Father.

In Jesus' Name,

Amen.

If you'd like to welcome Jesus into your life for the first time, or just again, I'd be honored to lead you in prayer.

Jesus,
Thank You for Your sacrifice on the cross for me. I am blown away that You knew my name as You hung there in pain, dying for me regardless of the sin You knew I would walk into and through on this earth. Convicted and moved by Your reckless love for me, I confess all of my sin to You today. I lay it down at Your feet and submit all of my bricks to You. Cut me loose, Jesus, for I believe in You, that You came to earth and died for me. That You rose again and are now seated at the right hand of the Father. I have accepted You, Christ my Savior. Praise You, Jesus! I feel Your freedoms washing over me, saturating me with the Holy Spirit, who will seal me as Yours for all eternity. I look forward to hugging you in heaven when my time on earth is done, and pray Your blessing on my life today, and always. I will follow You all the days of my life. Imperfect on this earth, but perfectly and wholly loved by You. Thank You for salvation.
In Jesus' Name,
Amen.

(If you prayed that prayer for the first time, I would just love to know! E-mail me at sunnyandeighty@gmail.com so that I can praise God and pray for you.)

CHAPTER 3

SURFACE
UNLOCKING THE GIFT OF HIGH SENSITIVITY

THE STRUGGLE.
Wrestling Acceptance.

Though our friends donned their scuba gear alongside me in the cove, my claustrophobia couldn't let go of the air in my snorkel … nor close proximity of the surface. Still able to feel the sun warming my back through the soft water, I explored without taking any un-calculated risks.

Words are my buddies, numbers not so much. Highly sensitive, my intuitive calculations battled reality. I applied everyone's explanation of who I was. Every little compliment and critique stuck to a piece of my soul like Gorilla Glue. Noticing more than the average person, all of the nuances and expressive ways people communicate, in addition to words, hot-glued themselves to my heart.

Noticing is more intricate than paying attention. *Notice* is a warning. We place reminders where we will notice them, to warn us of our potential forgetfulness. Calendars, alarms, and now Siri, remind us to re-notice things. *Re*-noticing is an inevitable part of high sensitivity. Initially noticing substantially more, the *re*-noticing can be suffocating.

The Bible says to take every thought captive. *Every thought* is *impossible* for *anyone*. The gravity of my *20% of the population* thought-life forced me to succumb to my own inability to check each and every thought early on. Conscious and subliminal thoughts sank and set in. Thoughts stacked alongside moments, mistakes and unaccomplished dreams, *re*-noticed. Dreams are guide-posts to what God wants us to accomplish through us on earth. He is good, and His purposes manifest in fulfilled dreams of blessing and joy.

It was easier to cruise under the surface, just deep enough to pop up for real air vs. snorkel air anytime I wanted to without much of an effort. Dipping down was therapeutic for me, but to stop short of diving deeper cut my potential.

Fear is paralyzing. That girl I was with the flippers on, swimming below the surface with mask and snorkel, was terrified. But she didn't know it was fear. I didn't know I was terrified. In my whirring mind, I raced to cope with life as it happened to me. Adolescence just happens. It's never welcomed, and always cheered out of the building when it leaves. The growth between my ears during those years further expanded up on my coping mechanisms to stay "normal" amidst the sea of thoughts I could potentially drown in at any given moment.

The God of our Memories

Being underwater muffled confusion and magnified the clarity of His voice. But I failed to dive deeper and hear clearer, who I was in Him. I thought believing in God was enough. When we broke one of His rules, we confessed and served our penance. That was it. Move on to the next …broken rule. I sensed there was something broken *in me*. My earliest memories are crystal clear, including my thought-reel! Looking back all these years later …I *remember* re-noticing.

What a gift to realize brokenness, for we are all cracked in places. We look into broken and skewed mirrors for most of our lives, but God sees the beauty reflected in the pieces. He knows the whole person. My thoughts and reactions, coupled with the compliments and critiques (good *and* unfair) of others, morphed my self-image and broke open my theology.

God doesn't punish us for breaking the mirror. We are always forgiven, never loved less. Because of Jesus' death on the cross, before we confess, He's forgiven. Confession is for our own good and growth towards the dreams we *think* we've missed by a landmark mile. Every confession leads us to repent, because we don't *want* to repeat it! We *try* not to! I was attempting to erase my sins with penance, failing to embrace the fact Jesus had already demolished them on the cross. I fought with my sin instead of handing it over. But I never had the power to wipe my sin away by anything I *did or didn't do*.

"It is finished." John 19:30

The pathway to freedom begins at the cross. Continual release of our sin to the Father brings restoration. Restoration is freedom to dive a little deeper. Sin causes us to fear. We do what we know we shouldn't and get stuck in non-sensical cycles of fear. God is bigger. We can do all things through Him who strengthens us …so why was I stuck snorkeling in the shallows?

Restoration is a process only God can accomplish in our lives. I knew I needed to turn all of the re-noticing over to Him, laying it down at the foot of the cross. But I would remember. I would re-notice the re-noticing, and remind myself why I was afraid. I created detours, changed and readjusted to fit the practicality of my fear. Practicality can be fear in disguise. People who notice more should be out in the world doing more with the more they notice, but the fear of stepping out scared me.

Diving in …or not.

Going with the flow numbed all of my re-noticing, but it didn't address my fear of diving. The literal pursuit of learning to dive into the water is excruciating. I wanted to see where I was going, so I failed to put my head down. When we dive, we lead with our heads. Our arms are out front, but the direction of our head leads the way.

Belly smacker.

Every. Time.

It hurt so bad, and I couldn't understand why …at 13 …I still couldn't just put my head down and trust it to lead me into the water splash-less like everyone else.

"Maybe trying off the diving board will help, " they said.

It didn't. It just hurt *more*.

The direction we turn our head to leads us, inwardly and outwardly. We don't walk around life backwards. We face forward and stride towards our intended destination. My failure to lead with my head started with my thoughts. Our thoughts direct our vision, forming what we think about ourselves and where we are going. I believed I had to see first. I refused to put my head down.

Faith in Christ isn't putting a blindfold on and holding His hand through life, but forming our thoughts around His truth. It's kicking out doubts and fears that have lied to us throughout life. Things people have said about us, or "said" without ever saying a word. Thoughts that have disguised our strengths as dysfunctions, like my re-noticing.

There's something about watching younger people act braver that motivates a person, and after watching my little sister dive-in over and over with ease and joy, I began to believe I could, too. She almost drowned when she was little. I pulled her out twice. If she could dive unafraid, I could too. I re-noticed. I remembered. I finally dove into the water head first. Remembering in proper perspective is powerful and effective, giving us the confidence to put our heads down and dive-in.

Jumping into the water when she was little, my sister knew there was someone to save her if she couldn't touch the bottom. Eventually, she learned to dive and swim in the deep end with the comfort of knowing she was never alone. Because after you almost drown twice, no one lets you near the water alone.

When I dove in to the water, it felt like breaking through concrete with my head…but no belly smacker. After the first dive, I never forgot how to put my head down. Diving became easier. I wasn't worried about what I couldn't see anymore.

The thought of ditching my snorkel for scuba diving was scarier than just putting my head down. It was a whole new level of fear. Life is like this, but expanded upon for an HSP person. One fear down … and lifetime more of them to go. The simultaneous fear-facing and re-noticing is overwhelming. Over time, little quirks of coincidence helped me discover high sensitivity. It begin to surface and re-frame my memories like little red flags of redemption, restoring hope.

Forget about it.

"Do not worry." Matthew 6:25

I doodled *"Don't worry, be happy,"* not because I was the most positive person in life, but the most worried! I noticed EVERYTHING. I knew I shouldn't worry, but I couldn't stop. Somewhere in the HSP person that was yet to be discovered, God had lovingly built in coping mechanisms to help me.

I was afraid to dive deep. Ironic, to be afraid of the deep water, when as an HSP person, deep thoughts are my existence. I didn't know enough about what went on in my head, and why, enough to lead with it efficiently.

Assuming the rest of the world picked up on the same cues I did, I messed up and missed out on a lot of opportunities to clearly communicate with the people in my life. Failing so often to love them well, I spun relationships into knots like dock-lines. As a kid, I loved to create ornate knot combinations, but I suddenly saw something about myself in those pretty-looking knots. Much like the highlight reel of my life, no matter how functional and put together the lines looked …they were still tied in knots.

Knot- an interlacing, twining, looping, etc., of a cord, rope, or the like, drawn tight into a knob or lump, for fastening, binding, or connecting two cords together or a cord to something else. (Dictionary)

Knots secure and fasten, tie and tangle. Knots form joints, like the one between a boat and the anchor or a dock that keep it from drifting.

Divers tie knots. "In diving, knots can help attach a load to an anchor, secure a surface marker or dock a boat …there are many practical applications when it comes to knot-tying and diving, not to mention that these skills can also be useful in everyday life." (Reynaud)

I didn't know anything about diving knots, because I was too scared to scuba dive. My friends could have walked me through the process. But fear of what I could not see paralyzed me. What could we could unlock if we were willing to face fear?

Through adolescence, I learned to cope and numb and fit in, crying myself to sleep many nights. Every heartbreak hurt so much I thought I might die from it. The thoughts I noticed suffocated me in silence because I was afraid to let them loose. I still re-notice them and wonder what could've potentially changed had they been taken captive. But dreams don't die at the hands or our fears. What God sets out to accomplish in this life cannot be derailed.

Instead of living in regret, I learned to look back and re-notice *well*. I could choose to see knotted relationships, or the growth God pulled tight in every season of my life.

Knots to Steady Us.

Each knot reveals more of who I am *in Him*. Knots keep us safely docked and securely anchored in calm harbors. The wrong knots can tangle and twist us, anchoring us to people, things, strongholds and circumstances. Through the knot Jesus tied on the cross, we are connected to God. To avoid drifting aimlessly in the water of the world, we need to be tied to the Anchor. There is safe harbor in the

Living Water. The Knot fastens, twines, and ornately ties wisdom together as we stay attached to the Vine. And the wisdom we gain from each knot softens our hearts.

Whether an HSP person or not, discovering the depths, like we've been reading about in Jeremiah, isn't always about uncovering what we can *see*. We all have things hidden deep within us, to which only Christ holds the key. Even counselors who are gifted to surface things we've buried, and researchers who are brilliant at studying the mind from all perspectives, still haven't completely uncovered the human soul in it's totality.

Only God sees into the unknown and uncharted depths. We need an oxygen tank just to keep breathing while He uncovers what He knows. Like a diver sinks down slowly so as not to rupture their ears and insides, every layer of pressure we endure slowly produces strength.

For every layer of pressure we surface from there is a knot that's been permanently untangled and retied rightly. For me, discovering high sensitivity is one of those knots. Untangled, untwisted and re-tied to set a firm foundation of growth and good fruit. I don't know what it is for you, but I know if you're reading this book, this message is for you whether you are an HSP person or not. It's important, not only to love the people in our lives well, but to embrace who we are in Christ with godly confidence. God grows our confidence in the depths.

When we uncover the fears causing us to sink, we can release them to be retied into knots of revelation and growth.

Steady My Heart.

"…until he fully accomplishes the purposes of his heart."
Jeremiah 30:24 NIV

Taking Scripture a part to apply it situationally is not a good habit to get into, but deconstructing it to release the pressure of an entire verse one layer at a time helps us to dig into God's word ENTIRELY. As we continue to discover the Book of Consolation in Jeremiah, we've come to the end of Chapter 30. So far we've learned about who Jeremiah was, and why he was called the weeping prophet. We've discovered why God's people were in trouble, and what their consequences would be. We've also seen the grace of God, and a lot of Jesus layered into Jeremiah's prophesy. Somehow, in a Biblical book full of woe and predicted destruction, God's love reigns. We've tied some healthy knots about who God is. Let's continue to dive a little deeper into this prophetic message to see how it can help us submit and surrender our tangled up knots to be retied.

When we consider our accomplishments, we think about things that are finished or completed. But in the context of the above snippet of verse 24, it means *to rise*. (Brown) It's the establishment of our stance. We aren't finished until we hug Jesus in heaven. True accomplishment on this earth releases human restrictions to walk out the fulfillment of God's purpose in our lives.

The purposes of God's heart imply His discretionary plans to carry them out. (Brown) He presses ballast and knots out of the messy, painful, and confusing parts of our lives, for His glory. Whether we get ourselves into our own messes, or befall on bad circumstances, there's only one Way to untangle the knots of fear and sin that so easily entangle us. 1 John 4:7 says, *"Everyone who loves has been born of God and knows God."* (NIV)

Our love is not God's love. Our love is the Greek word, agapao (Thayer). It means to welcome, entertain, be fond of, or love a person dearly. It's the same word we used to describe our pleasure or content with things. God's love is agape love (Thayer), brotherly love. Family. Agape love is affectionate, good willing, loving, and benevolent. The root word for agape is agapao.

Made in the image of God, we all have a certain tinge of high sensitivity. The gift of HSP people to interpret the depth of feelings, wisdom, and intuition is remarkable. Why we aren't wired all that way is a mystery, a depth, and a layer uncovered. It's genetic, so we know our Author has everything to do with it. But it's a mystery, just like the depth of His love is to us. Some things, like a complete understanding of all He is, will not be answered on this earth. 1 John 4:16 reads, ***"And so we know and rely on the love God has for us. God is love. Whoever lives in love lives in God, and God in them."*** NIV

Love in 1 John 4:16 is agape love. We rely on God's love. It's our oxygen tank. Living in love means we live in God …and God in us. The gift of Living Water is granted at salvation. He is our refuge under the water. Our Ballast, stability, and steadiness. In the constant journey of untangling and re-tying, Love is unchanging. 1 John 4:8 says, ***"Whoever does not love does not know God, because God is love."*** NIV

The first *love* in this verse is agapao love. If we don't love others with the kind of love we are capable of extending and receiving on this earth …we don't know God. For God's agape love drives us. God loves us abundantly more than we deserve. All we need to love on this earth flows from Him. God's love for His children is irreplaceable.

"God is love. In his essential nature and in all his actions, God is loving. John similarly affirms that God is spirit and light, as well as righteous, holy, powerful or great, faithful, true, and just." (NIV Study)

God's love is deep. It's no wonder we're called to put our heads down and dive. Jesus' command to love above all else makes perfect sense through Love's filter. (1Peter 4:8)

The Power of Answered Prayer.

Before God promised to fully accomplish the purposes of his heart in Jeremiah 30:24, he assured Jeremiah:

"For I know the plans I have for you," declares the LORD, "plans to prosper you and not harm you, plans to give you hope and a future." Jeremiah 29:11

This is popularly quoted verse. It's not my life verse, but it is my father-in-law's. A reserved man, he told the story after his wife's passing. He had just gotten out of the Air Force, and his sister had set him up on a date. On the way, He prayed to God for a wife to spend his life with. That night, he met the woman he would be faithfully married to for over fifty years. OVER. FIFTY. YEARS. Of marriage. MARRIAGE. (And all the married people said …AMEN.)

Marriage is one of the hardest things we'll ever dive into on earth. Trying to love and be loved with agapao love. The same love for "I love french fries!" Impossibly stacked against us from DAY ONE. Yet, over fifty years later, my father-in-law could barely speak through the pain of his gratefulness for God's answered prayer …of marriage.

I'll never forget that day, or see this verse from the same perspective. The one and only time I've seen tears in his eyes since the day his sweet granddaughters were born. The pain and heartache he felt in loss was nothing compared to the love he had shared with his wife this side of heaven. He's able to move past mourning with the hope of heaven and God's faithfulness in his back pocket. That's worth more than a fat wallet, a fancy house, or anything else this earth could offer.

Prosperous and good plans for a hope and a future involve a constant untangling and retying. It hurts. My in-laws walked through a time of sickness that almost took one of them to heaven before either one of them were ready. They said good-bye to family and friends together. They raised three people and led them to Christ together. They are the most gracious, accepting people I have ever met.

Their family loves to tell the story of Bucher Road. How generations ago, when the road was being paved, one of their ancestor's stood on the corner of his property with a shotgun and dared them to pave that road through his farmland. It worked, and the road still awkwardly turns around the spot where he stood.

Stubbornness is usually seen as a bad, or at best frustrating quality to have. Unless you know my in-laws. The are gracefully stubborn. Unmoved and obstinate in their faith. Accepting, loving, and peaceful. I want stubborn faith like theirs. The ability to love and accept people for who they are, right where they are at. I know this love first hand. It was my first impression of them.

I was fresh out of a failed marriage when I met them. Most people would be worried for their son's future, bringing home a girl like that. But they were not. They loved me from the moment they met me. No questions. No prodding. Just love. They were the extending arms of the love of Jesus to me when I needed to know most that God still had good plans for me. Plans for a hope and a future. Good plans.

When my mother-in-law passed recently, my daughters and I helped my sister-in-law go through her jewelry. There is a special healing that comes from remembering …re-noticing. It reminds us who she was, what we learned from her, and where she is now. The pain is somehow not as excruciating knowing she is with Jesus.

Our family trips to the top of the Mitten began with her legacy. The view from the top of the dunes, where we all feel a little bit closer to God, is a gift she passed on to us. Never, would I ever, have gone North on vacation if not for the love they showed me the day I met them. Who wouldn't want to spend more time around love and acceptance?

The pieces of God's love we experience on this earth are a fraction of what it feel like to be whole in heaven. Accepted and fully loved, with ballast and knots. Love pulls us through the plans God has for us. He promises they won't be easy, and there will be pain. Sometimes we think we have to say a lot about Jesus to be an accurate witness, but more than anything she ever said, through my mother-in-law's life, some of my most tangled knots were set right. He not only loves us for who we are, right where we are at …He uses us in the process to love others.

"The LORD appears to us in the past, saying: 'I have loved you with an everlasting love; I have drawn you with unfailing kindness." Jeremiah 31:3 NIV

Unfailing. We fail. It doesn't deter Him. Love never fails. (1 Cor 13:8) It's important to remember and hold on to the knots God sets right, because of the rest of the verse.

Unlocking the Ending …

"The fierce anger of the Lord will not turn back until he fully accomplishes the purposes of his heart. In days to come you will understand this." Jeremiah 30:24 NIV

The full context of the entire verse helps us see a what God is saying. He addresses this very understanding in the last part of this verse. There were false prophets everywhere in Jeremiah's time. Let's be honest, they are everywhere …now, and always will be.

Jeremiah 23:19 describes God's wrath as a whirlwind. A storm. Thunderstorms remind me of God's power. He is in omnipotent control beyond understanding. There is an un-explanatory respect for a God whose love is so big, and heart is perfectly just. We have a chance to untangle and tie on to Jesus. He died so we would not have to suffer the wrath our sin deserves …death.

"Why couldn't God's love have overcome his wrath? Because God's character demands that justice be satisfied. God does not vent his anger as a tantrum; his wrath is necessary to preserve the integrity of his holiness. God's wrath toward sin was ultimately satisfied by the death of Christ on the cross." (NIV Quest)

In a world full of "self-love" promotion, we need to clarify. Self-love is not OK if we're talking about putting ourselves, our desires, and our plans for life above His purpose and the great commission to spread the Gospel through the earth. We are put on earth to honor God with all we have, do and are.

Empathy is the way we identify with the feelings, attitudes, and thoughts of other people. We can't relate to others if we're too tied up in the wrong knots to understand them. It's crucial to love ourselves (recognizing who we are in Christ) in a healthy way. It helps us to be empathetic to others. Empathy is not apologizing for the way we are, or for what others are going through.

I began apologizing to everyone, for everyone, and on account of myself and who I was. This was a crack in my theology. I associated what I did and did not do with who I was, and it was preventing me from freely empathizing with my own heart in my relationship with Jesus, and the other people in my life. Sometimes we have to stop and remember we're forgiven.

We often hold ourselves hostage to un-forgiveness. I was so good at telling others to have compassion on people that hurt them, but not so good at applying the same attitude towards myself. Maybe you are hard on yourself, too. I empathize.

A heart full of empathy towards others has to be filled. Where does the ability to breathe compassion and empathy come from? Jesus. The guilt and shame I harbored had been causing me to stack un-forgiveness in my heart ...towards myself.

Highly Sensitive Person.

Everyone's journey is different, but we are all on a mission to unlock what is hidden in the depths. To love people well, it helps to love ourselves. So often we wrongly associate who we are with what we do …or do not do. No matter what, God has agape love for each one of us. It's who He is. Created in His image, we all innately crave a relationship with our Creator. He, in us, inspires us to dive deep and untangle knots. The more we seek God, the more we are promised to find Him. Every believer in Christ is on a course of constant change called sanctification. Agape change grows from every conviction, repentance, and restoration. Untangling and retying, He uses everything for good. All of me. All of You. All of us. Agape.

My youngest daughter campaigned hard for a puppy. I'm sure lots of little girls campaign for puppies, but not everyone's little girl is my HSP little girl. It tore her up inside to pass the puppy owner's walking their puppies. She is now known as *the girl who cannot pass a puppy.* Her three-year-old feet stomped hard on the ground one family vacation, face fully reflecting the heartbreak in her tone.

"I just really want a puppy! P.L.E.A.S.E.!!!"

She is my tantrum-prone girl, who would lay flat on the ground and remain in protest. There was no picking her up. She's tiny but mighty. She's also prone to nightmares, a tendency I can fully relate to.

Nightmares are worse than bad dreams. They are terrifying, detailed and convince every fiber of our being we will awake in grave danger. As I tried to wake up from these terrors, something in my subconscious leaves me with no way out. I have to be shaken awake.

I've had vivid dreams all my life, but they catapulted in extremity and frequency during seasons of drastic change, or loss. They were sporadic throughout my childhood, but started occurring more frequently when I moved off to college. Seasons of suffering strung together as my friends and I watched September 11th on TV. I didn't know anyone in those buildings. But the sheer trauma of what it meant to our country turned my nightmares up to max volume and continued throughout my twenties.

Sensory-processing sensitivity (SPS, the scientific name for HSP people) might underlie the unique symptoms and imaginative richness found in nightmare-prone individuals, and if they can have positive dreams, then this may be a case of differential susceptibility (experiencing both positive and negative more strongly.). -Aron

The more knots I let Jesus untangle and re-tie, the less nightmares I experienced. Long before I knew I was an HSP person, there was a construction project underway in my heart. Sometimes the answer to our prayers comes in a healing we don't even know we need. The disappearance of my symptoms is evidence of His healing hand. Ballast. Stability. Steadiness. Even in my over-active imagination while I slept.

My daughter still has nightmares, and I empathize. Because of what I know about who I am, I know a little more about her, too. My little HSP extrovert, just like her momma. Instead of shushing her and sending her back to bed, or telling her it's just a silly dream, I meet her watery eyes and snuggle her back to sleep. I get it. I know the terror. But I also know the power of a healing embrace. The safety of tying onto the dock, knowing we're safe for the night. I can be that safe harbor for her, because Jesus is for me. I learn from Him, and empathize with her. I pray over her, for her, and most of all let her know she's normal and not alone. These are things kids worry about. Loneliness, abnormality, and the dark. I can lead her out of loneliness, assure her she is who she is supposed to be, and show her the Light. I can be the channel of Love He uses to tie a good, healthy knot.

We have a sweet golden-doodle because of my youngest daughter. I joke even our dog is an HSP dog. I don't know if that's a thing, but golden-doodles are frequently trained to be therapy dogs because of their innate sense for people, especially when something is wrong. Do you see how our God cares for us? Before we knew we were HSP people, in the door bounced our adorable little doodle puppy. She has done so much to ease our emotions, just by being herself. My daughter knew she wanted a puppy …SO BAD …but I'd like to think we now understand a little bit more about the real *why* behind the reason she's ours.

Empathy Calls.

A positive environment allows HSP people to have self-empathy. I knew strongly I was called to be a stay-at-home mom. It was not an easy choice to leave my career behind, but the time allowed me to spend with my growing daughters led my empathetic intuition to inquire about their plausible high sensitivity. It took faith. The economy bottomed out at the same time I decided to stay home, but God never failed to provide for us.

He knew what I did not. Their positive environment has given them the freedom to experience themselves wholly and fully. I'm here. They have ballast. That's what we're supposed to be for our kids, whether we are stay-at-home or working parents …or a mix of both, which is what I am, now. Stability, steadiness and the tying of good knots.

Both of my kids ignored negative discipline. What worked for everyone else's kids didn't do anything but destroy and break hearts all over my house. I was sweeping up the pieces and mopping up the tears. I now know this is an HSP person thing. Sensitive people feel more rewarded by positive social or emotional cues, which they are more in tuned to in the first place. (Solo) When I had two kids under the age of two, positivity helped us survive the day. Laughter at the little stuff carried us through the crying spells.

Sensory overload happens for them in more than just disciplinary moments. We are constantly untying knots that threaten to strangle healthy friendships and mangle self-images. Some days, I spend so much time talking to and praying with and over my girls I lose my voice.

Overdone.

As a highly sensitive person, I don't get the same dopamine hit from loud external stimuli (Solo). I love my friends, but the constant tinging of a group text can sometimes be too much. Big parties of people, which I love, overwhelm me. Getting louder than all of the noise sometimes gave me a false sense of control over the massive wave of stimuli my mind attempted to process.

Distance running has been a refuge for me. A chance to proverbially swim under the water to muffle the noise, out on the road in the quiet of the morning. The miracle of my love of distance running is my insane tolerance for pain. I still can't figure out why that makes sense for an HSP person. All I can reason is somehow the mental relief is worth the physical pain. My body knows it. My mind knows it. "Mostly highly sensitive people are keenly aware that they have stronger emotional reactions than the people around them, and often notice emotional undercurrents where others pick up nothing." (Solo)

No one has a filter for incoming thoughts. They all come rushing in and we have to determine which are significant, distorted, and debatable. For an HSP person, emotions and sensory alerts flood our minds like those thoughts. No filter for the incoming. It's easy to drown in them. "If you're highly sensitive, this is not your imagination - you may actually have a brighter palette of emotional 'colors,' so to speak, because of the gene variant. And it directly drives the level of empathy and awareness you have for others' feelings." (Solo)

Highly sensitive people experience more than just their own emotions. We pick up on others, too, sometimes before they do. Talk about having trouble fitting in and sounding a little crazy. We're picking up on everything in our lives *and* what's bouncing off of others. Untangled and retied, I'm now equipped to empathize with others in a powerful way. Romans 8:28 says, ***"And we know that in all things God works for the good of those who love him, who have been called according to his purpose."*** NIV

"Only about 15-20% of the population is believed to be highly sensitive. Though it seems like a small number, that's two out of every ten people, on average. High sensitivity isn't limited to humans, either; the same trait has been found in at least 100 other species." (Solo) For HSP people, and those who work or live with them, effective communication is key. (Ni) We thrive in positive environments, so toxic relationships and broken communication welcomes implosion. Faith, counseling, and research on high sensitivity has helped me tie knots of stability in my everyday life. I'm learning to empathize with, rather than wear, everyone's emotions.

Scientifically, the genetics that help us understand what another person is doing (compassion and empathy) are called mirror neurons. (Solo) It's essentially like looking in the mirror every time we see or talk to people, and comparing/matching up their emotions with what we know about ours. HSP people empathize more because we genetically have more mirror neurons."Mirror neurons are both your superpower and, at times, more than a little inconvenient- like when you can't watch the same TV show as everyone else because it's too violent. But it's also what makes you warm, caring, and incredibly insightful about what other people are going through." (Solo)

The tendency to procrastinate is influenced by my high sensitivity. (Aron) Knowing there is nothing wrong with me for *that* is HUGE. We can tie healthy knots of skill into the fabric of our HSP gene, and really, any part of our personalities we are aware of. "It's just how I am" only takes us so far. Everyone has the capacity to seek steadiness, and untangle some knots. For HSP people in particular, emotional regulation happens unconsciously. (Aron) It's stacked upon the vast experience of our childhood. Positive or negative, we can work with the life we've been given. Knowing what we know about God, He's ready to meet us where we are at.

Since a lot of emotional regulation skills develop in childhood, it's possible layers of shame and hopelessness have been built into the fabric of our coping mechanisms. Knowing what we now know has hopefully begun the untangling any feelings of guilt and shame for who we are.

Shame and guilt are never from God.

We can see enough, now, to lead with our heads. Wisdom can break chains we've carried for years. As Christians, we have the all-surpassing power of the Holy Spirit flowing through the Living Water that sustains our souls. God is bigger than anything layered in our subconscious and all misunderstandings stacked up against us. Through counseling, and the great Counselor, we can heal and tie brand new knots of Love.

Stepping back gives us room to move. For HSP people, rest helps us process all we're flooded with on a daily basis. (Aron) Imagine the empathy from HSP people to other HSP people. When I step back from an assignment before I proof and submit it, I see it in a new light. If I don't get up and walk away from it, I start to hate what I've written, and contemplate deleting it. Stepping back is important. Rest is important. God built us in His image, and *He rested*. Six days of creation …and then rest. When I pause daily to remember who God is, worship Him, seek Him, and be with Him, it helps me remember who I am.

God places people purposefully in our lives. I guarantee, if you start sharing your story …your testimony, your high sensitivity, the 15-20% in your circle will start to surface. God knows community is important. He is our Provider. Look up and out for the HSP people in your life. Start a conversation. Start untangling and retying some healthy knots. Dive in. Romans 12:2 reminds, *"Do not conform to the pattern of this world, but be transformed by the renewing of your mind. Then you will be able to test and approve what God's will is- his good, pleasing and perfect will."* NIV

Paul, the author of Romans and a majority of the New Testament, knew suffering. Shipwrecks, jail, and beatings hurt him physically, but equal or added to physical pain was his mental anguish. The great commission to share the Gospel attracts some odd stares. It's not of this world. Paul explains in this verse, if we sit in that perspective for too long, we might be tempted to succumb to the pain of rejection. It hurts. We are people. Even introverts need people. *People need people.* But a transformed mind has a Christ-centered perspective. We are no longer living for this world. This one can be amazing, too! Full of blessings right alongside the heartache and pain.

Paul is charging his audience, and us, to think like citizens of heaven, children of the one True God. *Family.* We get our family. We don't have to explain ourselves to our family and our people. Remember what we learned about God as our Father? He's Family. He's always with us, through our salvation in Jesus Christ and the indwelling of the Holy Spirit. He stables and steadies us in a world set to rock and shake us. He will work in our lives, untangling and retying knots. When we seek Him, we will find Him. He will change us. Discernment is a fancy Christian word that describes how we know what to do, and what God is communicating to us. Daily time in the word and in prayer is crucial, not just to check it off our to-do list, but to discern His voice.

Every couple of years, the Olympics remind us what it's like to be a citizen of our home countries. We are proud of those associations. I am proud to be an American. I hope you are a proud citizen of the country from which you hail. The Olympics reminds us of the commonality of our nationality, but also of what we have in common as fellow human beings. Stories around the world are different, but we're all in this world together.

Scanning the screen full of athletes from around the world makes me want to run the track so badly, arm and arm with different corners of the world. Maybe I see a little bit of what God promises us in heaven. Diversity. Love. Unity. All Citizens of heaven. All children of the Most High God.

Hebrews 10: 24-25 says, ***"And let us consider how we may spur one another on toward love and good deeds, not giving up meeting together, as some are in the habit of doing, but encouraging one another- and all the more as you see the Day approaching."*** NIV We are God's church. The point of church isn't to check it off of our to do list, or show we have it all together. It's a gas station. We refuel, worship together in the presence of God, and then we go out into the world as the extended love of Jesus Christ on this earth. Citizens of heaven.

Much is developed in our unconscious mind. I still sleep with my bedroom window open a crack. I have to hear the outside noises. They muffle my thoughts. We'll never be fully healed this side of heaven, but we can have sustaining joy through the journey. I hope you are learning more about who you are and who God is. For my fellow HSP people, there is so much more to learn. I will share a lot more of what I have learned in the pages to come, and hope this book inspires you to discover more for yourself, too.

Father,

You are amazing. Thank you for bringing us this far and showing us how much you love us. We can't agape love, but we can love to the full capacity we are able to on this earth. Help us to appreciate the people You created us to be, and extend empathy to those around us. Forgive us for un-forgiveness. On account of ourselves and others. The unknown un-forgiveness, and everything else that is unknowingly lodged in our hearts. Give us the courage to dive head first into the deep end, and let you untangle and re-tie knots. Father, You are good. Thank You for Jesus. Thank You for all You are to us now, and all we have yet to learn, discover and experience. Bless and keep us safe in Your love, today and always.

In Jesus' Name,
Amen.

Chapter 4

SURFACE
UNLOCKING THE GIFT OF HIGH SENSITIVITY

THE SEARCH
Finding the Missing Pieces.

Headphones on and volume up, the twin engines roared as the boat whirred on top of the water. Music allowed my mind to set life's scene to a tune, as a child fighting to process everything around me all at once.

Like rocks tossed for centuries, the soundtrack to my life began to surface. Never any good at finding rare rocks, I started to pick up heart-shaped rocks along the Northern Michigan shoreline. Each heart God brought up from the depths of the deep, cold, blue lake touched mine. Just beneath the shallows, massive rocks laid surrounded by smaller versions of the ones in my pocket. The timing of our great God, and the scenes He sets, lie His omnipotent control and all-encompassing love.

Headphones on, volume up. I didn't understand why, but experiencing life with all five senses at once was often too overwhelming for me. Choosing the track and the volume gave me a sense of control.

Sun Up.

I look for God in the sunrise, and He meets me there. Pink and purple streak the sky and birds sing morning's melody. God's creation fills my lungs. I often run or walk along the shore-line as the sun peaks over the horizon. It's sacred ground for me. My favorite soundtrack. No sunrise is ever the same. Each day, the scene a little different. Every morning, God's equipping Truth is appropriate for the piece of life we are about to walk into.

The lighthouse perched on the pier's end remains through all four seasons of the battering Northern weather. Small in stature, it lights the way for giant ships. It is massive, sturdy, and dependable. Everything I feel I am not, God faithfully reminds me who I am in Him.

One particular dawn, the sun had already brightened the sky and the wind was still calm …as it so often is at sunrise. The great lake began to ripple and arise, and it's expansiveness held my awe. A single photograph, even in panoramic mode, could not capture what my eyes witnessed. To some just a sunrise, but for me, it was a piece of home.

Time with my Father drives me to wake up early and race to Him in His Word long before I lace up my shoes to stride the length of the pier. It's closeness to Him I crave. His voice is my soundtrack, cutting through my thoughts to hug my soul awake. A fresh day feels like a new lease on life.

Out under the expanse, rocks lie on the bottom. What was picked up in yesterday's NorEaster now sits upon the shore. Place purposefully, Our Creator put pieces of His heart in our hands. I collected a multitude of heart-shaped rocks when I needed to be reminded that He saw the season was in. God is thinks of me, goes before me, and leaves a trail for me to find Him, noticing me.

New Views of the Surface.

I pushed myself along the surface of the deep blue water on a stand up paddle-board. Just offshore, the depth had already dropped deceivingly. Enormous pieces of rock seemed like they could scrape my board, but in reality lied many feet below me. For such a great lake to be so calm in that moment meant everything to my tired soul. The quiet, swishing of the water replaced my handcrafted soundtrack. Dunes shot up to the sky on my right, and the water met the horizon on my left. I just kept paddling, a little nervous about how far I'd gone, but not enough to turn and re-enter the noise of the crowded beach on a hot August day.

Wholly submerged in the water, but standing atop it. Something so big, so expansive, so unexplainable. All of creation bows at God's feet. This day, as our conversation continued, I felt He calmed a bit of my chaos. To bring me closer to Him, He will speak my language, *water*. In ways I never expect, He continues to meet me through the water.

The scene He paints for me re-directs the current of my life when the bottom falls out, and I fall short. He celebrates all of the victories with me, big and small. Imagine my loss had I not surfaced from snorkeling to look around, or removed my headphones to let Him quiet my heart. My gift is nothing without His manual for operation. His ways are higher than mine. My high sensitivity is fascinating, but the way He revealed it to me along the journey of my life was nothing short of a miracle. A string of them, actually.

Your life is like that, too. Maybe it's not the water, but there is a thread of consistency running throughout every life, led by His orchestration. It's who He is. *Author. Perfecter. Love.* Romans 1:20 says ***"For since the creation of the world God's invisible qualities- his eternal power and divine nature - have been clearly seen, being understood from what has been made, so that people are without excuse."***

God's creation mirrors His heart. All of nature sways and bends in harmonious moments. We capture them in beautiful photographs and paintings. We want to take a piece of it with us, so the heart-shaped rock reminds us of the vast blue lake we held under our longboard for a moment in time. God speaks to us through His creations. Romans 1:20 reminds us He is clearly seen.

If we had no Scriptures to quote, all He made would be enough for us to know Him. His power trumps our ability to decipher what's happening. I can manufacture all the mix tapes my heart can muster for every mood I could ever possibly be in. I can set the soundtrack for scenes I want to imagine, live, or listen to alongside real time passing by. But the all-encompassing power of God trumps my every ability to muffle His presence. He permeates any and all volume I add or method I attempt to block out whatever I am not ready or able to process. As a highly sensitive person, the constant bombardment of more than I can process brings me to my knees. I get lost in His presence. In the water. In the sunrise. In Him. Life any other way is too much for me.

Land-locked.

I often joke about how I never would have left my college town had it not been land-locked. Water reminds me of the Living Water flowing through me. Much like I had to learn about high sensitivity, so too I needed to mature in my faith to understand the powerful influence of water on my life. My connection to it reflects my built-in desire to be close to Him. And I often need to be reminded.

When my neck cranes to see what's around the next bend of shoreline, my forty-year-old sense of balance threatens to knock me into the icy depths. I have to face where I'm headed to regain and maintain my balance. God loves me enough to thwart what threatens to knock me off balance. He will only let me push so far before He allows some real-life pain to remind me why He is the only way. The way, the truth, and the life.

God says I am no longer a slave, and discovering HSP was a freeing moment I never would have come to had it not been for the time I spent falling off of my longboard and climbing back on to find my balance. It's scary to fall into a piece of water where the bottom is illusive and the sheer shock of the temperature sucks the breath right out of my lungs. It's not a fall I want to repeat. I'll do what I have to do to get stronger and paddle smarter so as not to fall again.

But then, something pretty catches my eye. I strain to look out of curiosity. Before I know it, I'm not facing the direction I'm heading. Simple distractions can plant seeds of derailment. It's important to keep my body aligned with the board and face the direction I'm heading, not cater to the distractions.

Distracted Discoveries.

Highly Sensitive Person is not what I expected my counselor to say. It's not what I went there for. I sought clarity on some relationship fall-out in my life, and how to fix it. I didn't get the answer I wanted. While I could undoubtably always forgive, some godly boundaries were in order, because only God can change hearts. We can't restore, or take responsibility for reconciliation, and I was devastated. Gliding across the water on my longboard, I felt the stinging loss of friendship.

Acts 28:14 says, 'There we found some brothers and sisters who invited us to spend a week with them. And so we came to Rome." *NIV*

Brother's and sisters in Christ are essential channel markers in our lives. The reason I sought out Christian counseling was to make sure the guidance I received aligned with the wisdom of God. When we fall off the board, we need a healthy dose of wisdom to grow stronger and balance better. I learned to align the science of high sensitivity to my faith., but God stabilized the board. He gives us courage to hop back on the board after we've fallen hard. Faith focuses in the direction we are headed, though many things will catch our attention and tempt us to look away. Faith plays the soundtrack of Truth over the tune of lies threatening to re-write what God has already written about us.

God placed brothers and sisters in Christ along Paul's path of ministry. He went to some hard places and endured harsh elements and criticism. God knew those voices of encouragement mattered. He knows, if we're to stay on the board, we need to tune into voices aligned with what *He* says about us. Dive into the water, walk away, and remain in the soundtrack He has compiled.

"As water reflects the face, so one's life reflects the heart." *Proverbs 27:19*

I fall off the board sometimes. I lose my balance. I believe the wrong people and make the wrong decisions. The difference in growth comes in the reflection we see when we walk by the water. Do we see justification and bitterness, or do we see healing and restoration? Gliding along the surface that hot August day, I fully embraced the gift of paddle-boarding. I never realized how much gliding on the surface could match the feeling of swimming underwater. In continuing to get back up on the board, I had matured in my faith. The dune touched the sky to my right, and the lake drifted off into the horizon on my left. I stopped to sit down and breathe in every note of God's blessing.

Drifting for a moment, as He held me in a pocket of His creation, healing ushered in restoration. Broken relationships can only be restored to reconciliation when all hearts have been fully saturated by the healing power of Living Water. Making peace with unreconcilable differences is the hardest thing I've ever had to accept. To give the conclusion to God, and just wait. Holding out all hope for a full reconciliation, but not knowing how, when, where, or if it will come this side of heaven.

Keep meeting Him by the water, seeking, pressing in, getting quiet, and listening. Restoration *will* come.

High sensitivity can flip our perspective on who we are, and how we see everyone else. The reason it's important for us to understand HSP, whether we have the trait or not, is to know how to love people well. As Christians, we know our ability to love others comes from Christ. Anything blocking the flow of love in our lives will be flagged to our attention by the Holy Spirit's conviction.

Whether or not HSP people are aware of their gift, it has the potential to cripple them, even cause depression and hopelessness. It can be governor on their potential as people. God doesn't grant gifts to sit idle. He has good plans. And like He surrounded Paul with brothers and sisters in Christ, He surrounds us with community.

HSP or not, life without Christ puts a governor on our potential as people. Walking through the motions of Christianity without an active relationship with Jesus isn't the most productive, either. Under the surface is a power greater than anything we can learn, produce, or understand. Yet so often, whether we believe in Jesus or not, we sit on our potential. We bury it underneath all the voices of disqualification in our lives, instead of getting quiet and coming to Him.

God brings good of all things. All suffering. All injustice. All unfairness. Every mistake. Every ignorant judgement we cast and that which is cast upon us. We can run to Him with our suffering, confusion, and injustice. Keep Getting Up. Keep Looking Up.

"The Lord appeared to us in the past, saying:
'I have loved you with an everlasting love;
I have drawn you with unfailing kindness.
I will build you up again,
and you, Virgin Israel, will be rebuilt.
Again you will take up your timbrels
and go out to dance with the joyful.
Again you will plant vineyards
on the hills of Samaria;
the farmers will plant them
and enjoy their fruit.
There will be a day when watchmen cry out
on the hills of Ephraim,
'Come, let us go up to Zion,
to the Lord our God.'"

Jeremiah 31:3-6 NIV

The hand of Christ reaches down below the surface to yank us out of what we cannot shake. There is a limit to what we can do, fix, and accomplish on our own. That's when faith kicks in. The above verses from Jeremiah reminded the people of what God had told them in the past, and how it still reigned true no matter how disobedient they had been. No matter how short we fall, we are never left shattered and alone.

God reminds Jeremiah's rebellious audience that He has loved them before, throughout, and will continue to love them onward towards their complete restoration. When we can't figure out how to maintain our balance, we can run to Jesus. He is able to pluck us out of the water and onto dry land, no longer drowning and gasping for air, but fully restored and peacefully gliding on the surface of the water like we never dreamt possible.

In Jeremiah 31:3, God reminds us we've been drawn out. Like being plucked out of the water in our flailing, God has continued to love us. Drawn with unfailing kindness means to continue to love. (NIV Study) Psalm 36:10 says, *"Continue your love to those who know you, your righteousness to the upright in heart."* (NIV) *Love* refers to God's covenant love for His people. There's a difference between knowing and understanding. Knowing God's name in the context of *Psalm 36:10* is to understanding more fully who He is. God always remains faithful to His Word. (NIV Study)

We can apply this to our New Testament lives. Jesus is the Word. He is the New Covenant. No longer do we need to wait on restoration. He is readily available and waiting on us to come to Him and accept all He has done and sacrificed for our forgiveness. He sticks His hand under the water because He knows there is nothing we can do to earn what He has gifted us. The cross is our lifeline to the surface. Salvation is the acceptance of our Savior, and belief in who He is. Know Him, see His hand, grab onto it, and hold on for dear life. What He pulls us through will not always be easy. We're promised hard time in this life. The fate Jeremiah's people faced was grim. But they could hold onto what God had told them before. Nothing changes about God's love for *us, nor* negate Jesus' sacrifice for us on the cross. Grab His hand and let Him stand and steady the board. He is not only the balance that allows us to navigate, but the sturdy foundation which separates us from sinking. Jesus is the Longboard.

Jeremiah 31:4 says: 'I will build you up again, and you, Virgin Israel, will be rebuilt."

Calling Israel *Virgin* means God didn't see them as they were in their current state, but as His perfect creation. It also meant restoration. Jeremiah, in Chapter 1:10, says, **"See, today I appoint you over nations and kingdoms to uproot and tear down, to destroy and overthrow, to build and to plant." (NIV)** "The first two pairs of verbs are negative, stressing the fact that Jeremiah is to be primarily a prophet of doom, while the last pair is positive, indicating that he is also to be a prophet of restoration—even if only secondarily. The first verb ("uproot") is the opposite of the last ("plant"), and half of the verbs ("tear down," "destroy," "overthrow") are the opposite of "build." -(NIV Study)

Even though destruction was an inescapable consequence, there would be a hand to grab onto. Not just in the restoration of the line of royalty of King David, but the Messiah would come through his generational line. *Jesus.* Through a line full of real humans and all of their pain, came complete restoration.

A Foundation to Build on.

Build. The word expresses construction. We hate construction zones. We're impatient waiting for things to be built. The complex construction of our souls is safe only in the hands of our Creator. Christ, present at our beginning, is capable of building us into the people we were purposed to be. It's not a destination, but a journey, a process. A re-building we will not always like, embrace, or be patient with during long-suffering.

Building reminds me of my daughter's Lego's. She gets complicated sets for Christmas, and to everyone's amazement has followed hundreds of intricate steps to unveil amazing creations built in the cold days of winter break. It's a product of her tenacity to follow the directions that she's able to build such amazing things.

Her sister doesn't like to build by the directions. Her imagination runs wild, and the hours she spends building result in amazing things, too. But she is often the only one that fully appreciates the full scope of their majesty. The rest of us kind of wish she would follow the directions and put the set together the way it's supposed to be. Why don't we see the beauty in construction?

Both the set put together by following the directions, and the product of my daughter's imagination, carry the same weight of beauty to God. Some of us walk around following directions, and He loves us for that. But He also knows our struggles behind the smiles. The battle we wage mentally to maintain focus and push through towards the end goal. Some of us struggle with directional steps, for whatever reason. Our battles are more visible, and in some ways we wear them on our sleeves.

God knew what He built, and what He's building. He's already established the foundation, and started assembling the pieces. Some days, it helps to think of life as one more page of the instructions to follow. If we get it wrong, we can try again tomorrow. In God's eyes, we are His beloved creation.

Build in Jeremiah 31:4 means *to build and to rebuild* in the original Hebrew it was written in. (Brown) Build and re-build. There is nothing we get wrong that God can't re-write. If Jeremiah's people couldn't outrun the love of the Lord, neither can we. Jeremiah 31:3b says, ***"I have drawn you with unfailing kindness."*** (NIV) Unfailing kindness is goodness, kindness and faithfulness. (Brown) It's the faults and shame we cannot bear or shake that Christ takes on. All that threatens to drown us, He stands victorious over. That's more than just trying to be kind, as we see it. It's taking on all of our lack and sin, and literally killing it with His kindness. When have we ever looked at what someone else has done to us and let kindness cancel it out? We don't. We want fairness, justice, and answers. God doesn't need anything from us. He just wants us.

Timbrels (v4) were played on joyful occasions, often after a military victory. (NIV Study). When I experience a victory in my life, I dance down the pier at sunrise with praise ringing in my ears at maximum volume. God is reminded His people, in Jeremiah 31:1-6, of who He is, and who they are. He's instilled hope in the replanting of their land, and as God's chosen people. ***"Again you will plant vineyards on the hills …" Jeremiah 31:5 NIV***

Plant in the context of this verse is similar to building. It means to plant, as we think of a crop, and that's the visual God is painting. The restoration of their land. But He's also pointing towards something else. The word also means to *fasten, fix, or establish.* We associate *establish* with building. But *fastening and fixing* reminds us of the *re-building.* (Brown) The planting wouldn't reep an immediate harvest. The fruit of a tree could not be eaten until the fifth year after planting it (NIV Study). Normalcy would return, but the planting would be a process.

In our lives, seeds are planted along the way, but the planting doesn't always produce immediate fruit. There's no way to rush life into existence, nor the growth of wisdom. Sometimes, it takes our hearts and souls what seems like centuries to mature into the kind of faith that throws trust to God as a reflex. Why does it take some longer to get there than others? Why do we perceive everyone else's journey to be shorter and easier than our own when life is pressing in hard? When the pain of our consequences, the outcome of a fallen world, or the hurt at the hands of others is bearing down upon us, we just want to turn the page. We don't want to sit and let God put us together, brick by brick. We want to break out of the mold and run away. We want the pain to stop.

Jeremiah's people, I am sure, wanted the suffering they eventually went through to stop. I wonder how they looked back at Jeremiah's directions after the destruction he foretold began. Life flips through faster in heaven than the years on this earth seem to pass. What seems to take us forever to piece together, God is working out for our good.

As Jeremiah continued to deliver the Lord's words of encouragement for the people, a few lines of God's prose pull off the page and peel back a layer of His heart. *"Sing with joy for Jacob; should for the foremost of the nations. Make your praises heard, and say, 'Lord, save your people, the remnant of Israel.'" Jeremiah 31:7 NIV*

Sing with joy. In the face of the unknown, God tells us to sing with joy. Many times in Scripture we're told of the power of worshiping God through trials and suffering. Basically, when we feel least like singing, sing. What is it God knows about singing that we don't? We tend to want to sing when we're in a good mood, but why does it feel so healing for me to fall apart with a wet face and arms up in worship?

I think He knows without the reminder of the joy remaining through the trial, we may never allow Him to pull us through it. *Save* derived from the word *Hosanna,* the praise people sang as Jesus entered Jerusalem on Palm Sunday.

*Sing i*n Jeremiah 31:7 means *overcome.* Overcome with joy. Surface with joy. Kick the bricks off, grab His hand, and let Him steady you. The Longboard. Gliding a top the surface in a way we never thought possible, He will be our Peace. Sing for He has overcome …for us. So that we may have joy. *"They will come with weeping; they will pray as I bring them back." Jeremiah 31:9a NIV*

Weeping Worship.

This is how I felt that day, gliding on the surface of the water, surfaced and steadied by God. This is how I feel, weeping in worship as I trust God with the process of pulling me through and untangling what I've so badly mangled. Prayer is our lifeline. God's people held on through a lifeline of prayer to a God they chose to ignore for so long. When we resist God, and the changes He is working in our lives, we are no different, no better. The second half of this verse reads: *"I will lead them beside streams of water on a level path where they will not stumble, because I am Israel's Father, and Ephraim is my firstborn son." Jeremiah 31:9b NIV*

Beside streams of water. Listen to what the notes say: "Israel is full of streams, but they are not always full of water. Rainfall is generally limited to the months of October through February. For the rest of the year, these 'wadis' (stream beds) are dry, and thus they are often used as walking paths." (NIV Cultural)

When we think we are land-locked and restricted from water, God knows something we don't. He knows when the water will flow, and His timing is perfect. He leads us to places we don't always understand, but we have to trust He knows where the water will be. *Living Water.* In dry situations we have paced back and forth upon, He can spring forth a stream of Living Water. He can restore relationships. He can refresh hearts. Living Water has the ability to penetrate the cracks of our hearts that have dried up the most and been dead the longest. *"They will be like a well-watered garden, and they will sorrow no more." Jeremiah 31:12 b NIV*

"I will turn their mourning into gladness; I will give comfort and joy instead of sorrow." Jeremiah 31:13b NIV Whirring along the surface, atop the flybridge of my parents boat, headphones on and volume up, I watched the world go by to the tune of my own music. We cut through the calm water that morning, on the way back from a

restoring trip to the cove where I could snorkel under the refuge of the water.

Other trips back from the cove were not so enjoyable. The great lake we hung out on can kick up in an instant, because it's so shallow. Those journeys found my feet spread far apart to brace myself as the waves caused us to sway back and forth past the point of comfort. There were no headphones on those days, but I still played a soundtrack.

Prayer.

The seeds planted deep in me of who I was and Whose I was always activate during tumultuous times. Whether it be a stormy day on a kicked up lake, or a tragedy in my life I had to walk out on dry ground, prayer always kicked in. It was reactionary, but not an accident. I had been taught to memorize prayers as a kid in Catholic school. Over time, my instinct to pray led me to drift away from memorized prayers and into the personal spaces in my journal. I practiced praying. I prayed a lot. As a highly sensitive kid, I can look back and say it was a key to my survival. Even more so than the emotional support system I found in my family, prayer kept me from drowning. I believed what I prayed. I believed God listened. I believed I could talk to Jesus like He was sitting next to me on that swaying flybridge. I knew He was there, undoubtably.

Perhaps it was my faith and rich prayer conversation with Christ that allowed me to embrace dangerous situations out on the water without fear. I loved all aspects of the water, even the parts to be feared and prayed into were exhilarating to me, a way to be extremely close to our very big God. Gliding across the water on my Longboard, I felt that same safety. I had forgotten how it felt for a while. Long seasons of suffering will do that to our memories. Cause forgetfulness. Don't forget the power and majesty of Living Water, or the impact a prayerful life has on a soul.

Putting the Pieces Together.

My faith has helped me put together the pieces of my high sensitivity. A rich and ritual prayer life has fed the parts of me that glare the most obvious signs of an HSP person. Have you ever had to prayerfully remind yourself that you're hangry? I'm not a researcher, but breaking things into categories makes things easier for us to understand, doesn't it? High sensitivity was overwhelming for me to discover, and especially in the way I like to line everything up to the truth of God, it is taking me a while to get through everything out there on HSP people. These three categories helped me to understand myself in a simpler way than attempting to apply a whole series of text book studies to my heart all at once.

The three factors of high sensitivity are: (Aron)
1. Aesthetic Sensitivity -
    *   being deeply moved by arts and music
    *   have a rich, complex inner life
    *   being conscientious
    *   Knowing what to do to make people more comfortable in an environment
    *   being aware of subtleties
    *   noticing fine tastes, scents, etc.

2. Low Sensory Threshold
    *   unpleasant sensory experiences
    *   reaction to bright lights and loud noises
    *   avoiding violent media.

3. Ease of Excitation
    *   being easily overwhelmed
    *   being negatively affected by having a lot going on or by being hungry.

Aesthetically, the arts were my basis of survival. My faith in Christ comes out through all I create, and I'm grateful for the deep sense

God has gifted me for it. My inner life is about as complex as it gets, and I'm conscientious to a fault. Life, overall, is a deeply rich experience. Even tastes of foods, which help me understand my own HSP child's picky eating habits. Subtleties are my second language, and although it's a gift to be able to come alongside people, it can be overwhelming.

Low Sensory Threshold. As compassionate as I am, I cannot bring myself to give blood, because it involves voluntarily succumbing myself to needles. If you tickle me, I may slug you hard just out of pure reaction. Weird little things like that. I also get super down during a long string of cloudy Ohio winter days.

Ease of Excitation. When I know where I'm headed, I'm fine. I embrace people. But if I'm out of my comfort zone, I start to squirm. I get angry when I'm hungry like anyone else, except it's ramped up a notch. Same way when I'm dehydrated. When I have a lot going on, yes, completely overwhelmed. I have learned to allow myself busy seasons with a long break to look forward to. That helps me cope without making everyone around me miserable.

All of these things make it seem impossible to picture a thriving suburban child, but that's exactly what I was. Because my family was secure and I had a good childhood, I was able to adopt different strategies (Aron) to feed the extroverted side of me, with enough downtime built in to recharge from the my high sensitivity in those environments. Extroverts can be high sensation seeking, in search of rewarding experiences, people being one of the best sources of the rewards. Having both of these traits "is like driving with one foot on the gas, the other on the brake." (Aron) These genetic traits are evolving! I can testify, as the way I am doesn't always fit into observable categories of behavior, but looking back I can see how I built a way to cope with how sensitive I am.

'Being extroverted or a high sensation seeker and being highly sensitive is a great blend to be. You can be a natural leader, once you learn how to express yourself to non-HSP's, who can find your insights amazing, but also strange or difficult to accept. " *Aron, Elaine N. Ph.D. "Understanding the Highly Sensitive Person; Extraverted HSPs face unique challenges."*

The small Catholic grade school I attended undoubtably fed my highly sensitive soul. It was there Father Abbot Jerome became a mentor to me, uttering three words I still cling to:

"Be a leader."

I took the charge seriously, and intentionally developed leadership skills throughout my childhood and into high school. Not the class president kind of leader. Not the leader of the popular pack at school. This kind of leadership was a product of a life lived in pursuit of Christ. I knew what he meant, even way back then. As a highly sensitive extrovert, I can see problems in other people's plans (Aron) and am not likely to stay silent about it. Personally, the guilt I feel in not saying something is way worse than the reaction when I open my mouth. It's taken a long time walking the path of grace to learn how to wield my words wisely. It's still a journey.

"When you see injustices and hurtful behaviors, like all HSP's, your strong emotional reactions kick in. But you are more likely than other HSPs to find yourself standing on a soap box trying to get others to understand the consequences of their harmful behavior. Then maybe someone says you are overreacting or being an oddball. You may retreat, feeling embarrassed, angry, or just overexposed." *Aron, Elaine N. Ph.D. "Understanding the Highly Sensitive Person; Extraverted HSPs face unique challenges."*

Not knowing what I didn't know caused a lot of my relationships to implode. For the good communicator I am, I assumed too often that everyone else was on the same intuitive page I exist on. Failing to give others the benefit of the doubt, I jumped to a lot of conclusions that probably weren't true. Jumping the gun of injustice, I failed to have compassion for the way everyone else was wired. I simply didn't know. In my mind, I was protecting myself from being taken advantage of, when in reality I was probably roping myself off emotionally because I didn't understand how to control ALL OF THE EMOTIONS.

My two tween daughters can testify to *soap box Meg*. I CANNOT wrap up a point in under thirty-five minutes. They can sense me warming up, and start to get comfortable. It's an "I hate what I do but I can't stop doing it" thing. I always apologize to them for not being able to follow my train of thought faster. It weaves in and out and catches applicable stories and new revelations along the way. I'm only talking because I care. I see something that could hurt the people I love the most, and I want to stop it so badly I will talk in circles until I find something that seems to resonate.

Most of the time I get glazed over eyes. Soon, they will not be so nice as to sit and listen. I get that. I'm trying to get wise with my words. It's such a process.

Thrill Rides.

The summer I returned from my job at the local amusement park, I became a novelty. Somehow, I STRUGGLE with Scripture memorization, but still cannot forget the "Welcome back riders," speech I delivered hundreds of times a day that summer. My friends thought it was hilarious. I would motion for imaginary shoulder harnesses and point to the exit. It was a hit every time.

I loved that summer. All of the noises, lights, and people in one of my favorite places. The local amusement park. For a highly sensitive person, one would think …nightmare and overload. It was, and I had my moments of breaking. Failure to pause and rest is my downfall, so all the work and all the people broke me a few times that summer. But I remember the best parts, like hiding from the supervisors as they walked up to bust me from starting the hokey pokey on the platform full of people waiting to ride. Or the chicken dance. I loved the microphone, you guys. LOVED IT.

Public speaking came naturally to me. I stood on the pulpit to read in church on Sundays, and loved a chance to give a good speech in class. I faced a lot of fears and learned a lot about the trials and errors of independence that summer. My family was nearby, so I got to rest and, yes, even visit the cove and get lost in a book now and then. It was enough to recharge from all the action, and was a summer I'll never forget.

High sensitivity gives me a chance to embrace life in details that are unexplainably overwhelming and emotional, but oh so enriching. I wouldn't trade this 30% of a 20% life for anything …except when it gets impossible and I feel like drowning.

Serotonin is a mood stabilizer, and serotonin transports are the on/off switch for it. HSP's have less serotonin. The actual name of this gene is 5-HTTLPR. (Solo) Genetically lacking a mood stabilizer? That's unfair. HSP people automatically lack the same ability to stabilize moods than the other 80% of the population. Slamming my door off the hinges as a teen seems to make a little more sense, now.

There is a difference in how we process dopamine, the body's reward chemical. (Solo) This is why I get overloaded by group texts. We get the same hit of dopamine from an incoming text or a like on social media that we do when we take a hit or a …*vape.* (eye-roll emoji …because, SRSLY? Are we doing that now?) It triggers something really odd and overwhelming in me, and because I'm an extrovert … I'm drawn to people but need time to withdraw. Group texts are INVASIVE. And social media is a whole different animal full of animals.

"It's likely that HSP's are less driven by external rewards, which is part of what rewards them to hold back and be thoughtful and observant while they process information." Solo, Andre. "This Is

Your Brain on High Sensitivity; These 4 profound brain differences make you a highly sensitive person."

So we're dealing with serotonin and dopamine …but also norepinephrine. It's a neurotransmitter that also helps with the body's stress response, and the variant common to HSPs turns the dial up on emotional vividness. (Solo) "For some less sensitive people, it's easy to tune out other people. But for an HSP, almost everything about the brain is wired around noticing and interpreting others." Solo, Andre. "This Is Your Brain on High Sensitivity; These 4 profound brain differences make you a highly sensitive person."

"How can you not be on facebook …it's AMAZING," I asked my sweet introverted friend. To which she immediately responded,

"Didn't you *invent* facebook?"

It was a spin on an old joke that I couldn't wait to be friends with everyone. (Which wasn't a joke, but a stark reality. And now there's a book called "Friends with Everyone" that I wrote. Real deal.) "If you're a highly sensitive person, it's not an exaggeration to say that your brain is among the most powerful social machines in the known universe." (Solo) Even though we're emotionally overtaxed, HSP people need people to survive. Healthy relationships fill us up!

Overgeneralized Use of the Word, "Sensitive."

High sensitivity and hypersensitivity are two different things. Hypersensitivity is plain old emotional fragility, (Smith) the behavior we walk on eggshells around, not quite sure how our words will be interpreted or taken. It's not what makes up an HSP person, though it's often lumped in with the term to excuse or explain behavior. High sensitivity is a biological predisposition, having little to do with emotional sturdiness.

Elaine N. Aron, Ph.D., has put together an excellent way to describe and determine high sensitivity, through the acronym D.O.E.S. This helps to differentiate HSP people from hypersensitivity. The following are firm genetic sensitivities that make up all highly sensitive people: (Aron)

Depth of Processing:
- Thinking, planning, imagining or in a creative flow without noticing the passing of time.
- Considering all variables or possibilities before going out. (Often remembering what others forgot to bring.)
- Wishing for more time to think about what we need to be prepared.

Over-Stimulation:
- The result of Depth of Processing
- Makes thinking less efficient, which we can sense.
- Wish for even more time to make sure we aren't forgetting anything.

Emotional Responsiveness and Empathy:
- Adds to Depth of Processing and Over Stimulation
- Worry about what might be forgotten
- Slows us down when we sense others need us to speed up.

Sensitivity to Subtleties:
- Sensitivity to subtle stimuli means noticing small things about what we are doing.
- Noticing things that need to be done while we're still involved in completing another task.

No amount of physical preparation or knowledge of my high sensitivity trumps my need for Jesus. I need to linger longer with Him during busy seasons. He's the source of all of my strength …all of my wisdom …all of my abilities. When He is pulling a revelation out of me during a busy season, He is faithful to strengthen and uphold me through it. He understands who I am and what I need. "Some feelings are inevitable, and only time will help. But many times, we must look deeply into our complexes in order to bring our emotions under control or at least tolerate them." (Aron)

My time in prayer and seeking God untangles wrongly tied knots of emotion, and ties healthy knots of stability I can use as footholds to climb up to the surface, completely healed. HSE people (highly sensitive extroverts) make up 30% of the 15-20% of the HSP population, approximately 420 million HSPs, but are often mistakenly lumped in with extroverted introverts, outgoing introverts or contemplative extroverts. (Aron) Dr. Aron has published an article via Psychology Today called *"Introversion, Extroversion and the Highly Sensitive Person."* In this article, she lists truths and misconceptions to help further the understanding of HSE people. "We are contemplative, introspective, kind, gentle, empathetic, creative, visionary, intense and perceptive," she says in the article.

My mind went straight to the surface of the lake, and understood why I saw the deep levels of that experience the way I did. I naturally crave deep experiences and quiet time to recharge. The conversation I start with God each morning rejuvenates and readies me to process all He has for me that day. Gliding atop the water, I have an understanding of my God and who I am in Him that allows me to confidently stand for what I believe as a natural leader, even though I don't like the spotlight. I crave deep and authentic conversations and relationships. "Feeling misunderstood, excluded or invalidated is a recurring theme for the sensitive extrovert as well. The HSE identified as feeling things deeply, being emotional, caring deeply about others and the world at large." (Aron)

Imagine all of the beautiful experiences and layers of empathy and compassion HSE people are able to contribute and detect in the world. Excited to share it and help others, knowing what they know can make a difference in the lives around them. It helps us to love people well, and counsel, teach and lead others to love the people in their lives well!

Life as an HSP or HSE person is as amazing as it is challenging. The threat of isolation due to the downtime we need to process things is dangerous. Balance is key. Staying on the Longboard of stability, facing in the direction I'm headed, helps me love the people in my life well, and inwardly appreciate who I am.

Whether you are an HSP, HSE, or neither, take the time to honor the life you've been given. Respect the lives of others, realizing we are all on a journey to discover who we are in Christ. The scientific knowledge He allows us to discover and learn from helps us solidify our inclinations and categorize our genetic capabilities. On every application, we're asked to provide both our strengths and weaknesses. Search for authentic answers. Be on a quest to be genuine. Write them out proudly and know who you are.

No person is a mistaken creation. Don't confuse mistakes as definitions of character. The wrong we do does not encompass the full scope of who we are. We live in a fallen world full of sin that entangles us. Oh, how I wish we could see each other through the filter of compassion and equality. All celebrating and suffering at the same time. Searching and finding. Learning what love is and how to love and be loved.

We need a Savior, and thanks to our Great God, Jesus is ours. He died for all of us, despite all mistakes. The Longboard we glide across the surface of the expansive great lake on. Paddle-boarding only requires one paddle, but we have to keep switching sides lest we paddle in a circle. Walking with Christ is making the constant adjustment to keep moving in the direction we're headed …straight to His embrace in heaven.

CHAPTER 5

SURFACE
UNLOCKING THE GIFT OF HIGH SENSITIVITY

STIRRED UP
Finding the Surface.

Spring reveals the great lake's true potential, as ice gives way to bright blue hues. Before long, mucky sediment is kicked up by the wind to stir up brown, murky water.

The set of a boat's anchor reveals activity beneath the surface. Sand is often too slick to hold the anchor. Rocks grab hold initially, until the movement of the boat dislodges them. Mucky mud sucks the anchor into deep veins of clay. It can be tough to pierce at first, but once set, it's secure.

When we jump in for a swim expecting a soft sandy landing, our first reaction to squishing and sinking is *not* relief to have found a steady place to anchor. Another word for *muck* is mire, or mud. As a verb it means to make dirty; soil. To sit idle; waste time; loiter. Our souls get kicked up when we're working through something. Conviction and revelation are akin to mud and mire, stirring us up like muck from the lake's bottom. Though the anchor sets perfectly in the muck, our *feet* flounder for balance in it. We pull our feet instinctively back up to avoid sinking in the sliminess.

Submission is the result of obeying a good stirring. When we need to get out of the muck, but can't find our footing, it's difficult to determine the direction of the surface. How can we become clean in dirty water? Why is the process of submission …of surfacing …so hard, dirty, and stirring? Submission is giving up control, trusting we're not going to sink, and allowing God to pull us out of the muck.

Some days, the cove with the clear, soft, Canadian water was subject to a wind-shift that made anchoring and snorkeling less than ideal. On the other side of the point, biting flies abounded. Why one side and not the other, I don't know. I'm sure there is an ecological reason, but we rarely attempted to tolerate them. That side of the cove often sat empty. Small, biting flies chased full grown people away.

Tiny Temptations.

Tiny temptations can chase us away from submission. Think about biting flies for a minute, and how ANNOYING they are. They are too fast to smack, and it's impossible to cover every square inch of our skin in bug repellent.

One particular day, when chased away by the wind and the biting flies, we anchored instead in a Northern cove cut out of a small island. We cruised in, and anchored out deep, due to the rocky chop in the water. A compromise to my snorkel, but still clear blue water, I jumped into the waves with life jacket on, anticipating the relaxing embrace of the lake on a hot summer day.

What happened next is legend in my family. Previous to this anchorage, we'd been trying to spook my little brother with tales of the Lake Erie Monster. Well, we'd apparently done such a good job describing it, that when a patch of seaweed entangled my legs upon entry into the water …witnesses say I might have walked a couple of paces on top of it to get back out!

The tangling of my feet in the seaweed caught me off guard! Some days, we fight nature for the experience we feel entitled to. But no matter what is thrown at us, whether biting flies or a patch of tangly seaweed, God always provides a way out. A way to cope. A path of growth. Maybe not the kind of day we wanted to have, but the ailment to our current struggle. It might not look like the band-aid to fit the wound we can see, but God knows us. He knows we have trouble leaving our comfort zones. He also knows we must be pushed out of them in order to grow. He will allow the water to stir, the flies to bite, and the seaweed to entangle. He allows life to be life, and for us to live it. Not forcefully, but by the waypoints we put down as we learn and grow in life, and in relationship with Him.

Chased off of the big blue lake, but better than sitting idle at the dock, we anchored in the bay at a sandbar. During certain wind shifts and cycles of low tide, a massive bar of sand emerged for all to play on and anchor around. *All.* As in every boat on the bay when it was too windy and rough to venture out the channel to the lake.

Ironically, the sand bar isn't completely sandy. There are patches of muck everywhere, enough to create an overall murkiness to the whole body of water. Even if one is lucky enough to anchor with enough room not to hit another boat, person …it's not good for snorkeling. The sheer number of people compared to the zero number of bathrooms is almost more than I can take, and defiantly eliminates all underwater exploration.

Mire is wet and slimy …deep mud. Miring is plunging and fixing, sticking fast, involving, entangling, and soiling. We often hear the expression to sink in the mire or mud, but it also means to stick. In the dirty, disgusting water, full of muck and mire, we are forced to stick things out.

When sweltering, any refreshing splash of water or gust of cool wind seems acceptable. Though conditions in our lives may not always be ideal, God is ever present. He's not just in the clear, soft, comforting and restoring water. He's in the muck and mire, too, restoring and comforting the places. We often hear God makes good of all things and out of all situations. God can restore through clear or dirty water, situationally.

The dirty water I complain about is still much cleaner than many have access to in the world, not just to cool off but to bathe in, drink and do life with. The muck and the mire makes me appreciate the clean and clear water that typically surrounds and refreshes me. When we are taken out of our comfort zones, change sparks an opportunity for growth. But tiny temptations will attempt to lure us away from walking through hard changes …every time.

"He lifted me out of the slimy pit, out of the mud and mire; he set my feet on a rock and gave me a firm place to stand." Psalm 40:2 NIV

No one lands in the muck and mire deciding it's a great place to stay. The very nature of it doesn't allow anything around it to settle. The only thing that seems to be able to pierce through the muck for traction is an anchor.

To pull something out, as Psalm 40:2 suggests, there has to be a planting ...a setting ... a firm base upon which to stabilize weight in order to pull. It reminds of tug of war with my sorority sisters during Greek Week, and how hard it was to plant our feet in the slippery mud in order to pull the people tugging opposite from us over the dividing line to our side. Winning the tug of war had more to do with planting our feet than pulling the rope.

Christ is our Anchor. He is set, firmly planted, and unmoving. Christ is God's hand reaching down from the surface to pull us out of the muck. He is firmly rooted in Heaven. Seated at the right hand of the One True God. He's unmovable. What He did for us on the cross is not erasable.

The Anchor.

I've been entrenched in the muck. Tried to find footing and been entangled in muck and mire. I didn't feel anything soluble sticking in those seasons, I just felt stuck. But Christ was involved the whole time. In the mire. In the muck. The more I learn to submit to Him, the more stable my feet become.

Conviction and revelation begin a stirring of our reflection. We're turned up-side down and our perspective is shaken like a snow-globe. Jesus flips us upside down. Anchored in Christ, He pulls us through sanctification, a slow but sure changing of our hearts as we begin to reflect His. The kicked up bottom begins to settle. David penned this lifting out of the mire in the Psalms 30:1, *"I will exalt you, Lord, for you lifted me out of the depths and did not let my enemies gloat over me." NIV*

The decision to look up is the choice to allow God to lift us from the depths. There's a miring in removing us from the muck. The process isn't something we see clearly while we're going through it, just like we can't see through the murky water when the muck underneath is kicked up. But anchored in Christ, He becomes our stability and our ability to push through life. It's His hand, piercing through the surface of the water that pulls us out of the depths.

"The vivid imagery that associates distress with 'the depths'- so expressive of universal human experience - is common in OT poetry." (NIV Study) Depth is linked with silence, darkness, destruction, decay, dust, mire, slime, and mud. Those reading David's prose would have pictured pits dug for water (NIV Quest). A well, a hole dug for water. Going down to the pit meant to die without hope. (Encyclopedia) He intended "pit" to describe calamity, and God rescued David from a desperate, hopeless situation. Christ, Living Water, rescued us eternally from ours. Our hope lies in salvation through Jesus, our Anchor.

Settled and Sanctified.

To *set our feet upon a rock* means to fulfill and establish, arise and maintain. To be proven, validated, fixed, or built. (Brown) *Firm* means to be stable and prepared, directed towards, settled and secure. (Brown) Through Christ, we are firmly established and forever forgiven. We are set firmly and formed into the beautiful creation we are in Christ, not for our glory, but to honor God and make Him known. When we have faith in our Anchor, we grow wiser, closer, and more reflective of Him each day.

"I waited patiently for the Lord;
he turned to me and heard my cry.

He lifted me out of the slimy pit,
out of the mud and mire;
he set my feet on a rock
and gave me a firm place to stand.
He put a new song in my mouth,
a hymn of praise to our God.
Many will see and fear the Lord
and put their trust in him."
Psalm 40:1-3 NIV

The way we react to the miring matters. It's our testimony. If we complain and condemn the wind and the waves for making it less than ideal to anchor in our favorite bay, and fight to find a way to get *our* way, we testify an impatient, restless, and unwise soul. But if we can stop our motion, quiet our thoughts, and embrace the miring, we will then be able to see what God has in store for us. When we praise Him in the miring, "many will see and fear the Lord and put their trust in him." Being set on a rock, tied to the Anchor, allows us patience and perseverance. Paul encourages us to strive for and allow God to develop: *"whatever is true, whatever is noble, whatever is right, whatever is pure, whatever is lovely, whatever is admirable - if anything is excellent or praiseworthy- think about such things."* (Philippians 4:8 NIV)

God was faithful to place brothers and sisters in Christ along Paul's path, wherever he traveled. He does the same for us, placing people purposefully, even in the miring, to remind us Whose we are. They will pray for us, and hold us accountable. When things don't go our way, our natural inclinations are not to patiently wait in the muck for Christ to move. God-placed people remind us to look up when we are tired, and remember His arms are stronger and more capable than our feet.

We praise God through new Light, realizing what a true gift the respite of calm water is. But we aren't clinging to the calm in desperation, afraid of choppy days and mucky bays. We're content, whatever the weather. Christ steadies us, through all kinds of weather …and whatever.

When we decide to look up, we find wisdom to lead us. God is active, alive and bolstering our faith as we throw our gaze upon Him. Choose to follow His voice and repeat His promises. Praise Him in the muck and the mire. Sometimes, He requires our stillness while He works out what is weighing us down. We may need to rest before making difficult decisions. Activate faith before panicking at the sight of cloudy water, or a windy forecast.

"Rescue me from the mire,
do not let me sink;
deliver me from those who hate me,
from the deep waters."
Psalm 69:14 NIV

Conflict with people can feel like trying to find our way out of the muck. It's cloudy water. The bottom gets kicked up. We're living alongside imperfect people. All of us fall short, but so often we hold each other responsible instead of accountable. Sometimes, the people we think will rally around us leave in the middle of the miring. *"But some of them became obstinate; they refused to believe and publicly maligned the Way. So Paul left them. …" Acts 19:9 NIV*

There are unyielding, stubborn, and inflexible hearts hardened to God's Word. The most effective way to reach people with questions about God is to make sure they know God welcomes questions. He's not hiding. He can handle our inquisitiveness. "God wants to be found. he does not will for any to miss Him, and He is so gracious to show up right where we are looking- so He can take us beyond anything we've ever seen." (Moore)

We can answer for our faith by the way we live our lives. Paul shared the Gospel obediently, even to those who were not willing, or ready, to listen. He trusted seeds planted by God, and chose to spend his time around ears ready to listen. Time was ticking for Paul. Time ticks for us. Only God can change hearts. He's ready, willing, and able, but He won't force it upon us. *"God doesn't wait for people to come to Him. he goes to them and desires to intervene right at the point of the need." (Moore)*

Jump in, anyway.

Jumping into the water, the muck split my toes and I sank deep into the bottom. Even with no traction to push up towards the surface, my legs instinctively tried. They split and slid out to the sides, pushing me further down into the water. My eyes popped open, even though my mask and snorkel remained in the hull of the boat. The murky water stung. The watery canopy was dark, brown and murky. I shut my eyes again. Lost under the water, I began to panic. I didn't think the water was that deep! I jumped in to cool off. Missing the clear water of my favorite cove, hopelessness began to set it. I felt lost, alone. Would I drown?! The first gasp of breath was lingering closer to my mouth, which would surely lead to ingesting the mucky water. I felt nauseated.

And then I remembered to choose.

Choosing the Light, I reached up with my arms, believing my faith would pull me to the surface. A hand grabbed mine, and my body broke through the water. I felt the light before I saw it. Treading the water as hard as I could with my legs, I brought my hands up to my eyes and squeezed the muck and mire out of them, opening them back up to the sunny day I had left behind.

The Anchor held the boat in the same spot. I swam over to the platform and pulled myself up onto it. Belly flopping awkwardly, desperate to evacuate the water, I swung my feet around and pressed my back against the stern. My panicked breathing began to cycle with the boat bobbing up and down. From the surface, everything looked as it had before. Only I was privy to what just almost happened. Laughter floated on top of the water and down the sandbar. My toes were evidence to just how far down I had tried to dig with them for traction. I looked towards the sky as tears pushed more of the mire out of my eyes.

"Thank You, Jesus," I whispered.

Jeremiah's people would soon be covered, every crack and crevice, with the miring of God's discipline. But the hope He gave them was the promise of a hand. A Savior, who would pull them back into the Light of God's presence. Restoration would come.

This is what the Lord says:
"Restrain your voice from weeping
and your eyes from tears,
for your work will be rewarded,"
declares the Lord.
"They will return from the land of the enemy."
Jeremiah 31:16 NIV

Work refers to the bearing and raising of children. (NIV Study) I grew up babysitting, and would collect mental notes about how to be an awesome mom. My summers were full of crafts and adventures as I rode my bike to babysit and signed up to be a day camp counselor. When I began my own journey as a mom, it challenged me to grow into the mom of faith and wisdom my daughters needed me to be. They, and I, have a favorite babysitter that brings crafts over and takes them on adventures.

I love how life circles around like this. Soon, my oldest daughter will be old enough to babysit …and EEK ..the excitement I have for her as the circle continues. A line of great mothers, and wonderful babysitters. I'm aware not everyone's story looks like this, and that its seems like a terribly long side trail to start talking about Jeremiah 31:16, but I wanted you to feel my appreciation for children and parenthood, and to stir that up in your soul, too.

The joy of birth and life might have been far from the minds of Jeremiah's listeners as the destruction he foretold loomed down upon them. But the promise of life is powerful. From the moment I saw the word "pregnant" appear on the tiny little test stick, joy took over. Suddenly, there was no pain I wouldn't endure on account of my children.

2 Chronicles 15:7 mirrors Jeremiah 31:16: *"But as for you, be strong and do not give up, for your work will be rewarded." (NIV)* In all this talk about the ancient people of God, we must not lose track of New Testament wisdom. We're told to run the race (Hebrews 12:1-2) and never give up. Jesus has come and we are given eternal hope in Him, but we still need strength to endure life. Parenthood is a good testament to where God's strength begins and ours ends. We can set a good example, live a good life, and tell them all they need to know, but only God can shape the finality of their hearts.

Many would lose their children in the captivity Jeremiah foretold. This section of Scripture reminds them of every parent's worst nightmare. But the unthinkable would turn into joy, once again, with the reestablishment of life after destruction. In the verse before, we witness the weeping of mothers: *"A voice is heard in Ramah, mourning and great weeping, Rachel weeping for her children and refusing to be comforted, because they are no more." Jeremiah 31:15 NIV*

I'm consistently taken aback by child trafficking. It's the closest I can bring my mind to imagine my children stripped from me, never to be seen again. Not to say a final good-bye or know where or if a final resting place has been established in their honor. The agony and evil in this world is flattening. Some things happen to us consequentially, but other things just happen to us because there is evil this fallen world. And they pin us under the water trying to find our footing in the muck. Where is the miring and sanctification in such tragedy?

"They are advised to moderate that sorrow, and to set bounds to it: refrain thy voice from seeking and thy eyes from tears. We are not forbidden to mourn in such a case; allowances are made for natural affection. But we must not suffer our sorrow to run in to an extreme, to hinder our joy in God, or take us off from our guy to him." (Matthew Henry) How do we put a boundary on our sorrow? In the thick of life, when we have incurred the shocking loss of loved ones or our health, jobs or our dignity, how do we pull ourselves out of the muck and mire? We're all for learning from our mistakes and becoming sanctified and closer to Christ, but what about when life's hurt paralyzes us? Sticking our arms up towards the surface, we can throw all of our trust in God. Every last shred of ugly, messy, hurting humanity. He will make good out of all the miring.

"Though we mourn, we must not murmur, nor must we resolve, as Jacob did, to go to the grave mourning. In order to repress inordinate grief, we must consider that there is hope in our end, hope that there will be an end (the trouble will not last always), that it will be a happy and- the end will be peace." Matthew Henry Commentary.

There are moments in life laced so thick with grief we remain under the water for a while. It takes time to restore our hope and heal from the physical and spiritual pain of a trial. It's often in the toughest times of life we receive a crappy weather forecast. When we think, "If I can just get to the cove of cold, clear, water ....if I can just put my mask and snorkel on and swim beneath the surface ...I'll be OK. If I can just get there."

Tragedy Can't Make Choices.

Choosing to look up is hard. We will learn things about ourselves along the way that will tempt us to hide in shame and regret. Some things are too painful to realize, remember, and face long enough to allow healing to take place. Mourning the loss of children brings a deep sorrow to all of us, parents and beyond. Every time a school shooting shocks our world, we all mourn the loss of innocent lives and unfair circumstances. It's hard to find compassion for those responsible for fleshing out the evil propensities in this world.

Compassion becomes a discipline, a reminder, and an act of obedience to trust in what we don't feel like believing, hoping or trusting in.

"'So there is hope for your descendants,'
declares the Lord.
'Your children will return to their own land.'"
Jeremiah 31:17 NIV

For those that have lost children, I'm unable to fully empathize with that realm of pain. I can only say I am sorry, and in my best way, assure us all that through the unimaginable pain in this life, God is there. In the muck …the cloudy water …the mire. *"There is hope concerning children removed by death that they shall return to their own border, to the happy lot assigned them in the resurrection, a lot in the heavenly Canaan, that borer of his sanctuary. We shall see reason to repress our grief for the death of our children that are taken into covenant with God when we consider the hopes we have of their resurrection to the eternal life. They are not lost, but gone before."* Matthew Henry's Commentary.

"There is hope for your future," declares the LORD, "And your children will return to their own territory." Jeremiah 31:7 NAS
The Hebrew word for *hope* in this verse, the number one definition, is *cord*. (Brown) The root word infers a wait, looking for, and expectant hope, but it also means to bind together or collect. The Anchor Line.

Our hope is tied to Christ. When we follow the threads of our heart's desire, it's leads to Him. No matter the pain put on us, the consequence we bring upon ourselves, or life just being life …He is unmoved in the shakiest and murkiest waters. Firmly set on the bottom, anchored and bobbing in the wavies. Reaching down to pierce the surface, and pull us up. Christ is our Living Hope.

Sets of Waves.

Loss is some of the most acute pain we feel on this earth, and trials come in sets of waves. Out on the water, waves often come in sets of three. Stuck in heavy seas, I remember counting them with my dad…

"One …Two …Three …" and then we would collectively breathe, rush around to stable what had been shaken loose by the waves, and brace ourselves for the next set. All of us are born with a sensitivity to the waves of life. This book is purposed to meet you in the middle of yours. Science doesn't have every personality perfectly represented and revealed yet. It's a constant process. Even in looking towards answers to who we are, we need to elevate Christ in us before all knowledge. Our minds are futile, and heavily influenced by our feelings and emotions …for better and worse.

Christ-centered hearts don't suffer pain any less. In fact, we are told to batten down the hatches, because the waves will come in sets. Why? Because He is with us. In our very bones, filling the fibers of our souls that elude answers. He *is* the Why.

Personality tests are everywhere, promising answers about who we are. We want to know which Enneagram number we are and what that means. Then, we want to know what number the people in our lives are, so we can tell them why they are the way they are and why they aren't what we need them to be for us.

I discovered I am an Enneagram #2. The Helper. I then wanted to know if I was an extrovert or an introvert. This particular test said 'neither,' and instead categorized me as an *ambivert*. (That's all the people wedged into the 2/3 of the population that aren't introverts or extroverts.) If we're not careful, we'll start throwing our lives into categories, determining our futures and re-writing our pasts to the tune of them. It can get mucky in the midst of all of those personality tests, but I think it's worth the fight to find out how God has wired us to wield our emotions. It helps us love the people in our lives well, and that's what we're all built to do. Love is paramount. Knowing how we're wired helps us give and receive love. However, it's wise to take all of the test results to a professional for assurance, and wiser still to meet our Maker in prayer for clarification.

Helpers are perceptive, sympathetic, and nonjudgemental; lighthearted but tremendously deep. These are some of the testimonies listed of people who have befriended Helpers. (Wagele) Some of the characteristics listed in "Are You a Helper?" via Psychology Today are:

- People say I am overly emotional
- Watching violence on television and seeing people suffer is unbearable
- I try to be as sensitive and tactful as possible
- Be gentle if you decide to criticize me

These are just a few of the characteristics mentioned, but I pulled them out because they ran right alongside HSP person characteristics. I resonated with the childhood behaviors of a #2, and I had to laugh a little because we call my youngest daughter #2 … and her HSE tendencies mirror a #2 Helper: (Wagele)

- They may get their feelings hurt easily
- They try to be good at school, perhaps by helping the teacher
- They often try to get attention by pleasing or by showing off
- They may be attracted to there children or animals with problems.

- 2's are people people. They think about others a lot and want to be popular.
- They are sensitive to disapproval and criticism.

My personality is adaptable around different people, which becomes stressful when there are many people with richly different personalities in the same room. I find myself switching channels, so to speak, in an effort to empathize with all of them. This is where the HSP person differentiates from just a plain old #2. And where we leave the test results that say ambivert for HSE genetics. Ambiverts actively choose when to come and go from extroverted and introverted situations. HSE people have to transition from one to the other, and undergo a rich immersion in sensitivity to stimuli. (Aron)

HSP's are born seekers. (Aron) Seeking takes time. Down time, and active seeking time. Because of my rich and deep faith in Christ, and the Biblical definition of the word *seeking,* this brought the core of who I am into sharp focus. Maybe it does for you, too.

Being set on a rock - a firm foundation - this has helped me determine the difference between hurt feelings and frustration in being misunderstood or not listened to, filtering stimuli through the solid core of values that uphold my emotions. The coping skills I have developed over time have solidified this firm foundation. (Smith) I like to call it …wisdom. There's no shortcut to it, the work required to acquire it, and the maturity it takes to develop and remain obedient to the wisdom accumulated. This is true of anything in life. For me, Christ sets my firm foundation. No one can move or tear it down. Only I can allow the hurt to crumble me if I forget who I am in Him. "HSP people are no less capable than anyone else of developing emotional resilience and reliable coping skills. The common wisdom that we are pre-disposed to emotional injury simply isn't true. Biology is difficult to change, but skills are easy to add." (Smith)

We can have the most amazing personality traits built into the fabric of who we are, but without unlocking and developing them, we'll never reach their full potential. Evolutionary advantage (Aron) or not, HSP is the same as any trait or talent we are gifted with on this earth. Some people are natural gymnasts, while others can crunch numbers. Different genetic pre-dispositions are like talents. If we treat them with the same respect, they can take us far in our lives and relationships. If Love drives those traits to help us love others, I conclude they are important matters to unearth, acknowledge, and develop.

Re-Discovering.

"Sensitive people (and animals) are able to pick up on more environmental cues, recognize things others don't, and make smart decisions in seemingly new or unusual situations." (Solo) Imagine having a gift that can change the world, but sitting on it. What if the prophet Jeremiah would have sat on the prophetic gift God had given him? Jeremiah 29:14 says, *"You will seek Me and find Me when you seek me with all your heart."* (NIV) Are we seeking God for what we want, or what He wills? (Brown) To seek God we give up what we want to see, in exchange for what God wants to show us. The world's wisdom is fleeting. We want God's wisdom.

"It is certain that being insensitive is an undesirable trait, but does that mean that the opposite, 'being sensitive,' is a desirable one? Apparently, in our Western society we cannot make up our minds: We consider either being insensitive or being sensitive to be unfavorable. Society demands that sensitive people develop thicker skin, and that insensitive people be more considerate." Marwa Azab Ph.D. (Azab)

Ambiverts enjoy a mixture of being with people, and being alone; talking and listening. They are capable of small talk, but don't enjoy much of it. (Riggio) Many HSP people are mistaken for ambiverts, and other combinations of extroversion and introversion. HSP people have genetic predispositions, as opposed to social preferences. Some people simply fall somewhere smack in between extroversion and introversion.

Dr. Aron's research concludes that HSP is not the same as ambiversion. She explains, "Ambiversion implies one can choose to go out, engage in social activities and enjoy themselves without the kind of over stimulation, deep processing, or awareness of subtleties that HSPs encounter." (Aron) She also notes ambiversion does not encompass the characteristics of the D.O.E.S. acronym for HSP people. "There is a sense of transition or turmoil between extroversion and introversion for the HSE." -Aron

Before I discovered my high sensitive extrovert gene, I thought my lack of tolerance for fake-ness was increasing with the onset of age. Many of my friends talk of this experience, of cutting time with fake friends to spend more with genuine and authentic people. I find this to be true about many areas of my life, and I was encouraged to know it's a part being and HSE person. I prefer face to face conversations over text monologues, seeing my friends eyes and hugging them in person. Little snippets of conversation, though, are crucial to keeping me connected to my people during busy seasons and hectic days.

HSE people typically don't care for social media as an outlet for our personal lives, but will share them in conversation with a trusted friend quite easily. (Aron) I have learned to put up safeguards and boundaries on social media. It's not an accurate measurement of my whole life. It's not 100% highlight reel, but I am not going to rant, vent, or pour out my personal sadness on social media. It's just too private, and only authentic friends are trusted with that part of my heart. I unfollow people who vent, rant, and pour out their sadness in a consistent manner on social media. It's not personal. I care about those people, and their vents, rants, and poured out sadness …but the empathetic stimuli absolutely overwhelm me. I keep my posts positive and encouraging, and follow positive and encouraging people.

Follow is a funny term. I don't "follow" any of these people, I follow Jesus. But I do try to love the people in my life well, and some of those people are connected to my life through social media. That can be a good thing, with boundaries, limits, and real life face to face authentic friendships to go along with it.

All of the People.

On a life long quest to be friends with everyone, I've learned that not every friendship is active in every season of life (Friends with Everyone.) HSE people enjoy small talk in the confines of close friendships and authentic conversations. (Aron) Thank you to the friends who have lent compassion and empathy to me while I try to find my way to the surface. You are God-placed angels in my everyday life.

This world can be a repressive place. I've felt the sting of being misunderstood. I'm sure you have, too. Feeling misunderstood is a normal human experience. How could a world full of imperfect people be expected communicate clearly all of the time?

The lesson in discovering sensitivity is to yield to empathy. Try not to look upon others harshly, for we never know the struggle they are enduring. People are walking around wounded, and we're snickering about the ways they are falling a part. The youth of this generation is following our lead, having no mercy for their peers' mistakes or failures.

Every life is a gift. Some of the most misunderstood people were the most creative and change inducing souls the earth has ever seen. The world is hard on everyone. We all hold the ability to be compassionate to others. Why are we waiting to activate it until they are drowning in the mire? Why do we have to know something is wrong with our friends before we pray for them? Why are we only nice to someone after we find out they have cancer? Flippantly, why are we so apt to join the crowd of mockers, meanies, and bullies?

The answer is most likely fear. We are halfway through this journey of unlocking sensitivity. We've learned so much about who we are and how to love each other well. HSP people see through staged kindness.

High sensitivity is an amazing gift. We can love other people enormously well with this gift. Authentically compassionate souls, HSP or not, are direly needed in this world. Spend time in the mire and muck to work out all the kinks and be able to appreciate the joy of the journey. Take care of and love who you are. You be you. You are needed. You are loved. You are purposed.

Congratulations on making it half-way through this journey! In the last half of the book, we will continue to discover deeper levels of high sensitivity, and how it is different from other personality traits. We will also continue to unlock the love of Christ, through the hope Jeremiah delivered to his people amidst devastating news. No matter what we face, we are always forgiven and never loved less. We are the chosen people of God, and the promises recorded in the book of Jeremiah are still alive and active in our lives today.

Father,

You are AMAZING. Deserving of all praise. The glory of your creation reflects Your majesty. The simple return of the birds after a long winter speaks of new life and new hope. God, you promised your people they would return after devastation and destruction, that they would be Your people, and You are their God.

Your intricate care in our everyday lives amazes us. You know our hearts. In the direst and most rebellious of states, You choose to love and encourage us. Discipline for our sin is a consequence You allow as a good Father. Bad things happen to us in this world, and at the hands of other people. Natural disasters and every day tragedies surround and engulf us, Father. Through it all, You are unchanging, sovereign, omnipotent, and just. You are our Defender.

Father, thank You for the murky water and mucky bottom that suck our feet in when we need miring. Thank You for caring enough about us to answer our prayers according to Your great and good will for our lives, not our selfish and shortsighted goals and plans. Father, thank You for being available. When we seek You with all of our hearts, we will find You. Search our hearts, Father, and clear out any shred of sin blocking the line of communication. Wipe the dirty water out of our eyes so we can gaze up and mutter a "thank You" as we surface.

Self-discovery is something You delight in. God, You do not hide. You smile when we discover the intricate ways You've created us. Creator of all, One who stretches minutes and holds hands when we are afraid. Faithful Father, You have journeyed through this life with us, and we are so grateful and thankful. Our hearts overflow with gratitude for Your faithfulness. Thank You for sending Your Son, Jesus, to save us. His hand has broken through the surface of the water many times to pull us up from drowning in the depths of murky water. You make all things new, and meet us in the most personal ways, the way only the Creator of our hearts could.

Jesus, what You mean to us is hard to put into words. You are Life, Love, and our EVERYTHING. Always forgiven, never loved less. That is Your anthem to us, and we sing it out to the world at the HIGHEST VOLUME we can muster. We loft YOU high. We exist to honor You. Holy Spirit, convict our hearts. Stir up the muck and mire. Make our hearts new.

Bless these pages, this prayer, and unlock sensitivity, Jesus. Give us the ability to see it as you intended it to be understood and utilized. Bless every note of research that has poured out of the hearts of those gifted to seek answers. Help us to use every gift for good, to honor You, and bring glory to the Father of Heaven.

In Jesus' Name,
Amen.

CHAPTER 6

SURFACE
UNLOCKING THE GIFT OF HIGH SENSITIVITY

STRENGTHENED
Creating Room to Breathe.

The bubbles flitted and floated instinctively towards the light at the top of the water. Some giant and floppy, while others tinier than a pin-head. They raced to join the rest of the air in the atmosphere. Every breath eventually returns. A peace replaced the breath I released. It turned to bubbles that danced and made their way to the surface.

There are pit stops along the path of sanctification. Beautiful, deep breaths of peace and tranquility. A taste of the full restoration that will never fade once we step onto the front stoop of heaven.

Bubbles let us know something is alive under the surface. Gliding through the clear water, I felt more alive than ever before. My reflection …scarred and aging …appeared more beautiful than I had ever able to see.

My shadow swam along the bottom of the sandy cove, following and then leading. I felt another hand in mine. So vivid was His grip, I could feel wrinkles separate the different sections of His fingers. The realness of His humanity squeezed my hand with His scarred one. A hole right through the middle of His palm hadn't affected the strength of His grip. His scars made Him stronger. *His* scars had defeated death. I floated along with Him near the bottom of the cove, assured a purpose to all the pain.

I caught a glimpse of my daisy tattoo, and felt His fingers wipe the tears from the eyes of my heart. "This, too, will be for good …not evil." The how's and why's were too hard for me to sort through, as I pictured the girl who let go of hope too soon. The squeeze of His hand led me to the surface. Instinctively, my gaze drifted to meet His. A smile full of peace washed over me as I broke through alongside the bubbles …to breathe.

Someone reading this today needs to know He fought for them, won for them, and now calls them His. No one can loosen His grip on their hand. Nothing can loosen His grip on their life.

Hold Hands.

Halfway through this journey seems like the wrong place to surface, but it would be misleading to paint a picture of life with only one hard fought battle or submerging season. Remember the story of my sister jumping into the pool in depths over her head more than once? Why, after the first near death experience, would she try that again? We, too, are sometimes tempted to jump into the deep end again. On days it doesn't seem as deep as it was the last time, or moments we are caught completely off guard. Sometimes we are dragged into the depths and pulled underwater by this world and the imperfect people we live alongside. Other days we jump in expecting to push off the sandy bottom and instead get stuck in the muck. Or, maybe we fall off the longboard and into the icy depths.

We may not feel a strengthening happening when we're gasping for air, but we can be assured of it. In a seemingly never ending season of long suffering, there will be moments we come up for air. There will be pockets of air to breathe. During these moments, we must stay focused, remain grateful, and be sensitive to what God is speaking into our lives. In these moments of respite God prepares and emboldens our hearts. *"He has so much to give us. Yet His greatest riches are those things that are conformable, not comfortable." Beth Moore, "Portraits of Devotion" (Moore)*

Conformable is corresponding in form, nature, or character; similar. Compliant; obedient; submissive. ***Romans 12:2 says, "Do not conform to the pattern of this world, but be transformed by the renewing of your mind. Then you will be able to test and approve what God's will is -his good, pleasing, and perfect will." (NIV)***

Conformity often comes with a negative connotation. We're told it's not good to be a follower, or a copy-cat. When we witness someone trying to fit into a crowd like a square peg to a round hole, it makes us cringe. Let's be honest, when *we* are that square peg trying to fit in a round hole, we make *ourselves* cringe. Yet, we still follow a lot of biting flies down the road to those awkward shaped peg-boards, don't we? Why is it sometimes scary to be ourselves?

We fight change. We want things to settle down so we can set our bearings and implement processes to cope with what's going on around us. God knew us before we were born, before *we* knew us. The right way to embrace change is to seek God's perspective through it all. He gives us the ability to understand the constant shifting and submitting. The more we seek and obey Him, the closer we get to our God-planted purpose.

We are Citizens of Heaven. That's what Paul is pointing us towards in Romans 12:2. Salvation unlocks the gift of sensitivity. Christ is the filter through which we see life to the full, as the Creator intended it to be. A life submitted to Christ shifts in perspective like a rogue wave. He knocks us off our feet, drenching us in wisdom and revelation. Who we are becoming has everything to do with who Created us, and the Savior who watched our lives drawn out in the great plan of God's purpose and Kingdom agenda. When we unlock our sensitivity, whether *highly* sensitive or not, our perspective changes.

What does it mean to be transformed by the renewing of our minds? To allow them to be conformed to Christ. Romans 6:11 says, ***"In the same way, count yourselves dead to sin but alive in God in Christ Jesus." (NIV)*** We can live in a new way, to the extent we embrace by faith our new identity as those united with Christ. (NIV Cultural) Counting ourselves as the righteous children of God, and embracing His truth. Ancient philosophers, and modern society, convinced people to set aside their beliefs and feelings for the truth about reality. God is calling us to the opposite. A life full of answers, even scientific ones. God is not afraid of our questions. We can go to God with any inquisition.

Christ lived life on earth. Some days suck. They do. Life isn't always fair. He gets it. But are we conformable. Are our ears open to listen? In the moments we get to breathe, are we looking up with a peace-ruled smile and heart full of gratitude? Do we expect and feel entitled to a fair shake at life and an explanation to all we want to know, or have we allowed our minds to be transformed ...conformed to the patterns of Christ? Allowing God to reveal who we are in His time? Are we patient enough to wait for Him to reveal the answers we seek? Have we accepted His love?

By faith, we are to live in the light of His truth. "True believers are 'in Christ' because they have died with Christ and have been raised to new life with him." (NIV Study) Comfortable. Content and undisturbed. At ease. More than adequate or sufficient.

"When I felt secure, I said, 'I will never be shaken.'" Psalm 30:6 NIV

This verse seems to speak of the positive nature of being comfortable at first glance, but it's part of a larger picture. Psalm 30 is a public song of praise for the Lord's deliverance, most likely due to illness. (NIV Study) In the NASB translation, the word *prosperity* is substituted for *security. Prosperity*, in Hebrew, means ease, *to be at rest, quiet. To have quiet, to prosper.* (Brown)

Simply, Breathe.

When we are given a moment to breathe this side of heaven, we must be so careful not to get to comfortable. A feeling of rest and ease can come when we are working hard for the Lord, and the resulting joy is so intoxicating we can't believe we get to do it. Quiet moments mustn't be wasted mindlessly. Comfortable moments can be deceiving. My highly sensitive mind knows this more than most.

Quiet is a time to process, observe, and align what I've just come through with where I am and what the next step is. To be easy and at rest is to allow our thoughts to fall down like the tokens in a good game of plinko, applying them and appreciating them in due process. Sometimes, it is helpful to simply revel at what we've witnessed, how far we've come ... and what we've survived.

Little will flatten our ability to make ourselves comfortable in this life more than illness. Even a common cold steals more comforts of daily life than we're willing to part with. We complain, angst, and pray for healing.

The following version of Psalm 30 is a paraphrase, but it captures so beautifully the notes of comfort found only in becoming conformable to Christ. Look for Him in this, and all Old Testament passages. The Living Word pops off of the pages of Scripture and into our daily lives.

"I praise You, Eternal One. You lifted me out of that deep, dark pit and denied my opponents the pleasure of rubbing in their success. Eternal One, my True God, I cried out to You for help; You mended the shattered pieces of my life. You lifted me from the grave with a mighty hand, gave me another chance, and saved me from joining those in that dreadful pit.

Sing, all you who remain faithful! Pour out your hearts to the Eternal with praise and melodies; let grateful music fill the air and bless His name. His wrath, you see, is fleeting, but His grace lasts a lifetime. The deepest pains may linger through the night, but joy greets the soul with the smile of morning.

When things were quiet and life was easy, I said in arrogance, 'Nothing can shake me.'

By Your grace, Eternal,
I thought I was as strong as a mountain;
But when You left my side and hid away,
I crumbled in fear.

O Eternal One, I called out to You;
I pleaded for Your compassion and forgiveness:
'I'm no good to You dead! What benefits come from my rotting
corpse?
My body in the grave will not praise You.
No songs will rise up from the dust of my bones.
From dust comes no proclamation of Your faithfulness.
Hear me, Eternal Lord- please help me,
Eternal One- be merciful!'

You did it: You turned my deepest pains into joyful dancing;
You stripped off my dark clothing
and covered me with joyful light.
You have restored my honor. My heart is ready to explode, erupt in
new songs!
It's impossible to keep quiet!
Eternal One, my God, my Life-Giver, I will thank You forever."

Psalm 30 (VOICE paraphrase.)

A Christ-led life is conformable to His heart. Remaining
conformable is not to rest at ease in moments of comfort, but to
embrace the restoration fueling us for the next round of miring. It's
learning how to grasp Peace and Joy through all seasons. To learn
wisdom and constancy, reigning in our thoughts, and letting them
fall down into the proper categories of God's perspective.

A Memorable Mark.

Clean lake water is clarifying. Sometimes it's stirred up simply
because it's shallow. We need to tread deep water to learn

dependance on God's strength. Dirty water needs to be settled. Sediment is eventually pressed and packed back down to the bottom as the wind calms and the lake sets. The water is clearer in the spring, because the winter ice has spent months chasing the sediment from the surface. Before we drink water it has to be purified. Contaminated water can be deadly.

Distorted thoughts can convince us of a drought of Living Water. We live in a society where young people are increasingly convinced to take the advice of their naysayers, and bow out of this life at their own hands. 436 kids committed suicide in the United States in 2016. It's the second leading cause of death in our country for people age 10 to age 34.(NIH) There's been a troubling rise in suicide in children younger than age 12. (O'Donnell) "We all own a piece of this. It takes a village …some how we failed." Fay (O'Donnell)

We have failed to accept each other. We have failed to love one another well. The evidence is mounting, especially with the younger generation. The more vocal we get about it, the worse it gets. From small towns to big cities, the anthem for un-acceptance and hate is "go kill yourself." And some kids do. And when they do, sometimes the cruelty doesn't end there. Those left to mourn the loss are sometimes encouraged to join them.

Somehow suicide has become the mantra for the misunderstood. The hate is palpable …beginning in elementary school. But we fail to recognize the problem for what it is. I'm reminded of this fresh tragedy everyday when I gaze at the small daisy tattoo.

Every thirteen-year old looks up to the cool high-school kids in their lives. I was no different. While I couldn't bring myself to pop my head above water, she was harnessing the power of it wind-surfing. That's about as brave and beautiful as it gets through a thirteen year old's eyes.

A handful of times in my life, my mom entered my room with a certain look on her face. After the first time, I knew what it was all about before she uttered a word. She would sit on the edge of my bed and hug me while we cried. Death is a hard thing for a kid to understand. That cold January day, that girl left this earth by choice. There wasn't any windsurfing the following summer, and nothing - for any of us -was ever the same. How a life so beautiful and precious couldn't strain to see her worth was beyond me ...until I started to grow up into the world she left behind. It's hard, cruel, and unforgiving. The water is mucky and dirty, and the fight to breathe is very real, many days.

There were many times I stood in my room wondering what my purpose on this earth was. We have to do what we have to do in this life to remind ourselves that the pain won't last forever, and the misunderstanding will eventually melt away.

"If we make it," we vowed to each other, "nothing can hurt that bad."

Five collegiate freshman cross country runners vowed to bravely give the tattoo artist a piece of canvas to paint on if we could make it through our first season. We made it, and we did it. My tattoo represents a kind of pain I came to honor in deep layers. The small daisy reminded me I would survive every race, heartbreak, failure, and tragic loss.

Highly Sensitive People can be more prone to suicide and suicidal thoughts just like they are prone to feel anything ...good or bad ... more deeply. The D from D.O.E.S., Depth of Processing, causes our minds to filter through all of the consequences of depression automatically, wrongly considering ending life on this earth or relieving those we love of the burden we feel we are. HSP people tend to be intellectually gifted, and the level of perfection we expect of ourselves and assume others expect can topple us over into hopelessness.

Different is hard. It's tiring. It seems unfair. HSP people can become "sick of feeling different, 'weird.'" (Aron) They have been so deeply misunderstood for so long, and "easily devastated by criticism from those important to them, who then see them as too touchy, criticizing them even more." (Aron)

But the "D" is probably what saves us. It causes us to pause and process …deeply. It gave my mind time to usher in the windsurfer when I wanted to let go and just go home to that hug in heaven. The water is murky, but we have to hold on to the hope that it will eventually clear. We are living in a world saturated with scientific research to help all those who are marginalized for genetic differences. Knowledge is powerful. But long before we know, we can hope.

Jesus endured the most suffering and unjust pain this side of heaven. There will never be a hurt that cuts deeper than the cross. We are not citizens here. The pull of Home and Him on our hearts makes the world feel foreign, because it is.

Headed Home.

"Spiritually, we all have doubts about our path, but when the doubts win, all meaning can seem lost, and therefore our ultimate support. The mast snaps. The ship sinks." (Aron)

I had witnessed first hand the devastation suicide left behind, but sought clarity on the other side of the mire. Highly sensitive people are wired for hope. This is why HSP isn't just for the 20% of those who carry the gene. Unlocking sensitivity helps us to understand ourselves, and how to help those around us. God has placed us in communities, commanded us to love, and given us family and friends. We can be brave, speak authentically and genuinely, equipped with an empathetic heart capable of coming alongside those who have been placed in our lives …and loving them well.

No matter the level of sensitivity, disability, color, the piece of geography we call home, or the language we speak …we are all people. We were all loved equally by God, and His greatest command is for us to love Him …and each other. Bits of those who have been precious to us settle into a shard of our reflection.

If you or someone you know is having suicidal thoughts or are in a crisis, please contact:
1-800-273 TALK (8255).

All Kinds of Pain.

Sensitivity towards suicide, and an HSP person's ability to fully feel and embrace that emotion in depth of processing without acting upon the finality of it, melted me to tears. HSP people are perhaps the most well equipped to help those suffering from suicidal thoughts. God is our first line of defense when the bottom falls out of our world, or tumbles on top of us. Acts 20:19 says, *"I served the Lord with great humility and with tears and in the midst of severe testing by the plots of my Jewish opponents."* (NIV)

The importance of Paul's tears is two-fold. They represent the urgency of his message (NIV Study), and yielded the appreciation and attention customary to respond when such suffering on another's behalf was mentioned. (NIV Cultural) He did everything to get their attention, and point it towards the Gospel.

"You know that I have not hesitated to preach anything that would be helpful to you but have taught you publicly and from house to house." (Acts 20:20 NIV) Paul felt compassion and empathy for people who did not know what he knew. He was not shy about droning on night and day in the hopes his words and his tears would find a place in the hearts of those he loved in order to move them to Gospel freedom. We have the opportunity to be a life-line of love to someone in danger.

"And now, compelled by the Spirit, I am going to Jerusalem, not knowing what will happen to me there. I only know that in every city the Holy Spirit warns me that prison and hardships are facing me."(Acts 20:22-23 NIV) The Holy Spirit may not be warning us of prison and hardship, but Jesus guarantees trouble in this world. When we feel alone and misunderstood, remember our Savior who suffered the most. If we spend enough time looking around us, paying attention to what's going on in the world, we'll see those suffering alongside us. We are never alone. Not figuratively, literally, or spiritually.

"I consider my life worth nothing to me; my only aim is to finish the race and complete the task the Lord Jesus has given me- the task of testifying to the good news of God's grace." Acts 20:24 NIV

Paul was wise enough to know the purpose of his life didn't revolve around self-seeking answers and achievements. For as much as Paul talked, the goal wasn't to draw attention to himself. Had it all been for himself, I'm pretty sure he might have tapped out at shipwreck followed by deadly snake bite. If not then, surely prison. But he wasn't doing anything for himself, yet to honor God and share the Gospel of Christ. He was so changed by Christ, He let the Living Water charge through his being and throw him upon whatever shore God needed him to preach to. This perspective allowed him to see joy throughout his journey. In the midst of pain and sacrifice …and an ailment he never was healed of …Paul wrote some of the most inspiring literature known to man. But he suffered for it. This is why we need to hold on, in good faithful assurance, that days of clarity will come this side of heaven.

"Now I know that none of you among whom I have gone about preaching the kingdom will ever see me again." Acts 20:25 NIV

This was Paul's last chance to get his point across. He knew this was good-bye. What if we treated every conversation and chance meeting like our chance to make sure the last impression we left on everyone God has placed into our lives is one of hope and love?

"I know that after I leave, savage wolves will come in among you and will not spare the flock. Even from your own number men will arise and distort the truth in order to draw away disciples after them. So be on your guard! Remember that for three years I never stopped warning each of you night and day with tears." Acts 20:29-31NIV

What can be done about all that cannot be undone?

No one purposely chooses death when they have a clear understanding of life. We fight and scrape and claw through this life, and we do the best we can humanly do. Guilt and shame are never from God. Loss is tragic and painful. Humanity has limits, boundaries, and frailties. We are living in a broken world.

WE. ALL. FALL. SHORT. (Romans 3:23)

Paul said there were wolves coming …savage wolves. It's a metaphor for cruel, greedy, rapacious, destructive men. (Thayer) But the origin of the Greek word for *wolves* here is *luke …light.* The savage wolves have whitish hair. Savage can look beautiful.

"Now I commit you to God and to the word of his grace, which can build you up and give you an inheritance amount all those who are sanctified." Acts 20: 32 NIV

Grace is our line of defense against the wolves. Against destruction, and the imploding of our own poor choices. Grant grace to the wolves, for they don't know what they don't know …and that's sad. Have compassion for those who resort to cutting others down, because they are the walking wounded. They may be able to navigate this world, but the world intends on eating them alive. We must pray for our enemies.

"In everything I did, I showed you that by this kind of hard work we must help the weak, remembering the words the Lord Jesus himself said: 'It is more blessed to give than to receive.'" (Acts 20:35 NIV)

We are already equipped to help those around us, just by extending arms of love and words that foster peace. Paul poured his heart out to them for three years. We are to invest in those we love, and genuinely want the best for them. For our enemies, it can be a struggle! But for our loved ones, our children, we do certainly pour out tears …and lengthy monologues …in the hopes enough truth about who they are and who Christ is will sink in to save them from some of the pain and heartbreak of this world. Or, at least cement their hearts in the mold of His love to carry them through it.

HSP people are peppered throughout our world, placed perfectly to make the impact only they are capable of making. In this flawed world, we will be marginalized and misunderstood, because that is simply the way of this world. To convince us we are abnormal and unfitting, undeserving and terminally flawed. Flip it out. Choose to see beautiful people and find the good there. Be the good there. It's not enough to fix anyone, or the world. That's not our job. The purpose of our lives is to love people well enough they can see the One who can heal us, and the world. The One who has conquered death, for good. The One who reaches down, breaks the surface of the water, and pulls us up to breathe.

Jeremiah's message of death, displacement and destruction surely sent some people into a hopeless tailspin …if not from his prophesy I'm sure it all sunk in deeply as the water began to stir and get murky while it became the truth they experienced. Will we be able to breathe again? Who is our defense? *"Restore me, and I will return, because you are the Lord my God." Jeremiah 31:18b NIV*

No matter where we are in the restoration process, God is God. Whether we are still running away, barricaded behind our stubbornness and hardened hearts, or returning in repentance, God's love is God's love. Unlike us, there are no benchmarks or standards to earning or losing God's love. If religion has delivered that message to your inbox, delete it.

"When people fall down, do they not get up?
When someone turns away, do they not return?
Why then have these people turned away?
Why does Jerusalem always turn away?
They cling to deceit;
they refuse to return."
Jeremiah 8:4-5 NIV

None of this changed God's love for them. *Turn away* and *return* mean the same thing in Hebrew. (NIV Study) Love is a verb, not an accolade. Before talk of restoration and return, the beginning of verse 18 reads: ***"I have surely heard Ephraim's moaning; 'You disciplined me like an unruly calf, and I have been disciplined."*** *(Jeremiah 31:18a NIV)*

To understand what it means to be disciplined like an unruly calf, we have to define stubbornness God's way. Hosea 4:16 calls the Israelites stubborn. Nehemiah 9:29 records God's people "stubbornly" turning their backs on God. Zechariah 7:11 says they "refused to pay attention; stubbornly they turned their backs and covered their ears." The same word for stubborn is used in all three of these verses (Brown), and the definition points to rebellion. We don't usually consider stubbornness akin to rebellion, but rather obstinance, like that of a two-year old laying flat on the ground in refusal to follow directions. Nor do we consider the *gravity* of rebellion. God's people choose to turn their backs to Him, out of stubbornness, and rebellion. (NIV) But how did God care for them:

"I led them with cords of human kindness, with ties of love. To them I was like one who lifts a little child to the cheek, and I bent down to feed them." Hosea 11:4 NIV

The moaning of God's people is grieving. (NASB) Grieving has a sound that permeates beyond simple sadness and disappointment. We grieve loss. Spiritually, we grieve loss at the hand of our own stubbornness sometimes. *"Though I often speak against him, I still remember him. Therefore my heart yearns for him; I have great compassion for him." (Jeremiah 31:20b NIV)*

Not all wolves are savages. They are fascinatingly beautiful creatures, both visually and in their behavioral adaptations. How do we know which wolves to turn our backs towards? Jeremiah 31:21a says, *"Set up road signs; put up guideposts. Take note of the highway, the road that you take."* (NIV) *Road-marks* are *signposts, monuments, or markers*. From a conspicuous angle, the root-word in original Hebrew means *to be bright, excel, preeminent, perpetual, enduring.* (Brown) My daisy tattoo is a guidepost. Inside my heart, the truths of Scripture are layered and woven into markers.

Jeremiah 31:21b says, *"Return, Virgin Israel return to your towns."* (NIV) Return. Restoration. When we have a moment to breathe in this life, leave a trail to find the way back. All we have to do is make it back to His hand. The one with the scar, covered with crevices dividing the parts of each finger. The grip that tightens in compassion and understanding. Christ is our guidepost. He is the road back Home. Jesus is the bridge to God. Jeremiah 31:31 says,

"The days are coming," declares the Lord,
"when I will make a new covenant
with the people of Israel
and with the people of Judah." (NIV)

Jesus is the new covenant. The old covenant shed the blood of animals, the new covenant shed the blood of Christ. (NIV Study)

"This is the blood of the covenant, which is poured out for many for the forgiveness of sins." Matthew 26:28 NIV

Moments of clarity *will* come. Christ already defeated death on the cross. Any and all pain on this earth is temporary. Even if not revealed or healed this side of heaven, upon entering the embrace of our Savior, all of this world's drama and trauma will dissipate. When we hold His hand and wholly believe, eternity awaits. There is no pain, no suffering, no sickness, and no death in Heaven, rather a reunited people with their Father and King.

"I will put my law in their minds
and write it on their hearts.
I will be their God,
and they will be my people." -Jeremiah 31:33b NIV

Through the Holy Spirit, the new covenant is written on the hearts of all who believe in Christ. This is how He dwells with us, and how the Spirit is able to take over in interpretation and action when our humanity fails us. Matthew 5:17 says, *"Do not think I have come to abolish the Law of the Prophets; I have not come to abolish them but to fulfill them." (NIV)* At the time of Jeremiah's prophecy, it would be a very long time before the New Covenant, by human standards. But it would, in fact, come. He would, in fact, come.

"No longer will they teach their neighbor,
or say to one another, 'Know the Lord,'
because they will all know me,
from the least of them to the greatest,"
declares the Lord. -Jeremiah 31:34a NIV

Scripture assures us every ear will have a chance to hear the Gospel before Christ's return. Those who have chosen to stay ignorant and barricaded behind rebellion and stubbornness will be weeded out. This isn't just book knowledge, but the experience of God. (NIV Study) Christ-led hearts. Christ-centered lives. Through all the murky days, the miring, and the repression and oppression of this world, a day will come when Jesus returns and we all go home.

"For I will forgive their wickedness
and will remember their sins no more." -Jeremiah 31:34b NIV

Always forgiven. Never loved less. Strengthened until the day we arrive Home, with moments to breathe along the way. We can all feel isolated and alienated, misunderstood and tired of being "weird." It's not easy to understand high sensitivity, let alone try to explain it to others. Don't give up on your gift, whether it's high sensitivity or not. Flip all the negativity and choose to see it for what it is. God's people faced devastation for turning their backs on God. Christ died to set us free, to usher in the New Covenant, which we still live under.

God put the Book of Consolation in a book filled with destruction and sadness to encourage them. We, living in New Testament times, can be assured He goes *OUT OF HIS WAY* to encourage us. *Psalm 34:18 says,"The Lord is close to the brokenhearted and saves those who are crushed in spirit." (NIV)*

God is sensitive. Made in His image, we all have a shred of sensitivity. I believe we unlock the full potential of it when we live a Christ-centered life. It's through His strength we find the capacity to love on days of both clarity *and* cloudiness. It's a different capacity of love.

He knows us. He sees us when we are wrecked and broken, rupturing, or shattered into pieces. (Brown) God is close. *Crushed*, in the original Hebrew, means *dust*, taken down to the place where we started. It also means *contrite* (Brown), the overwhelming guilt and shame we feel, and the sincere remorse and repentance that follow or motivate it. God is sensitive to all of it. He doesn't just see and sit idly by. He SEES us, all the way through, and gets involved in our lives. He's intricately involved in every heartbeat of life on this earth.

A Different Capacity.

HSP people benefit from emotional regulation. It's a skill competently learned over time, and has helped me to process the onslaught of stimuli flooding my life each day. A friend of mine advised me to stay level while my girls went through tween and teen years. She moved her hand like the train of a roller coaster, describing what hormones and life in general do to tweens and teens. I work hard to create to contain everything I notice and observe. Wisdom is ineffective when drowned in too much emotion and too many words.

Emotional regulation is consciously or unconsciously influencing what emotions we have, when we have them, and how we experience or express them. (Aron) Regulating our emotions happens naturally for all of us, to some extent. HSP people just have more to regulate. Especially tricky to handle are the negative ones. Like any healthy habit we hope to instill, there has to be a good note of wisdom backing it. The following five increase the effectiveness of emotional regulation.

1. Accept your feelings.
2. Do not be ashamed of them.
3. Believe that you can cope as well as others do.
4. Trust that your bad feeling will not last long.
5. Assume there's hope.
(Aron)

The world is tough on us, so while HSP people attempt to regulate the larger scope of good and bad emotions, society plays tug of war, causing anxiety and stress. This doesn't necessarily mean HSP people are more susceptible to low-self esteem. We assume, because others feel more it means they are sad more, without leaving room for the other side of the pendulum. "Many HSPs are happy, confident people who have managed to hone their sensitive qualities to their advantage. But there are also HSPs who struggle with how they feel about themselves, not as a result of their high sensitivity, but as a consequence of living in a less than sensitive world." - Deborah Ward, "High Sensitivity, Low Self-Esteem." (Ward)

Mirror neurons in HSP people are part of the scientific stuff helping us to understand how other people feel. They do this by observing the behavior in another person, and then relating back to a time when we behaved the same way. We literally mirror them to figure out what's going on. (Solo) This is why we are able to relate to so many different people on so many different levels.

Funerals are terribly overwhelming for me. The sheer attempt to empathize with all of the emotion in the room is tiring. I almost always revert back to my childhood coping mechanism of laughter. It's so embarrassing, but I do this! I find myself finding a way to smile and laugh …even in the most somber of moments. Inevitably, when the line to hug the family mourning a loss fades to a stop and the service begins, my sorrow has no escape. It's as if I spend so much emotional time processing everyone else's emotion, I'm finally left to process my own when I sit still. It comes like a flood. As if I've absorbed all the sorrow in the room like a sponge.

Ongoing research can help kids who are highly sensitive. If kids don't' know what they don't know, they run the risk of depression. One particular study, "Sensory-Processing Sensitivity Predicts Treatment Response to a School-Based Depression Prevention Program: Evidence of Vantage Sensitivity," noticed a positive difference in 11-12 year old girls. (Aron) Knowing what we know about positive childhood environments allowing highly sensitive kids to embrace and thrive in their gifts, positive parenting matters.

Reminders and Guideposts.

Seeing the bottom of the lake is having a moment to breathe. For a moment, there's no mystery as to what the depths hold, and I can see everything from top to bottom. It's clarity at it's finest. I'm amazed at the depths at which we are able to peer straight through to the bottom.

The great lake I grew up on is temperamental, at best, and shallow most of the way through. A clear day to see straight to the bottom can be elusive. I was lucky enough to find a cove where the view straight to the bottom was prevalent. Clear days were many. Or, maybe I just let them outweigh the murky ones. Clarity has the power to shift our perspective. It allows us to capture Light from different angles, and revisit and replay certain circumstances we've already been through.

It's been a long time since I allowed my heart to fully embrace and revisit the wind-surfer cutting though the cove. I surely realized then it was a profound and marking moment, but I don't think I understood why, or just how much of an impact it had on my young life back then. Four decades later, I can look back with astonishing clarity to see the channel marker it became in my life.

A reminder. A guidepost.

When the people we love are hurting, we'll do almost anything to stop it. We all have marking moments in our lives, moments when we can come up for air, and take stock of all that's happened. Everything we go through has the potential to save a life out of love. God uses everything for something good. Not one life is ever wasted. No hurt aimed in our direction will ever go unnoticed by the God who defends us, and promises to be close to the broken hearted.

Many souls have fought the good fight of faith. Swimming through all of the air bubbles, I feel them surrounding me. Their cheers from heaven make the hairs on my arms stand up. They are rallying for us. Cheering us on. Jesus, Himself, prays for us. Never leaves us. There are brilliantly gifted minds set on this earth to discover new knowledge about the way we are created.

To unlock the gift of sensitivity we need to tap in to who we are. Ask questions of science. Ask questions of God. Wrestle with the curiosities that bug like a biting fly. Get to the bottom of it! Knowledge is powerful, and along the way, we'll not only find out how to love ourselves better, but the people in our lives, too.

Every life serves to honor God. From sunrise to sunset, each day carries a weight and a purpose. Don't waste these minutes this side of heaven. We don't know how many we will have. Remember Paul, and the tears he shed on behalf of those he preached to. Each day could be a "good-bye" day. Send each one out with a bang. Make sure the people in our lives know we love them. Strive to honor the best parts of those who are no longer with us. Make sure we know who we are. And Whose we are.

Everyone is sensitive. We all perceive things through our senses, are affected by what influences us, and respond to other people's feelings. Sensitivity is our ability to react to stimuli, but also the capacity to receive, and tendency to be emotionally affected. Impressions are therefore left upon our intellect. Notions, memories, or beliefs leave marks. Layers of knowledge are pressed down into our minds by way of natural and acquired abilities.

Our minds have a natural pre-set ability to do all of this, but we have to choose to tap into it. Highly sensitive people are not the only ones gifted to notice when others are suffering, or take time to listen and process emotions. We all have the ability to affect change in this world based upon our experiences and perceptions. Hate is a cover up for a lack of confidence. Intolerance puts instability on display. Cruelty to others reflects a massive case of self-doubt. No one is innocent, here. No one can claim the "I'm just not sensitive" card or the "I'm too sensitive" one. We all have a level of sensitivity built into the very core of our humanity. And at the very basic level it allows us to notice when we hurt someone, and acquire the necessary knowledge to prevent the roots of ignorance from growing into massive trees of prejudice. We are not victims, on either side of the sensitive pendulum. We are all created beautifully …wonderfully made. ALL.

Unlock the gift of sensitivity.

"If we love and serve God, our lives will be a great adventure. he'll never take you anywhere He hasn't already prepared for your arrival. Keep trusting Him." Beth Moore, "Portraits of Devotion" (Moore)

Father,

I choose to trust You. I choose to believe You will compose and string together beautiful and good notes out of every painful and unfair melody of life this side of heaven. I pray today, for all of those who have lost someone to suicide. Bring comfort to them, Father. Rush Your love over them like a raging waterfall, and allow it to gurgle and wind through every hurting part of their heart. I pray today for all those who have had, and are having suicidal thoughts. Bless and encourage their hearts, and stir them into action in search of counsel and Christ.

Father, we live in a broken world, with a lot of hurt people walking around …hurting people. Please bind the wounds of those who spread hate around like it's free candy. Let Your voice boom louder than any other in the ears of the victims of bullying and badgering. Highly sensitive people aren't the only ones walking through the world wounded. There are many injustices, prejudices, and intolerances that cause us pain, and You to weep for Your children. You promise us You will defend us and love us unconditionally. Your love is enough to conquer all injustice and heal all wounds. Today, we pray for an end to injustice and hate. Show us how to start a spark of love amidst the people in our lives.

Jesus, thank You for staying with me, always. For holding my hand and praying for me. Thank You for Your sacrifice, and for choosing to fully feel the pain of this earth and death on the cross. You felt it all. When this world hurts more than I can bare, I want to remember to lean on You. I trust You with my life, and live every day of it to honor You. I not only know You, I experience You. Thank You for the gift of high sensitivity. What a wonderful gift, to be able to extend Your love through awareness and empathy.

For every experience I am blessed to feel, I am extremely thankful. It brings me to my knees, to realize the special care You have created me with. In this life, given the gift to notice more, I promise to give all the glory to You. Bless the world, Father. Show me ...show us ... our place in it. How can we help reduce the hate? How can we care for those hurting and alone? Show us these people in our neighborhoods, and around the world. Let our lives symbolize Your love.

I think the water is Your most amazing creation. You teach me so much from its many angles and experiences. Much like the water, the inspiration I find in Your Truth, Your Word, and Your Love, flows out without end. How could I ever learn all there is to know about You in a single lifetime? I will continue to press on, as a scientist faithfully researches. I will never stop seeking you. I will keep the conversation going ... Thank You for this book. If only it is a journey we share together, that's more than enough for me. I love to walk out words with You. Thank You for inspiring me, speaking to me, teaching me, and holding my hand through this journey.

I love You with all of my heart.

In Jesus' Name, Amen.

CHAPTER 7

SURFACE
UNLOCKING THE GIFT OF HIGH SENSITIVITY

STABILIZED
Adopting a Peaceful Perspective.

The river softly lapped boat hulls as my socked feet creaked down the dock in the dark, still dawn. The reeds sang in the slight breeze, as I sunk my tanned feet into a beat up pair of running shoes. The scent of freshly caught fish wafted up my nose, as a live one plunked off the edge of the hollow metal container wall lining the channel.

The sky bloomed into day as I breathed deeply. The gravel crunched under my feet, echoing the familiar rhythm of my stride. The gulls called me crazy as I set off to reach to the sun-risen sky.

Benches scattered the wooden boardwalk alongside the shipping channel, and two C's with an arrow carved through a plank let me know I wasn't the only one who liked to stride past this stretch of fresh water. I stopped to watch the pink morning sky, adorned with the deep fuchsia and scarlet hues sailors take head of. Purple cut through the dark blue of night, dragging it back to bed. Pastel beginnings yielded to orange and yellow as the sun pierced the horizon. The entire scene changed by the second. It's a shame we have to blink. Lamentations 3:22-23 says, *"Because of the Lord's great love we are not consumed, for his compassions never fail. They are new every morning; great is your faithfulness."* (NIV)

Always a Sunrise.

God's compassion as purposeful and personal as the sunrise sky every morning. Psalm 30:5 says, *"For his anger lasts only a moment, but his favor lasts a lifetime; weeping may stay for the night, but rejoicing comes in the morning."* (NIV) Isaiah 54:7 guarantees, *"with deep compassion I will bring you back."* (NIV) Again in Isaiah 33:2: *"Lord, be gracious to us; we long for you. Be our strength every morning, our salvation in time of distress."* (NIV) And in Isaiah 30:18: *"Yet the Lord longs to be gracious to you; therefore he will rise up to show you compassion. For the Lord is a God of justice. Blessed are those who wait for him!"*

The trail God's love and encouragement followed the tracks my tears. Psalm 88:13 says, *"But I cry to you for help, Lord; in the morning my prayer comes before you."* (NIV) God paints His Word onto the canvas of my heart at sunrise. He communicates to each of us in our own personal language of love, lacing the hope of *every* life with His Truth. Psalm 143:8 says, *"Let the morning bring me word of your unfailing love, for I have put my trust in you. Show me the way I should go, for to you I entrust my life." (NIV)*

The morning ..."salvation from the present 'darkness.'" (NIV Study). Entrusting my life to God meant more than being plucked from enemy attack. I raced to the sun-risen sky, each day one step closer to the Light. I have experienced the Living Water in such depth, I fail to find words eloquent enough to describe the experience.

The early morning view refreshed my perspective on life. The long, quiet moments strengthened me as I found stability in the stillness. Every note of nature palpable, sharing a laugh with the ducks. They have no qualms about breaking the tranquil morning silence. Genesis 1:5 says, *"God called the light 'day,' and the darkness 'night.' And there was evening, and there was morning- the first day."* (NIV)

What we call each other matters. Whatever God called something, it became ...including us. He said, "Meg ...you are Meg." And I am who He tells me I am. I'm not you. I'm not them. I'm me. I'm who He says I am. Every morning, I'm still that girl. Though the world may take it's toll on a body and a mind ...we are still His. We grow and change over time into the people He purposed us to be. We don't love our kids when they are officially adults, or when we decide whether or not they've grown up to their potential as human beings in our eyes. We love them immediately and always, as our God loves us. We fall in love with our children the moment we discover they are to be born! No expectations or benchmarks. No standards or scoring system …just love. God feels the same way about me … about you …about all of us.

Jesus didn't just notice the people who had it together, He saw the ones falling a part. The outcasts, diagnosed to die, and ashamed of their mistakes. He never once made them feel undeserving of His love. He saw who they were, not what they had done, what had happened to them or how the world had battered them. We have a mixed up view of religion and a backwards understanding about love and life telling us and others to earn it. There's no earning love. Love is love. Jesus meets us right where we are at, right now …and loves us completely. And He paints the sky at sunrise to bless us … because He can and He's God and He is LOVE.

Clouds make for the best characters at sunrise. On this particular summer trip, I picked up a framed picture of an angel-shaped cloud at sunrise and a book mark to match. Something about that picture resonated so deeply, and I planned to be reminded of it consistently. One sunrise, fresh off of the biggest mistake and heartbreak my life will hopefully ever speak witness to, there she was. Majestically displayed across the dawn sky, reflecting off the water. Isaiah 58:8 says,*"Then your light will break forth like the dawn, and your healing will quickly appear; then your righteousness will go before you, and the glory of the Lord will be your rear guard." (NIV)*

Light is the joy, prosperity and salvation of the Lord. Healing is the promised restoration of His people. He will go before us and guard us. Isaiah's listeners remembered the way He led their ancestors out of Egypt. He will lead *us* out of whatever is enslaving us. The glory of the Lord leads us. The exact text most likely refers to the pillar of cloud and fire in the wilderness by which He led His people out of Egypt. (NIV Study) God's people, in Isaiah's time, had just witnessed destruction. They needed hope. They needed to know God was still who He said He was. The same God that led their ancestors out of Egypt. Amidst great suffering and decades of darkness, we, too, need to be reminded of Hope. Of Christ. Of healing to come.

Isaiah 60:1 says, *"Arise, shine, for your light has come, and the glory of the Lord rises upon you."* (NIV) The sun rises and brings light, day after day. God wakes us daily with the greatest gift …life. For as long as He wills, the sun continues to rise, and light shines through all of the cracks glued, pieced and remolded.

I had leaned into my old coping mechanism to catch the early morning sunrise as the bottom fell out of my life the day my bookmark angel showed up. The little girl in me that God loved laced up her shoes again in the hushed hours of morning, racing to the end of the street for a seat watch God orchestrate the sunrise. Just underneath a branch blocking my full view of the sky …the cloud-shaped angel streamed across a bright salmon-red sky.

God is close, and He is personal.

The shelly sand attached to my shoes always littered the floor of my house. Tiny flat pieces, impossible to sweep or vacuum up. I liked the reminder of the sand …the beach …the end of the street …the sunrise …and the bookmark angel in the clouds.

Breathing was always easier for me along the shoreline at sunrise. As a little girl, I watched the sunrise come up over the valley through the screened blocks of bedroom windows. That view was important to me. I took photographs of it, back when we had to wait until the whole roll was finished to take them to be developed. Without fail, every roll of film held the promise of a sunrise picture or two. Those pictures took me right back to sunrise moments.

My life is littered with them. Before social media, sunrise pictures filled my photo albums and found their place on the wall of my bedroom, and then college dorm room, alongside the goofy faces and memories that reminded me who I was and who I wanted to be.

The morning keeps coming. The freshness of a new day rejuvenates the tired places of my body and clears the dust out of the sleepy corners of my mind. The sunrise pushes me to get up in the morning, and it's taught me to appreciate the protective coat of darkness in the last minutes of night as I relish the anticipation of what I know is to come.

John 4:24 says, ***"God is spirit, and his worshippers must worship in the Spirit and in truth."*** (NIV) True worship isn't a place we go to …but a Spirit and truth. (NIV Cultural) Worship isn't a show, or a Sunday morning church attendance record. Church is important, because we are placed purposefully in a community of believers to accomplish greater kingdom purposes together than we could ever accomplish on our own. But worship is also personal. It's spiritual. I close my eyes when I worship at church because I don't want to notice what everyone else is doing or wearing …I only want to notice God.

Worship is the sunrise, and the language spoken in layers of His wisdom stacked into the core of my soul and embraced with Love. True worship is almost indescribable, because it's so personal. Like trying to capture a single sunrise fully and accurately, or effectively enough to represent all of them. It's simply impossible …too big to fit all of the stirrings, stimuli, feelings, and prayers layered into the levels of the atmosphere in one frame. *"The place of worship is irrelevant, because true worship must be in keeping with God's nature, which is spirit. 'True worshippers' must worship God in the power (enablement) of his Spirit and in accordance with truth … truth is associated with Christ, a fact that has great importance for the proper understanding of Christian worship." (NIV Study)*

Christ made a way for us to connect to God. I'm overjoyed to look back and rediscover what my high sensitivity allowed me to experience and remember. But my faith? Christ? Everything is different through *His* filter. Richer, better, more beautiful. Purposed, planned, and perfectly orchestrated by His sovereign hand.

Some mornings I can just feel a good sunrise brewing and I can't wait to meet Him there. I'm still sneaking around in the morning, trying to keep it all to myself while everyone else sleeps peacefully in the darkness before dawn. The only company I want is God and the sky …and a stretch of water.

There is stability in the sunrise.

"He set the earth on its foundations; it can never be removed."
Psalm 104:5 NIV

God called the sky the sky and it was the sky. He called the land the land and it was the land. He called the water the water and it was the water. Light is light. Darkness is darkness. None of this shifts or changes without His command. And He has commanded it to stand firm. As the sun rises over the horizon, the separation of water and sky, to me, signifies the power of God. When He says it's time, it's time. And the Creator of time can stretch minutes miraculously. What we view as days dragging by are mere heavenly moments.

Since I was old enough to remove myself from the rest of the family in the early morning hours, and especially since I discovered my love of distance running, the sunrise and I have had an unspoken date along the water at sunrise. Highly sensitive people need time to process, and at the shoreline at sunrise I meet my Counselor. I look to the sky, and He meets me there. Our conversations are never audible or the same. Without spoken words, the mainframe of my heart somehow communicates the message it needs to process with my Father, and He shows up to make Himself known to me EVERY. SINGLE. TIME. If I will slow down and stop long enough to breathe, He makes a point to hug me with the morning sky.

Every time it's time to say goodbye to a stretch of shoreline I have grown to love, I shed tears as if parting with a close friend. Long distance relationships are hard to maintain, and although I vow to return to the same spot, I rarely make it back. Transitions aren't easy for me, but exploring and discovering new stretches of shoreline is part of His plan.

Quiet Change.

"And you, my child, will be called a prophet of the Most High; for you will go on before the Lord to prepare the way for him; to give his people the knowledge of salvation through the forgiveness of their sins, because of the tender mercy of our God, by which the rising sun will come to us from the heaven to shine on those living in darkness and in the shadow of death, to guide our feet into the path of peace." Luke 1:78-79 NIV

This, in part, is Zechariah's Song. He lost the ability to speak because he let go of his faith to believe God for the impossible. When his son was born, against the odds of he and his wife's old age, Zechariah's silence ushered in clarity. His voice returned to a tune of prophecy. His son's name was John. John the Baptist.

The sunrise is often the most peacefully quiet time of the day. Many days, the great lake sets down overnight. Morning colors sprinkle its mirrored glass with pastel hues. The stillness reminds me to get quiet. On the days when the North wind roars, I'm reminded of the Dark Decade of days I neglected to quiet my soul.

As a highly sensitive person, there's no way for me to control the way I notice things. But I can allow myself peace and quiet to process it all. These are sunrise moments, and in those moments, I find clarity. All the inner workings and outer stimuli settle in like sediment as my thoughts and prayers drift up into the clouds to meet God in our daily conversations. Over time, I craved more time. And after a while, I didn't need the sunrise by the shore anymore. I just needed Him in the dark hours of dawn. He is the Word. I needed more time with Him in the Word because that is how He communicates to us aside from His creation.

I still love the sunrise. I'm up before it most every day. I love the quiet stillness of everyone else sleeping and the world waking up slowly. I don't have to be as near as I can physically be to the sunrise to know it's coming up. I trust it's there, and I see the pink hue coming through my window as I follow curiosities and revelations through the Bible. I started reading a little devotional paragraph each day before I ran out to catch the sunrise, but after a while one little paragraph wasn't enough. Five minutes wasn't enough. The beauty of each new day starts with the promises of God.

Growing up in the valley, watching the sun come up over the beautiful of changes in elevation, my soul's compass instinctively faced the shore. My family camped together and then boated together. Destinations and discovery were always on the horizon. We didn't participate in a lot of the same activities as other kids did growing up, because we were too busy exploring …having adventures. For a creative kid …it was heaven. I never missed my friends or the activities I didn't participate in. We named our boat after us, *Five Alive.*

Boating, for me, was an outlet to get lost in an adventure. Safely surrounded by my family, I was free to explore ….dream …read … and be at peace. As soon as the winter melted away, I packed a bag before school every Friday I didn't have a track meet, and darted onto the highway after the last bell rang. The hour drive took an eternity, but being the first of the weekenders to the marina was always worth it. I found the independence I craved in the water. By the water. And especially in the morning sunrise.

For a time I survived on that promise, hung on every word of forgiveness, and prayed for restoration.

Rinsed Hull.

"But whoever does not have them is nearsighted and blind, forgetting that they have been cleansed from their past sins." 2 Peter 1:9 NIV

Cleansing can feel like drowning. Some kids like baths …others are convinced we are absolutely drowning them as we pour the water over their heads to rinse the shampoo out. My oldest would instinctively jump up every time the water rolled down over her face. It was just a bucket of water, but to her it felt like a raging waterfall. The process of getting clean takes a good scrubbing. The things that drag us to the dirt, and the messy choices we make, need to be cleaned. When we run from the bucket of water, it's like we have forgotten what it feels like to be clean. We're so dirty we can't smell ourselves, and thought of leaving our comfort zones to get all wet and drippy doesn't seem worth it …because we've forgotten. Or, perhaps we truly understood.

1 John 2:11 says, *"But anyone who hates a brother or sister is in the darkness and walks around in the darkness. They do not know where they are going, because the darkness has blinded them."* (NIV) It's blinded them. It blinds *us*. Darkness is deceptive. We don't *aim* to be dark. Hateful. If we're not daily drowning out the yuck with a good scrubbing, we're living in denial and probably harboring hate …towards ourselves, towards others, and towards God. We all harbor hurts we don't even know about. How can we come completely clean if we're not willing to give all of ourselves over to Christ, who baptizes us with Living Water? Able to seep into every crack where the light shines through and heals all of the hurt, shielding us from the propensity to give in to the hate.

My memories often floods with film capturing my childhood and teen years *(which are now further away than I'd like to admit)*. I like to revisit those memories. In between them and the reappearance of my bookmark angel, I almost drowned. More than once. Being a highly sensitive person, everything that happened to me in the decade in between probably should have killed me, or at least left me for dead. At most, depressed and lost. I shouldn't have survived, and don't deserve forgiveness for a lot of the decisions I made. Not knowing who I was through it all makes it excruciating to watch that reel of memories. It's painful. I would much rather sit by the water and watch the sunrise, reminded of the new life God promises each day.

Paths and Routes.

"The path of the righteous is like the morning sun, shining ever brighter till the full light of day." Proverbs 4:18 NIV

The godly have all the guidance and protection they need, and are able to lead others to righteousness. (NIV Study) But the righteous Word of God requires our participation. The reason I experienced the water with such vivid clarity is a tribute to my high sensitivity, but I can go back and see Christ's hand on my life through the lens of His unfailing love. The foundational bricks of His stability and strength formed in the first two decades of my life pulled me through the third.

Psalm 130:6 says *"I wait for the Lord more than the watchmen wait for the morning, more than the watchmen wait for the morning." (NIV)* The Voice paraphrase of this verse is, "My soul waits for the Lord to break into the world more than the night watchmen expect the break of day, even more than night watchmen expect the break of day." I often wonder if anyone saw my struggle. The sun still rose every morning, but I rarely made it out there to witness it. Days became years since I'd gone out to meet God at sunrise. The Truths buried in my heart began to collect dust on my nightstand. I questioned God. I was mad at God. I defied God. I ran from God...

"When Jesus spoke again to the people, he said, 'I am the light of the world. Whoever follows me will never walk in darkness, but will have the light of life.'" John 8:12 NIV

Something inside of me broke in transition. But Jesus said, *NEVER* walk in darkness. The Son of God was still living in me. In the middle of the night when I woke up terrified, He was there. *THE WHOLE TIME.* At the end of it all I landed at the end of my street, sitting on my favorite stretching rock, gazing at the real life version of the bookmark angel. Stability returned as I focused on the majesty of God more than the mistakes I made, and chose to amplify His voice over all others. As sure as the sun rose a little differently each day, so were the changes God stirred in my heart. I'm a walking miracle in so many ways, protected, healed, provided and cared for as only my Father and Creator could master …and only my Savior could redeem.

"His splendor was like the sunrise; rays flashed from his hand, where his power was hidden." Habakuk 3:4 NIV

The stretching rock wasn't always uncovered by the tide of the sand enough to sit on. That day it was. As the clouds floated across the sky I noticed the bookmark angel. I pushed the volume up on my iPod. I instinctively looked to my right and leaned my head toward His shoulder, slightly smiling through the tears. My hand felt all of the wrinkles where His fingers separated into sections, and despite the gaping hole in the middle of His palm He squeezed mine.

"Jesus Christ is the same yesterday and today and forever." Hebrews 13:8 NIV

Jesus Christ doesn't change. Not with our perception or belief in Him. No trial or change in our lives redefines Who He is. We can get angry. We can run. *He remains.* When we get quiet enough to notice His hand in our lives, we realize He's been holding ours the *WHOLE TIME.*

"Even in darkness light dawns for the upright, for those who are gracious and compassionate and righteous." Psalm 112:4 NIV

The darkness is a metaphor for calamitous times, (NIV Study) like the dark, obscure, secret places (Brown) Jeremiah spoke of. The deep and hidden places. Even there, the sun rises. Christ-led lives find their way to the Light. We see Light in the darkness, and we see it in people going through darkness. There is little bit of Him in all of us. Goodness. Love. Sensitivity. Though it's so dark in this world, Light is there. Under the surface, sensitivity is waiting to be unlocked. For some of us, it will change everything. For others, it's an awareness of the HSPs in our lives, and an opportunity to unlock and develop the little bits of sensitivity we are all born with as children of the One True God.

HSPs have a genetic sensory experience they cannot shut off, and are positioned to help the rest of the world see what it cannot sense. We need each other to illuminate the best versions of ourselves. We often write out the hard parts of our stories because we don't see beauty and growth in our seasons of suffering. Horrible choices and hurts happen. But the sun still rises despite our mistakes, losses, and hurts.

Meet Him there.

Empty Graves

"Very early on the first day of the week, just after sunrise, they were on their way to the tomb …" Mark 16:2 NIV

The empty tomb was discovered in the morning, at dawn …in the light.

"At daybreak, Jesus went out to a solitary place." Luke 4:42a NIV

Maybe I'm not the only one drawn to the quiet of the morning or the canvas of the sunrise. Jesus got up in the morning to find solitude. Maybe the connection I feel when I'm on the edge of the shoreline looking at the sunrise is even deeper than I understand. Christ, too, gazed at the sunrise. He looked into the heavens at the same angle, and undoubtably had conversations with His Father only they truly understood. Our God is so good to us. He leaves much a mystery, but the parts He reveals *BLOW MY MIND*.

In the silence of the morning, can you imagine what Jesus was able to hear? As He stands with me each morning, He is seated at the right hand of God. Knowing another day will bring the threat of darkness and the promise of Light all at the same time. Christ knows the perspective is blurry from where we stand, but He faithfully brings it into clarity bits at a time. I love that He meets me there. Whether I'm standing on the edge of the water watching the sky dance at dawn, or figuratively watching Him paint the canvas of my life with His living and active Word, He is there. In the quiet of the morning and the still before the dawn.

"The people walking in darkness have seen a great light; on those living in the land of deep darkness a light has dawned." Isaiah 9:2 NIV

Jesus is the Light Isaiah prophesied would shine in the darkness. He would be present at the dawn, breaking through the darkness with piercing light. Matthew quotes this verse in his gospel, "the people living in darkness have seen a great light; on those living in the land of the shadow of death a light has dawned." (Matthew 4:16 NIV) They were talking about the Gentiles, important to note because they were not God's chosen people. The Gospel is universal. Jesus didn't just come to be a light to some, but to all.

"And you, my child, will be called a prophet of the Most High; for you will go on before the Lord to prepare the way for him, to give his people the knowledge of salvation through the forgiveness of their sins, because of the tender mercy of our God, by which the rising sun will come to us from heaven to shine on those living in

darkness and in the shadow of death, to guide our feet into the path of peace." Luke 1:76-79 NIV

John the Baptist, about whom this passage begins, came to prepare the way for Jesus, *the rising sun*. That word, in the New American Standard Bible …is *sunrise*. It means a rising of the sun and stars. It refers to the east, the direction of the sun's rising. The word's origin means to cause to rise, to arise, to rise from …be descended from, of the sun moon and stars. (Thayer) Zechariah was talking about more than just a sunrise, but of Christ descending from heaven. The Messiah, the Savior of the world, would rise.

John paved the way by giving people knowledge of salvation and forgiveness of their sins, by baptizing them in water. Being immersed in the water one person, and coming back up new. Born again. Once Christ came, a true baptism of the Spirit would become a reality, and never again would we have to live without the Light.

"Very early in the morning, while it was still dark, Jesus got up, left the house and went off to a solitary place, where he prayed." Mark 1:35 NIV

Jesus got up, wound through what was most likely a crowded house, and made his way down to the …shoreline? *Maybe.* "Most homes were highly packed together; and villages along the Sea of Galilee were often close together. Finding privacy with so many people desiring attending required rising before others did (in that culture, normally at sunrise)." (NIV Cultural)

The Greek word for *place* simply means a portion of space marked off. But if we shine a little light on it …and look a little deeper …we notice it's also a metaphor for opportunity. (Thayer) Jesus made an the effort to get up early in the morning in order to have the opportunity to speak with His Father. He wanted to hear God, in the still quiet space of the dawn before sunrise. He forged a path to watch the sun rise, as the rest of the city awoke and the sun danced off the Sea of Galilee. God is not as far off as we often put Him. He is close, and extremely personal.

No longer underwater.

The sunrise over the water eventually became the permanent replacement to the cove and my snorkel. For HSP people, the adjustment of transitioning is magnified. We'd rather get used to the water one toe at a time verses jumping right in. No matter how prepared we are, life doesn't always transition according to our plans. Regardless, the sun always rises in the East.

Growing up, I found it comforting to face the direction of the water, even if I couldn't see it. Now, I face the Living Water. Which, when I'm having trouble transitioning or just having an overwhelming day, lies off in the horizon to the East …at sunrise. He's always there. He's always in me, but some days I just need more of Him. And He is faithful to meet me there.

I wanted to be friends with everyone, but neglected to be-friend myself. My high sensitivity had hijacked my sense of reality, processing everything whilst empathizing with everyone around me. Not knowing what I didn't know, still immature emotionally and spiritually, I didn't build in time to process or hold myself accountable to read my Bible and pray every day. But though we fail to put our armor on before walking out into battle, God is still our Defender. He will take down to dust what needs to be remolded. Jesus will always grip my hand when I need to surface.

Labels can be leveling, or they can set us free.

Ancient and Timeless Light

"This is what the Lord says, he who appoints the sun to shine by day, who decrees the moon and stars to shine by night, who stirs up the sea so that its waves roar- the Lord Almighty is his name: 'Only

if these decrees vanish from my sight,' declares the Lord, 'will Israel ever cease
being a nation before me.'" -Jeremiah 31:35-36 NIV

Jeremiah pointed people to the light. Genesis 1:16-18 says, "*God made two great lights- the greater light to govern the day and the lesser light to govern the night. He also made the stars. God set them in the vault of the sky to give light on the earth, to govern the day and the night, and to separate the light from darkness. And God saw that it was good.*" (NIV) Why would the Lord instruct Jeremiah to remind the people about the light? They were about to enter a dark time. Their Dark Decade, so to speak, but it would extend long past a decade. Though they would be entrenched in the dark, they were never to forget who God was. Author of the stars and Determiner of the Day.

It is against everything in God's nature to be anything but just and good. This was crucial, and probably why the sun and moon are not named verbatim in this passage (NIV Study). Some worshipped and feared the sun and the moon, but God's creations were not to be worshipped or feared, only God Himself. Recalling the truth of who God is would allow them to survive the depths of despair. Healthy fear of God is a sense of respect and trust in Him for who He is. In the same way God orders creation, He promises His people will always have descendants. They will continue on.

Remembering who God is will always pull us through suffering. He has made a way for us all.

"Only if the heavens above can be measured and the foundations of the earth below be searched out will I reject all the descendants of Israel because of all they have done,"declares the Lord. - Jeremiah 31:37 NIV

As our journey with Jeremiah continues, (Jeremiah 32) God tells him to buy some land. It's land that he has coming to him, except that disaster is about to destroy it. Jeremiah obeyed though he surely didn't understand. It was a reminder of God's promised restoration, like my bookmark angel was to me. The God who goes before us, knows what we will need.

"Ah Sovereign Lord, you have made the heavens and the earth by your great power and outstretched arm. Nothing is too hard for you." Jeremiah 32:17 NIV

The land was meant to point Jeremiah to a hope past even the restoration of it. The picture I bought didn't come full circle until I sat down to feel His hand on my life. The cross is our purchased piece of land. Jesus is our hope.

"Great are your purposes and mighty are your deeds." Jeremiah 32:19b NIV

That's not an easy thing to proclaim in a Dark Decade.

Jeremiah was honest with God in asking *why* regarding the command to purchase the land. *"See how the siege ramps are built to take up the city."* (Jeremiah 32:24a NIV) Siege ramps were to help them bring up battering rams and scale Jerusalem's wall. (NIV Study) *"And though the city will be given into the hands of the Babylonians, you, Sovereign Lord, say to me, 'Buy the field with silver and have the transaction witnessed.'"* (Jeremiah 32:25 NIV)

It's OK to wrestle with God. He can handle our questions, and knows we have a limited understanding of His ways. I think in many of the darkest times of my life, I slid even further away because I didn't understand this concept. I didn't know how to wrestle with God over the reality of my pain. It's much different to know what you believe and live what you believe. Living through darkness is excruciating. We're not even thinking straight because it hurts so bad. It's hard to have the strength to wrestle well, even for the spiritually mature.

The more positive the childhood an HSP has, the more they are able to regulate emotion and have a healthy self- control. My mom doesn't seem to remember me being overly scared or shy, nor a child prone to outbursts. That foundation was like the field Jeremiah bought and the bookmark angel I purchased long before I needed it. Promises of restoration, despite the Dark Decade. But HSP has little to do with emotional sturdiness. It's a biological pre-disposition. (Smith)

"Differential susceptibility is a theory that individuals vary in the degree they are affected by experiences or qualities of the environment they are exposed to. Some individuals are more susceptible to such influences that other- not only by negative ones but also to positive ones." (Mitchell) Instead of choosing to pick and wade through every negative experience in my childhood, I chose long ago to obey God and honor my parents. For reasons I didn't even know back then, it allowed me to focus on the positive. HSP's benefit more from a better childhood. (Aron)

My life hasn't been perfect, but I love God, and the people in my life, too much to dishonor them for being …people. There are many who blame their parents for every dysfunction and problem in their life, and I just simply refuse to. Pray for your enemies, honor your parents. Safety, counseling, and forgiveness are paramount goals in those situations.

"Although high sensitivity is genetic, there's not just a single gene that causes it …remember: your genes alone are only a part of who you are, and every HSP has grown up with different experiences." (Solo)

No matter what we're given, we have the opportunity to unlock the full potential and purpose we were put on the earth with and to accomplish. For HSPs, that's a balance of understanding what about our trait is biological and out of our control, and what we can do to cope and create healthy processes to work with our biology. *"The greatest work of the Highly Sensitive Person (HSP) will be to fall back in love with his sensitivity." (Gujral)* Coming out of a Dark Decade, I had a lot to learn about who God made me to be.

I've been a writer and creative soul my entire life, but forums, networking, and building a social media platform overwhelm me. It wasn't fear, but overstimulation. In her article, "6 Decisions a Highly Sensitive Person MUST Make," Namita Gujral unlocks the key to understanding the difference:

1. Call it overstimulation, not fear.
2. Don't try to "overcome" over stimulation. You'll just add more to it.
3. Let go of your need to be like the non-HSP.
4. Find ways to bring yourself back to your optimal range of stimulation.
5. Introversion helps.
6. Forgive your past by reframing it. (Gujral)

Not so long ago, as I was discovering I was a highly sensitive person, I discovered a letter from my Grams. She passed during the Dark Decade of my life, but holding onto the pieces of paper she wrote on while I read her handwritten words through misty eyes made me feel her right next to me. I have always joked that I am a product of prayer, but she really did pray for me. She taught me how to pray, and she listened to me more than anyone ever listened to me. When I wanted to talk, there was no stopping me. I just talked and talked and it took forever because I had a lot to say about EVERYTHING I noticed. She was a big part of the positive emotional thread that allowed me get through those formative years.

Prayer pushes me to express and process everything. I'm thankful to my Grams for teaching me how to get quiet to talk, where to go when things go wrong, and grateful she saw and embraced me for who I was on such a deep level before any of us had a clue what high sensitivity was. I bet, if we all strain to look back, we will find we've been surrounded by people who have loved us well right alongside those that have failed us or hurt us. Where we decide to stop our focus is key, no matter if we are genetically gifted to notice and be effected by it more or not. Love always wins.

Colossians 1:-9-11 is part of a prayer for knowledge and insight that can only come from God. (VOICE)

"Since the day we got this good news about you, we have not stopped praying for you. We ask:
Father, may they clearly know Your will and achieve the height and depth of spiritual wisdom and understanding. May their lives be a credit to You, Lord; and what's more, may they continue to delight You by doing every good work and growing in the true knowledge that comes from being close to You. Strengthen them with Your infinite power, according to Your glorious might, so that they will have everything they need to hold on and endure hardship patiently and joyfully."

CHAPTER 8

SURFACE
UNLOCKING THE GIFT OF HIGH SENSITIVITY

STANDARDS.
Exchanging Experience for Wisdom.

Stop clinging to the cause of the sinking.

My grip on the tow-line had finally given way, and my body flailed for a moment and then smacked the water. Instead of bobbing to the surface, I was pulled under like a torpedo. The water cleared the air out of my lungs and shot up my nose. My mind went black with panic. Instead of releasing, my skis clung to my feet like an angry vacuum.

Suddenly, everything stopped. My feet were still stuck. Everything was still dark. I couldn't find my bearings, breathe or think clearly enough to find my way through the water. Unsure if I was floating up to the surface, or being dragged beneath it, the stillness enveloped me.

Boats take a minute to stop. They don't have breaks like cars do. All I could do is wait.

Skis are designed to let go of your foot when you fall. Mine didn't.

My parents loved to ski. They, like most parents who wait for their children to be able to do things, were excited I was old enough to try it. The trainer skies were bright yellow, orange and tiger-striped, tied together and hooked to the boat by a yellow ski line. I had gripped the white handle while tucked and bobbing, tips pointed up. Having everything tied together made me feel safe. But it's the very reason why, when my feet didn't pop out of the skis, the boat pulled me under.

It still makes my dad nervous to this day to tell the story. It never became funny to him over time. He was driving the boat that pulled his precious kiddo under. I know my dad's heart pretty well, and can only imagine the terrified look of concern as he watched the water, waiting for me to come back up to the surface.

I hated my life jacket. I understood why I needed it, but it suffocated me. I felt like I was choking and dying and restricted. I made all kinds of excuses why I couldn't wear it, or at the very least needed it to remain unbuckled.

That day, as I bobbed in the water trying to balance and keep my ski tips up, I LOATHED that life jacket. It was creeping into places I don't want to talk about because they made sure *ALL OF THE STRAPS* were fastened nice and tight. It crept up to the bottom of my chin threatening to steal every last bit of room to breathe. I bobbed in misery. Every fiber of my being wanted to be back on the boat, but I also wanted to ski. It looked so freeing and fun.

The boat yanked me right out of what was probably a prayer not to die coupled with the repeated directions of my parents to keep my tips up and sit back a little. My little twiggy arms were not prepared for the tug on ski line that popped me up. The sheer speed was impossible for me to process into the next step of balancing on top of the water, and my twiggy's sent the handle right back up into the air.

Under the water, I clutched my lifejacket as it hugged me through the torpedo of gushing water gurgling around me. And ...then stillness.

Absolute stillness.

I don't remember floating to the surface, but my dad does. I can't remember being pulled back to the boat or getting out of those skis and the water. But I remember being pulled under.

My lifejacket saved my life. The very object of disdain in my life saved it. How many times do we fight the very things that are meant to save us.?

Once all chance of dying had been ruled out, I returned to my natural coping mechanism ... laughter. I somehow found a way to rally and make light of my near-death experience …and, like any good big sister, I turned to my siblings and said, "Your turn to try!"

We tubed a lot after that. I HATED tubing. The only thing fun about clutching to a tube while someone tries to knock you off at high speeds is being the one in the boat belly laughing as the scene unfolds.

The lessons we learn strengthen us, and the skills we get from practicing what we're passionate about make us stronger. When we come through near-drowning experiences, it's never for nothing. There's a lesson to learn, share, and apply. The first thing my dad did when we returned to the dock after "Trainer-ski-geddon" was cut the yellow ski line off with his pocket knife. I vividly remember him detaching all the ways those skis were attached, and putting it all back together in a way that wouldn't drown us.

The Nature and Nurture of Kindness

"She is clothed with strength and dignity, and she laughs without fear of the future. When she speaks, her words are wise, and she gives instructions with kindness." Proverbs 31:25-26 NLT

Kindness. To be kind is to be of good nature or disposition. Titus 3:3 says, *"At one time we too were foolish, disobedient, deceived and enslaved by all kinds of passions and pleasures. WE lived in malice and envy, being hated and hating one another."* (NIV)

Can you imagine someone trying to ski without power? Or without holding onto a line to be pulled? It would look ridiculous. Paint that picture right now. No tow line. No boat. Just skis on our feet. We jump into the water or off the dock, and then what? We're not going anywhere, and we certainly aren't swimming very well with skis on our feet that want to float to the surface of the water. This is the depth of foolishness Titus 3:3 is talking about. This is how silly it looks to "try" to "act" kind without a proper understanding of what it is.

Now, picture this. We are sitting in the water, powerless, the boat bobbing a little ways off. The tow line is in the water, just a few yards away. All we have to do is grab onto it, but for some reason, we are trying to figure out how to get up on skis without help. Humans deceptively assume we can do things on our own power. Please don't try to ski without a boat or holding onto a line. And if you must, please were a lifejacket.

It's a silly analogy, but we are silly to assume complete control over God-planted virtues. Our hearts need to be propelled by the one who Created them. He's right there, ready to rev up the engine at our thumbs up. The tow line is almost within arms' reach. But there we sit, trying to force our own solution. Our own way. And when it doesn't work, non-sensical as it was in the first place, we get mad. We look around at everyone else who, in our distorted view, seems to be able to ski without boats and tow lines, and we become envious because we don't see the line they are holding onto and the boat pulling them. Ephesians 2:1-3 says, *"As for you, you were dead in your transgressions and sins, in which you used to live when you followed the ways of this world and of the ruler of the kingdom of the air, the spirit who is not at work in those who are disobedient. All of us also lived among them at one time, gratifying the cravings of our flesh and following its desires and thoughts. Like the rest, we were by nature deserving of wrath." (NIV)*

Grab the Line

There is evil in this world that custom tailors temptation to deceive us. What looks like a skier zipping across the water without a tow-line is really a blue line blending into the water, or a line attached to their life jacket while they go no-handed. The boat popped behind part of a cove, but for the moment we were looking, it appeared as though the skier was just zipping along the water on their own power. The misunderstandings and misconceptions that occur in our daily lives are often custom tailored temptations to deceive and drag us away. And when that happens, we are sitting dead in the water. Frustrated, blinded, and bobbing aimlessly. The devil wants to isolate us, so we'll feel detached instead of purposefully placed.

"As for you, don't you remember how you used to just exist? ...the prince of the power of the air -oh, how he owned you..." (Taken from Ephesians 2:1-3, The Voice Paraphrase.) He owned us ...creepy. To think we could be so deceived by darkness. That is how we drown under water even though we've tied extra lines to our skis. If we're being towed the wrong, we simply get pulled under and away.

In our frustration, bobbing instead of flying across the water without a line, we grab for one. Though the right one sits just a few yards off, we grab for the first one we can reach and give the thumbs up. Pulled onto our skis, we are still thinking about how frustrating it is to have to compromise and grab a line. By the time we start to appreciate being up on our skis, we realize we're being dragged by the wrong boat. We panic, looking around to realize we've been pulled into an unfamiliar stretch of water. To let go would mean to try swimming in skis ...or popping out of them and swimming to the nearest piece of shoreline. But who was this pulling us? And would they allow us to swim away? And what about the other boats and skiers zipping around the water ...would they see us?

Oh, how he owned you ...

To get away from what is dragging us into a good drowning, we need the perspective to see and grab onto the right Line. That happens with rebirth. Titus 3:4-5a says **"But when the kindness and love of God our Savior appeared, he saved us, not because of righteous things we had done, but because of his mercy."** (NIV) *Kindness* meaning moral goodness, or integrity. (Thayer) Kindness isn't *rooted* in our actions. We treat kindness as a learned ability, or something we do because we think we should. But the fruit of kindness begins in a heart rooted in the right kind of love.

Raise the Right Hand.

In a recent room full of kids, most raised their hands when asked if they are kind people. But the missed connection is clear. The kids who are bullying and picking on others are raising their hands. We've misunderstood kindness to be something fleeting …an add-on adaptable to justify our behavior. Kindness stems from the heart. If we neglect to develop that part of our hearts, nothing our intellect or actions can do will cover up the lack of authenticity.

Benevolence isn't a word we often use. It describes a genuine love of mankind, and concern and kindness towards the people in our lives. It's the source from which we are able to love the people in our lives well. But no one is wearing buttons or making signs that say "Be Benevolent." A benevolent person operates out of the goodness of their hearts. Not for show, and not to gain anything but the fact they have contributed charitably to help others. It's a desire to help others for *their* benefit. Goodwill towards men. Goodwill is to have a friendly disposition. To be cheerful.

Kindness is a virtue built into our character. Paul said in Galatians 5:22-23, *"But the fruit of the Spirit is love, joy, peace, forbearance, kindness, goodness, faithfulness, gentleness and self-control. Against such things there is no law."* (NIV) Kindness is a fruit. From the new life we have in Christ, the Holy Spirit dwells in us. In us, the seeds of all of these virtues are planted. The product of living a Christ-centered life is fruit. We are kind because of who we follow, and Who is in us. We don't want flashy kindness that goes no deeper than what we know we're supposed to do. We want to operate from a place of kindness like a kiwi …it's fuzzy and brown on the outside, but when you cut it open it's beautiful, bright and green …with lots of seeds. We want to be kiwi's. Not flashy and shiny, hard to cut open and sour on the inside, but giving all the glory to God. Not to be noticed by what we do, but effect change because of who we are …and who we're becoming.

When water skiing, if we let go of the line we immediately start to stop. Kindness is the same way. If we let go of Christ, we lose the ability to operate out of genuine kindness. Kindness can flourish in the most messy of people. In fact, messy and imperfect people make good fertile soil for God's fruit to grow.

When we're desperate for Him, white knuckling the tow line, the Holy Spirit takes over to accomplish more than ever we could on our own power. If we truly want to make a change, *we* have to relinquish control. If we genuinely want to move, we have to hold onto the Line and let Him pull us into who we are supposed to be. ***"He saved us through the washing of rebirth and renewal by the Holy Spirit, whom he poured out on us generously through Jesus Christ our Savior, so that, having been justified by his grace, we might become heirs having the hope of eternal life."*** (Titus 3:5b-7 NIV)

Nothing we do earns or inaugurates salvation. God's mercy saves us. ***"For it is by grace you have been saved, through faith- and this is not from yourselves, it is the gift of God- not by works, so that no one can boast."*** (Ephesians 2:8-9 NIV) We are a personal pursuit, and our salvation begins the moment we stop trying to ski on our own power and grab onto the Line. It's a personal relationship. A surrender. A choice to grab on and continue to hold our grip to Him throughout life.

In Christ, we are new people. It's because of these virtues, we are brand new. Things we could not genuinely do without Christ, we can now do because His Holy Spirit dwells in us. And why? What's the point? Authentic faith has the power to effect change. To change people. *We* can't change anyone. *We* can't even change *ourselves!* It takes a continuous hold onto the Line! God places people purposefully in our lives, to witness the change. People are naturally drawn to genuine kindness.

God's kindness and love choose to save us. He *is* Kindness. He is Love. He is our Savior.

All-Inclusive Kindness.

"For the grace of God has appeared that offers salvation to all people." Titus 2:11 NIV

God's mercy is all-inclusive. It's not a contest to see who can do salvation the best, or grow the most fruit. He's pulling us all with the same amount of power.

Waterskiing shows amaze me. Probably because I can't master it, so I am fascinated by others' ability to glide across the water at top speed! Professional skiers make it look so easy! Anyone who has skied before knows the soreness that sets in afterwards. Time spent behind the tow-line has made them strong.

Same with our faith. When we first start to ski we are awkward. We don't really know what we are doing, and all of the new muscles we are trying to activate are sore from not being used in that way before. The more time we spend behind the Tow-Line, the stronger we become. To others, it might even seem like we are cutting through the water effortlessly, but we know the struggle behind the strength. Accumulated strength allows us to apply and adhere to God's standards.

The part of the show that most amazed me happens when people are stacked on top of the skiers in formations. Sitting in the right spot, I could look right at the person at the top of the formation on the same level. I remember looking down and calculating just how high up they were, and being absolutely AMAZED.

Tow *LINES*. Multiple lines attached to the same boat! All of the lines received the same amount of strength and speed from the power of the boat. Just pulling up one skier blows my mind to bits …but several …stacked precariously on top of one another?

This is how God pulls us. Christ's sacrifice on the cross was for *ALL* of us and is powerful enough to pull *ALL OF US* at the same time, even if we're precariously stacked together at times until we're strong enough and sure enough to let go of others and grab the Tow-Line for ourselves. There's a handle waiting for every person. Who has a boat powerful enough to pull all of us? God. And who made it possible to connect to the boat? To hold onto the line? Christ. And the muscles we develop to hold on despite all of the factors that beg us to let go and fall down …the Holy Spirit.

Owning ALL OF IT.

When we're pulled in the right direction, we experience Holy Spirit power. Galatians 2:20 says, ***"I have been crucified with the Anointed One- I am no longer alive - but the Anointed is living in me; and whatever life I have left in this failing body I live by the faithfulness of God's Son, the One who loves me and gave His body on the cross for me."*** (VOICE) The ability to do things humans cannot do on their own. Kindness is more than convenience. It's a way of life we choose to walk in, through celebration *and* suffering. The celebration part can easily lead us to arrogance and pride. The suffering to bitterness. Kindness alone isn't enough. It's all the other virtues simultaneously being grown and harvested right alongside it.

Christ-centeredness allows us to pursue the potential good and purpose for our lives. In Him and through Him, we experience life to the fullest, just as He died to give us. (John 10:10) Life to the full looks a lot like a fruitful harvest. Galatians 5:22-23 says, ***"The Holy Spirit produces a different kind of fruit: unconditional love, joy, peace patience, kindheartedness, goodness, faithfulness, gentleness, and self-control. You won't find any law opposed to fruit like this."*** (VOICE)

Living highly sensitive temps me to put a big *"not fair"* chip on my shoulders. It's hard to be different. Just look at the sacrifices people make in their character to keep from rocking the boat or making waves. It's easier for us to wrap our minds around fitting in, but we're fools to think the easy way is the path to a full life. Matthew 3:8 says, ***"Produce fruit in keeping with repentance."*** *(*NIV)

Church Flocks.

The church isn't a building, it's a movement. The world waves a deceptive a banner of acceptance that leaves us feeling lonely and lacking. Christ died to forgive our sins, and free us to live life to the full. When the congregation is released on Sunday, the extending arm of Jesus' love trickles through the community.

Forgiveness fights the good fight of faith. Un-forgiveness is like an ingrown toenail. It affects our stride and causes other injuries while we favor it. It makes us grumpy and irritable because it hurts and it's gross. Meanwhile, life goes on. Our toe doesn't care because it's *A TOE.* And other people will give us bandaids and ibuprofen but they don't want to get close to it because …*IT'S A GROSS TOE.* When we choose to forgive, and leave the rest in God's hands, we avoid walking around with a big ingrown toe-nail. Even if the only reason we can forgive is because Jesus forgave us, it's enough.

Forgiveness is the lifejacket we cling to when we're sinking under the surface. How many times do we fight the very things that are meant to save us? Forgiveness is a floating device.

Not knowing I was a highly sensitive person for the first four decades of my life, I can look back and attest to many life-jacket moments. I grabbed onto the Line long before I knew all of the answers. Everything we go through has the potential to strengthen us. No matter what happens, the mistakes we make, or tragedy that befalls us, we have the opportunity to tell a story that honors our

Creator. Proverbs 31:26 says, *"When she speaks she has something worthwhile to say, and she always says it kindly."* (The Message)

My Grams chose to have something worthwhile to say about her Creator. Her mother died before she was ten years old. Her father, just two years later, jumped into the water off of a boat they were on together and never returned to the surface. During the Great Depression, no one wanted another mouth to feed. She and her siblings were split up. Her brother, a pilot in the Air-force, died of a heart attack before he saw his fortieth birthday. She often showed me his picture as I grew up so that I would know who he was. She and my Grandpa, despite the many challenges of being married for decades upon decades and raising two boys, fulfilled their vow of "till death do us part," but not before my Grandfather suffered a massive stroke that robbed him of the ability to talk. Years after my Grandfather passed so did her sister, and then her oldest son, my uncle, almost died, leaving him without the use of his left side.

Grams was never bitter. If she was angry at God she wrestled with Him privately, maybe silently in prayer. She was always singing a mixture of Sinatra and church hymns, and joyfully went through an old shoe box of pictures telling story after story with a smile. Kindness. She knew the Source, held onto the Line, and survived many life-jacket moments. Grams chose to tell a story that honored God. This is how the church works. The Christ-redeemed stories of our lives, and the kindness and love that fuels us to live on in hope, spreads into our communities like wild-fire.

Dead in the Water.

Remember how we left Jeremiah wrestling with God over buying a piece of land about to be destroyed? It was a sign of hope that Jeremiah couldn't fully wrap his mind around. Think of it like sitting in the water with skis on …no towline, no boat. Jeremiah 32:27 says, *"I am the Lord, the God of all mankind. Is anything too hard for me?"* (NIV)

Wrestling with God is welcomed, but disobedience is dangerous. God is worthy of obedience. He is always faithful in fulfilling his promises. (NIV Study) In the following verses, we are reminded of the grim prophesy Jeremiah delivered. Verse 32 says, *"From the day it was built until now, this city has so aroused my anger and wrath that I must remove it from my sight."* (Jeremiah 32:31 NIV)

The promise of restoration would come through the Messiah. Jeremiah 32:37 says, *"I will surely gather them from all the lands where I banish them in my furious anger and great wrath; I will bring them back to this place and let them live in safety."* (NIV) Even though the people had stubbornly rebelled, God threw out the Towline. The Messiah would come, and make it possible for them to pulled back into God's grace. Jeremiah 32:38 says, *"They will be my people, and I will be their God."* (NIV) Will be. Not maybe. I *will* throw the Line and they *will* grab a hold and I *will* pull them back into grace. He didn't say, I *might* throw a line and then *maybe* will I will pull you back into grace. *The Line has been thrown.* Jesus conquered the cross. The Line is just a few yards away, and the Boat is sitting off in the distance waiting to pull all of us back into His grace.

We all have a chance to grab the Towline, and the expiration date is known only to Him. *"I will give them singleness of heart and action, so that they will always fear me and that all will then go well for them and for their children after them."* (Jeremiah 32:39 NIV) We are fascinated by the stories of addicts who have made a full recovery, and revel at those who have been abused can forgive those that hurt them and walk away free. Change sparks curiosity, and kindness spreads like wildfire.

Jeremiah 32:40 says, *"I will make an everlasting covenant with them: I will never stop doing good to them, and I will inspire them to fear me, so that they will never turn away from me."* (NIV) We all want to be inspired. The dictionary defines it as an animating, quickening, or exalting influence. *Animate* means to give life to; make alive. *Quicken* is to make more rapid; accelerate; hasten. *Exalt* is to raise in rank, honor, power, character, quality; to elevate.

We don't do these things. *We* don't make these changes. We have a *choice* to cooperate with the process. We make wise decisions when we pray about what God has prepared for us, trust who He created us to be, and remember He is not a God of coincidence. *Inspire*, in the original Hebrews, is the word *nathan*. It means to give, put, or set; to be given, bestowed, given up, or be delivered up. It also means to be put upon. (Brown) The NASB translation uses the English word *put* instead of *inspire*. Fear is reverence for God and respect for who He is. We *respect* those we *revere*. Jeremiah 32:41 says, ***"I will rejoice in doing them good and will assuredly plant them in this land with all my heart and soul."*** (NIV)

Direction is Everything.

Life will drag us under the water like a torpedo at times. God will always provide a way to pull us back to the surface. But we have to wear the Lifejacket in order for it to save our lives. *WE* have to grab and hold onto the Towline to be pulled in the right direction. We have a choice. God is sovereign, and Jesus made a way, but He allows us to chose Him.

Jeremiah 33:3 says, ***"Call to me and I will answer you and tell you great and unsearchable things you do not know."*** (NIV) We innately lean in to learn. God teaches in layers of wisdom, and a life of seeking. The longer we hold on, the stronger we get. We're going to fall, sink, and almost drown. Our faith is like our life jacket. Each clip and zip protecting something, guarding, and sealing something. Ephesians 1:13 reminds us, ***"when you believed, you were marked in him with a seal, the promised Holy Spirit,"*** (NIV). And Ephesians 6:13 tells us to ***"put on the full armor of God."*** (NIV) When we believe, we are strong. When we live a Christ-centered life, we put on the armor of God.

The prayers of God's people invite and assure His response. (NIV Study) God doesn't always answer our prayers the way we want Him to, for reasons we sometimes never understand. My HSE daughter was crying this morning, because somehow we got on the topic of things not going to heaven with us. The thought of leaving blankie bear and teddy behind while she went home to be with Jesus was just too much. Her bright blue eyes welled to the top with tears, and her cheeks became red. Pure sorrow filled her heart at the thought of it, and she clutched her most special possessions in all the world tightly.

I took a moment to remember what I know about God, and then I went over and sat beside her to hug her while she cried. I asked her how that made her feel, and told her how much I loved her. "You know, " I responded, "God tells us not to worry, and God is good."

"If God is good and He tells us not to worry, I can't imagine Him separating you from blankie bear and teddy," I continued, "Can you?"

She looked at me intently, searching not for answers, but for compassion and comfort. Far beyond memorizing Scripture and having all the answers is loving people. Having love and kindness sealed in our hearts, so when we give those moments to Him, His love and kindness shine through us.

"Do you know what I think?" I asked her. "We don't always have to understand everything to know God is good."

It's an overwhelming world for her, sometimes. It's an overwhelming world for all of us. A little sense of security goes a long way. All the way, actually, to heaven.

Sometimes, answers to unsearchable things lie in reminders of who God is. The people of Jeremiah's day could not imagine the way in which God would restore them. We cannot comprehend the answers to some of the questions we have for the Lord, but we will be blown away a few times on this earth by the answers He does allow us to find. Jeremiah 33:6-9 says: *"Nevertheless, I will bring health and healing to it; I will heal my people and will let them enjoy abundant peace and security. I will bring Judah and Israel back from captivity and will rebuild them as they were before. I will cleanse them from all the sin they have committed agains me and will forgive all their sins of rebellion against me. Then this city will bring me renown, joy, praise and honor before all the nations on earth that hear of all the good things I do for it; and they will be in awe and will tremble at the abundant prosperity and peace I provide for it."* (NIV)

Discovering Who We Are In Him.

Living four decades without knowing I was highly sensitive is *NOT AT ALL* akin to the suffering God's ancient people were about to witness. It's not comparable to the forty years the Israelites followed Moses through the desert and out of slavery. But realizing who I am after all this time is a relief. Though I've been holding onto the Line for decades, He's given me new life, again. A new discovery. An answer. A hidden thing.

HSPs have *emotional vividness*. "If you seem to feel things more strongly than other people do, it's probably not just in your head. HSP's are finely tuned to pick up emotional cues and react to them." (Solo) A highly sensitive perception notices things the average person does not, resulting in deep conversations. HSPs require a lot of downtime, but we also need to process all we perceive through conversation and creative expression.

Friends that share deep conversations and a rich sense of the purpose of life are much more engaging and fun to be around for HSPs. Though sociability (introversion and extroversion) is different than sensitivity, HSPs often can't handle the overstimulation that being out in a group comes with. My extroversion lets everyone in all at once, and I often fail to recognize the need for boundaries.

The Bible says everything we do flows from our hearts, and so we must guard them! I started to limit access to friends who only called me when something was wrong, and to allow space in my schedule between large get-togethers. HSP's sometimes avoid the overstimulation that can go with social interactions. (Aron). Learning to execute wise boundaries allowed for a healthy balance between my extroversion and high sensitivity. I've really come to love and embrace who I am more than ever! "With practice, all HSPs can learn to use their sensitivity to know just what to say, with just the right finesse to ensure that their voice and perceptions will be heard." (Aron)

<u>Walking Free.</u>

Standing in worship one Sunday, my hand in the air and tears streaming down my cheeks, eyes instinctively closed …a cracked moment in the presence of God allowed Him to reach down and comfort my brokenness. "Simply closing your eyes removes 80% of the stimulation to your brain …instant HSP downtime." (Aron) I remember this particular moment in time, because I began to discover my high sensitivity just a few days later.

As we seek God more, He strengthens us. Sitting in silence with Him makes us stronger. Jesus awoke in the morning to spend quiet time in with His Father. When we actively seek Him, we will find Him. He will reveal hidden things.

We are all created to crave God's presence. HSP or not, we are all sensitive to His pull on our lives. The most intimate experience I have with God comes through writing. It's miraculous, the connections He will make and truths He will reveal as I obediently type away. As I diligently dig, research, and work, He meets me there. I find myself praying a lot in those moments. They are sacred and special to me. If no one ever read my books, I would still write them, for the thrill of the personal journey I get to go on with Him.

"Come to me, all you who are weary and burdened, and I will give you rest." Matthew 11:28 (NIV) God knows all about HSP. He's Elohim, my Creator. The world cannot comprehend His ability to react to us, care for us, and love us perfectly. When we are weary and burdened, we can come to Him and rest. He sees us. He hears us. He knows what we need, and faithfully provides for us. I do believe, somedays, to others it appears we are skiing on top of the water without a towline or a boat propelling us …and maybe we are. Maybe those are the freeing moments when He ties the Towline to our Lifejacket and lets us live and exist in a moment of pure freedom in Christ. When we cannot hold on any longer, when our strength fails us, He is our strength. Matthew 11:28-30 says, *"Are you tired? Worn out? Burned out on religion? Come to me. Get away with me and you'll recover your life. I'll show you how to take a real rest. Walk with me and work with me- watch how I do it. Learn the unforced rhythms of grace. I won't lay anything heavy or ill-fitting on you. Keep company with me and you'll learn to live freely and lightly."* (The Message)

Highly sensitive people are often misunderstood. Brilliant and beautiful, they are being written off and shoved aside. Instead of being accepted for their deep and compassionate souls, they are bullied and beaten down. For an HSP, it feels a little like drowning to be ostracized in such a way. Start a ripple of change. We will be known in life for the way we have treated others. Are we loving the people around us well? Do we know how to define …Kind?

Father,
My heart breaks for all those who have been hurt and misunderstood. Not just HSPs, but ALL who have been marginalized and made to feel they are less than who You say they are. The burden is too much for us, Father. Sometimes, we need you to tie the line

onto our lifejacket, so we can throw our hands up in a moment of freedom.

Thank you for the gift of Grace. Father, sometimes in our quest to follow Christ we forget we are just people. High sensitivity is a high maintenance gift. Teach us to carve out time for rest. Remind us it's ok, and restore us in places we are cracking from pressure. You know what happens in our subconscious minds and beyond. Take control, and mold us into the people You purpose us to become this side of heaven. May every soul that brushes up against ours be witness to the Kindness driving our hearts. Help us to love the people in our lives well, with the gifts we have. Help us to see others as equally special, and give us the curiosity and care to help others discover their gifts, too. Help us to encompass Grace, walk with godly confidence, and rest in Your Peace.

Give us the strength to hold on ...to surface.
We pray this promise over our lives, and the lives that brush up against the borders of our hearts, today ...and always.

"Finally, be strong in the Lord and in his mighty power.
Put on the full armor of God, so that you can take your stand against the devil's schemes.

For our struggle is not against flesh and blood, but against the rulers, against the authorities, against the powers of this dark world and against the spiritual forces of evil in the heavenly realms.
Therefore put on the full armor of God, so that when the day of evil comes, you may be able to stand your ground, and after you have done everything, to stand.

Stand firm then, with the belt of truth buckled around your waist, with the breastplate of righteousness in place, and with your feet fitted with the readiness that comes from the gospel of peace.

In addition to all this, take up the shield of faith, with which you can extinguish all the flaming arrows of the evil one.
Take the helmet of salvation and the sword of the Spirit, which is the word of God.

And pray in the Spirit on all occasions with all kinds of prayers and requests.

With this in mind, be alert and always keep on praying for all the Lord's people."
Ephesians 6:10-18 (NIV)

Bless these words of Scripture to our bodies and write them on our hearts. Stir our souls to repentance and change, growth and the search of knowledge. Give us a fire stoked by Your love, and set our lives aflame with the Gospel. Jesus, thank You for dying on the cross, to be our Towline to hold to.

In Jesus' Powerful Name,
Amen.

CHAPTER 9

SURFACE
UNLOCKING THE GIFT OF HIGH SENSITIVITY

SHORE-BOUND
Discovering who we are in Christ.

The shore-line is closer than it seems ...

On a sunny day, sitting at the sweltering dock, I let the misery of a bad nautical forecast wash over me. I craved the clear water of the cove. Trapped, suffocated, and *STUCK AT THE DOCK,* I leveraged every argument and facial expression of disdain against NOAA Weather Radio. Our dock mates decided to risk it, and as they trolled out of the marina, I climbed to our flybridge.

A South wind gusted, infamously kicking up the channel leading out to the lake. I watched our dock mates cut across the bay, and into that channel. Barely able to make out the dot they were in the distance, I could clearly see the reason we had remained at the dock unfold.

The great lake kicked up *FAST*. Lake Erie is the shallowest, allowing the waves to build and chop quickly. I watched from the bridge as spray from the waves shot up and into the air ...and over theirs. The only boat wrestling the waves, spray leapt up over and over. On a chopped up day in the channel, the end of every wave is signified with a SLAM, leaving curiosity as to what was shaken loose and still in tack.

My dad taught me to study the horizon for bumps. On a calm day, when the stillness at the dock is deceiving, a peak off in the distant horizon can tell a more accurate story. If it looks bumpy from the dock, we're staying on the dock. I wish I could tell you exactly how large the waves were in the channel that day, but boaters exaggerate stories every time they tell them. In my mind, they're twenty footers by now.

When I was a kid, I didn't realize we couldn't just force the boat through all manner of waves without breaking it. I felt like I was going to break at the dock. Or melt. Or die of heat exhaustion and boredom simultaneously. I campaigned for peace, and the restoration I felt when we were out on the water and anchored at the cove. Watching our friends battle the waves launched a serious case of FOMO.

Until they turned around.

The worst part about waves like that is trying to figure out how to turn around and go back. Turning around is *TERRIFYING.*

The captain has to wait for just the right break in between sets of waves and spin the boat on a dime. If the bow doesn't whip around fast enough, the boat could get smacked in the side. In what I am sure felt like a *"Perfect Storm"* moment, they spun around …and survived. Walls of water escorted them back to the bay, as if to spit them out and call them crazy. As they entered into the marina, the bilge pumps ran constantly to clear the boat all the water it had taken on. Every inch and everyone was absolutely drenched. Shaky hands tied the spring lines back on, and we gathered to hear a first-hand account of the story.

Forces of nature can seem manageable, but they are still forces of nature. When the wind blows and the lake is angry, it's best not to brave her fury.

Living life highly sensitive without knowing it was a lot like trying to scale waves my hull couldn't conquer. From where I sat, the water was calm and the day was balmy and breezy. Christ knew what I did not, and on the most dangerous days, He kept me at the dock. Though I didn't know I was highly sensitive, He did. He placed people around me to protect me from what I, or they, didn't know could harm me. I've always been in good hands. Looking back at this journey solidifies my faith in Christ and trust in God. If He brought me all this way, leaving a trail of His care for my highly sensitive self, I can trust Him to lead me through all the unnamed things I am battling today.

Braving the Waves

On the day we crossed the lake to start our first journey Northward, the lake had a bad attitude. Determined not to let it deter all of our vacation planning, *on this day*, we risked it. The sun was out and the waves, though setting down, were still five to seven feet tall.

We tied everything down and set what we could on the floor. Since the lake was trying to settle, the waves weren't chopping us in to bits. They were rollers, *HUGE* rollers. Ironically enough, as the skyline full of roller coasters faded into the background, each one of those rolling waves left a pile of butterflies in my stomach. My dad had one foot on each end of the flybridge trying to steady himself, throttling up the waves and gliding back down.

Every once in a while, as we reached the bottom of a wave, the lake would send us through the rinse cycle. One of these instances popped a tie that attached a bike to the bow.

"I'll get it!!!" I volunteered. Minutes later, I tightened the straps of my lifejacket, popped the front hatch open, and stuck most of myself out of it to reach and tie the bike back on. I can't even imagine how my dad felt watching me dangle out of that hatch …laughing the whole time. A wave of water caught me off guard as I heard him tell me to brace myself. I felt the water trickle down to the rest of me that was still safely underneath the hatch, and when it passed looked up at my dad to share a giant laugh.

It takes a lot of bravery to try the channel on an impossible day, or to pop out the hatch in the face of a giant roller. Navigating the water requires us to keep our eyes on the horizon. Some of the biggest risks lie not just in the open water, but right offshore. That day, as we rolled across the lake, we kept our eyes on the shoreline. Watching it creep slowly into view gave us just enough hope and energy to push through the journey to the other side of the lake.

True North

In tumultuous times, we have two choices: push through and hold on for a breakthrough; Or, let go. Both require trust in God. Turn arounds can be terrifying. The moment before we spin the bow in between a set of waves, or stick our heads out of the hatch to face giant rollers, the anticipation is great …and the fear is overwhelming.

Navigating through life when my first marriage shattered felt like channel on an impossible day. The waves pummeled me. I clutched onto broken pieces, bobbing in my life jacket, until He me plucked out …shaken, scarred, and sinking.

I wanted to go back to that college dorm room and hug the girl in so much pain over a broken heart coupled with the unexpected death of her best high school friend. I scrambled to get a piece of my heart back *and* mourn a loss at the same time. The delicate balance of my coping mechanisms crumbled. I saw a counselor, one time. I can't remember what I said. Too painful to face it all head on, I remained my positive and fun self on the surface. No human could love me enough to heal all the pain. No amount of laughter could stop the pounding waves of grief. Everything blurred. Lines, morals, goals, friendships, and relationships. Sometime after my friend died I set my Bible down, let it accumulate dust, and gave my enemy a wide open space to work with.

There are two sides to every story, and only one is mine to share. Even still, I will leave most of it out to honor the person on the other side of all of this hurt. Married for two years, right on the heels of all the trauma that rounded out my collegiate years, my affair shattered all of our dreams. It's an impossible mistake to look in the eye, and a never-ending battle to out-run the shame. But, the Bible says if we don't look at it and talk about it, we delay our hearts from fully healing. Proverbs 28:13 says, ***"Whoever conceals their sins does not prosper, but the one who confesses and renounces them finds mercy."*** (NIV)

"How did I end up there?"

It's tempting to look back and wish for what-ifs. No one walks down the aisle on their wedding day and plans for it to end in dissolution. I never took time to heal. I never took time with God. People rallied around me and I let them make excuses for me. I made excuses for myself.

We live in a broken world. Through my shipwreck I learned there's no need to torture ourselves for the disastrous choices we make. I tell my daughters, 'it's what you did, not who you are," but I have often failed to apply that truth to my own story of salvation. There are consequences still fleshing out in my life from the wake of that season. I'm thankful, all these years later, to have forgiveness.

My *"how did I get here"* mess left me where Christ met me. In order to pick up the pieces, I had to accept Jesus' sacrifice, and forgive myself. He went to the cross knowing I would make that horrible choice and hurt another heart with my hurting heart. He knew me, all of me, and even still, *DIED* for me. For the first time in a long time, amidst the wreckage, I clung to His hand …with all the cracks where His fingers separated into their different parts …and He squeezed mine.

He had seen every hurt leading up to the wave that broke me into pieces. Highly sensitive people have an over active, rich inner life. I keep most of mine to myself. As I talked to family and friends over the course of writing this book, few recall noticing the pain I assumed they could see. I popped onto facebook a years later remarried with a brand new baby girl, but few knew the pain underneath the smiles.

To see me only for who I am today would short-change my journey, and dishonor the miraculous, saving power of Jesus Christ. Without the squeeze of His hand, I'm nothing but a collection of the mistakes I've made. In Him, I am loved; I am fearfully and wonderfully made.

Christ alone was strong enough to pull me out of the water and set me back on dry land. Unfortunately, we don't just learn from inspiring stories in life, and sometimes learn the most from the messes we make. For anyone who thinks that all is lost because of a mistake, an addiction, or a flaw...go to @sunnyandeighty on Instagram and see what restoration looks like. When we quiet our hearts and our hands bump into His, squeeze it back. Feel the lines, the strength despite the hole in the middle of it. That was for us. He is *FOR us*. Accept His forgiveness. Only then, can we truly say we accept Jesus Christ as our Savior. Live free and watch Him move.

Who am I?
Saved.

My authenticity is a product of His creative hand.
My obedience is made possible through His strength.
Everything I accomplish is to honor Him.
In Christ, even my memories are made new.
This side of heaven, all I do is to honor You.
Keep me facing the Shoreline,
A heavenly embrace at the top of my heart.
The squeeze of Your hand is only a small piece of the full experience of Your presence.
I'll always be thankful.
I'll forever look up and slightly smile.

Love redefined.
Saved.

Set A Course

No matter the bumps on the horizon or the days we have to sweat it out at the dock, we're on our way home. With every passing day, the shoreline is closer. When we've experienced the presence of Christ in our lives so profoundly, it creates an urgency in us for more. It's eternity in us, calling us Home to our Father in Heaven.

Let these Scriptures rain over and remind us who we are, and who God is. In our drowning moments, and in our victories, He is the same …and so are we. On this earth, we will age physically and grow in wisdom. Our Creator is the core of who we are. Proverbs 28:14 says, *"Blessed is the one who always trembles before God, but whoever hardens their heart falls into trouble." (NIV)* Don't let hardness form by running from what we cannot erase, and from what He has already died to forgive us for. Give it rightly to Him and accept forgiveness. He sees what we do not, and forgives our repentant hearts of sin because of the cross of Christ. No matter what mistakes or near drownings we've gone through, we can sing these notes of encouragement and wisdom over our lives:

"I waited patiently for the Lord;
he turned to me and heard my cry.
He lifted me out of the slimy pit,
out of the mud and mire;
he set my feet on a rock
and gave me a firm place to stand.
He put a new song in my mouth,
a hymn of praise to our God.
Many will see and fear the Lord
and put their trust in him.

Blessed is the one
who trusts in the Lord,
who does not look to the proud,

to those who turn aside to false gods.
Many, Lord my God,
are the wonders you have done,
the things you planned for us.
None can compare with you;
were I to speak and tell of your deeds,
they would be too many to declare."
Psalm 40:1-5 NIV

"Every word of God is flawless;
he is a shield to those who take refuge in Him. Proverbs 30:5 NIV

"Yet to all who did receive him, to those who believed in his name,
he gave the right to become children of God -" John 1:12 NIV

"So you are no longer a slave, but God's child; and since you are
his child, God has made you also an heir." Galatians 4:7 NIV

"Now if we are children, then we are heirs- heirs of God and co-
heirs with Christ, if indeed we share in his sufferings in order that
we may also share in his glory." Romans 8:17 NIV

"Praise be to the God and Father of our Lord Jesus Christ, who
has blessed us in the heavenly realms with every spiritual blessing
in Christ." Ephesians 1:3 NIV

"God made him who had no sin to be sin for us, so that in him we
might become the righteousness of God." 2 Corinthians 5:21 NIV

A promise beyond our understanding, to love and be loved. We were created to be authentically original, and are all called accordingly by He who knows us better than we know ourselves. Lean in to learn more, and God will reveal hidden things.

Hidden Fields of Blessing

Remember the field God instructed Jeremiah to buy? It held the hope of restoration, but Jeremiah couldn't see it yet. He had to trust God. Sometimes our lives are like that. Obedience to God doesn't always make sense. It's not always what we want, and we won't always know why.

God can make our memories new. He sheds light, even on our remembering. He shows us who we are by giving us glances of where we've come from or what He's done before. After we've grown another layer of wisdom on our hearts, we can look back with greater clarity and new perspective as God reveals what He has prepared for us. Questions and hurt, even mistakes we made …can be reaccessed and reassigned as we become a new creation in an ever permeable way. When Christ is the center of our lives, miracles can happen, even in our memories!

"Give thanks to the Lord Almighty, for the Lord is good; his love endures forever."
Jeremiah 33:11b NIV

All of the doom and gloom the people of God would endure gave way to praise. The promise of the Messiah hangs thick in this verse, and hope douses the darkness. The promise of joy resounded to a people who started to assume there would be nothing but darkness and desolation.

"Though weeping may endure for a time, joy will return." (Psalm 30:5) The last thing we feel like doing when we're drowning is unlocking our sensitivity. But HSP or not, it helps us to feel the reality of the above verse. Something in our sensitivity knows that despite all odds, we keep waking up to a new day. It's in all of us to crave Christ. Living in the New Testament covenant, we can look back and see God's faithfulness through the perspective of the cross. In our lives, we can look back and weep all over again for the painful drownings. Time will not completely erase those wounds for a reason. They leave scars to remind us of the promise of the future.

This too, we will get through. Through the eyes of the cross, we can smother forgiveness all over our mistakes, and reframe our shame with hope and grace.

We can praise Him in the hard times because He is unchanging. His hand is always there. His forgiveness is always there. We aren't going to choose perfectly all of the time. The humility it takes to share a story that is scary helps those who are standing on the dock thinking about taking the choppy and unpredictable channel on alone. Our mistakes are mistakes. They are not to be made light of, admonished, or encouraged in any way. They are not glamorous, they are in fact quite painful. No one wants to relive them, much less talk about them. We want to wipe the slate and move on and away from them. But acting like they never happened can hamper our healing.

Being authentic means wearing our scars, not hiding them. Giving our lives to God means to allowing Him to make marvelous, the madness. God uses the scars we are ashamed of to strengthen us and to serve others. This is how we love the people in our lives well.

Mirroring

We all have mirror neurons, helping us to feel empathy and compassion for others, HSP people just have more of them. The extroversion built into highly sensitive genetics helps HSP's connect with people on a deep level, quickly. My mistakes hurt, but my story, through the healing hand of Jesus, help people. We all have a natural level of sensitivity. Make a conscious effort to listen to others, and instead of thinking about what to say or how to fix their problems, search for common ground. No conversation happens by coincidence.

We honor the people in our lives when we recognize their gifts. We can become stewards of our words by filtering our thoughts through the lens of love before we speak. Ephesians 4:29 says, ***"Do not let*** *any unwholesome talk come out of your mouths, but only what is helpful for building others up according to their needs, that it may benefit those who listen."* (NIV) The Voice paraphrase reads, "Don't let even one rotten word seep out of your mouths. Instead, offer only fresh words that build others up when they need it most. That way your good words will communicate grace to those who hear them." The more we know, the greater the responsibility.

"Perhaps your most important gift as an HSP is the one designed to protect you: your brain is fine-tuned to notice and interpret the behavior of everyone around you. If someone is bad news, you know it. If someone is not going to treat you right, you see it coming. And if a situation isn't right for you, you know that, too." (Solo)

There's simply no way, in a fallen world, to completely avoid mistakes and suffering, but we can lessen some of our pain by taking care of ourselves. Self care is important for everyone, and even more so for HSP people. For me, it consists of quiet time with Christ, adequate sleep every night, eating healthy and restricting my calendar. When we pray for God to search the far corners of our hearts and remove anything hindering us from following Him completely, He is faithful.

Boundaries make people uncomfortable. Especially the people that benefitted from us having none. So, have patience while everyone adjusts. The people that love us will ultimately see how much more pleasant it is to be around us when we're allowed to step back. It's hard to be misunderstood and sometimes picked on for not fitting the normal mold of the social circle, but high sensitivity has a lot more benefits than drawbacks. We have to make peace with who we were created to be, and learn to love ourselves completely, as Christ does. There is a purpose for our lives. Let the natural abilities of high sensitivity take over and lend empathy towards others, and have healthy boundaries.

<u>Who We Are.</u>

The first paper on sensitivity was published in 1997. (Aron) That's the year I graduated from high school. How exciting to think we live in a time where we will come to appreciate sensitivity in a brand new way. We can be a catalyst for change by understanding how to explain it to others, advocate for ourselves and others that have the trait, and most importantly, raise the next generation of highly sensitive children to know, honor, and love their gift.

Highly sensitive or not, we all have a gift to share with the world. But in order to fully give the best of ourselves, we have to take care of ourselves. The Bible says, *"Above all else, guard your heart, for everything you do flows from it."* (Proverbs 4:23 NIV)

If we store up good things in our hearts, our words and actions will be good. "For the mouth speaks what the heart is full of." (NIV Study) HSPs are affected exponentially by their childhoods, and the good or bad memories there. We store up those memories, allowing us to thrive in our sensitivity and enabling us to be our best selves! We store up the good things, including the wisdom and revelation we learn from God's Word.

Proverbs 2:1 says: *"My son, if you accept my words and store up my commands within you,"* Counsel is advice and admonishment. Another translation reads, *"My son, if you will receive my words And treasure my commandments within you," (Proverbs 2:1 NASB)* Beyond just accepting, we are to be engaged in God's wisdom. (Brown) This is the relationship Christ died for. Personal, equipping, caring, and constant discovery of ourselves, the world around us, and the One True God. The good things we *store up* connect us to Him intricately. A love that cannot be accomplished by human strength alone, flows through us.

We are receiving more than just Scriptures and commands, but God's promise for us. The original Hebrew translation includes the word "utterances" to define God's word. Sure enough, if we trace the

Hebrew root of *"word"* in this context, it means to say, speak, or utter. The action of the Holy Spirit in our lives allows us to perceive the utterances of God. His answers, promises, and intentions travel into our thoughts and hearts through His care and power. (Brown) But we still have to be ready to receive them, and this is accomplished by our constant seeking of Him. It's relationship.

Storing up, or treasuring these commands means to keep them hidden. (Brown) God reveals things to us in accordance to the level we've unlocked our sensitivity to receive them, and Him. God personally reveals hidden things, meeting us right where we are at for a custom built message of love and encouragement.

The commandments God tells us to store up are threefold: commandments of man, commandments of God and commandments of wisdom. The root of *commandment* means to charge, commission, appoint, ordain, or give change unto. (Brown) The commandments of the Father, the Son, and the Holy Spirit, working good of all things in our lives. Even the deep and hidden things.

"My son, if you will receive my words and treasure my commandments within you," Pv 2:1 NASB

"My son, if you will ..."

We are children of God. Built, rebuilt, established, and caused to continue. Established, as in made permanent. (Brown) But we are not forced to obey God's commands. We can choose. That word *"if"* begs us to receive and store God's goodness in possible and impossible situations. Unconditionally, whether and whenever. (Brown) Since He is the One True God and makes good of all things, it is wise put our trust in Him! This is God's will for and calling on our lives, to *CHOOSE* His will over our own.

God makes good of all things. This means our memories can be looked upon through a new perspective of God's love. Yes! Even the most horrific and horrible choppy-channel days can be re-framed through Christ, our Savior. When we are able to look back upon a memory and see God's hand there, the change in our countenance often enlightens those around us. As a HSP, each miraculous healing in my life has grown my personal relationship with God.

This doesn't give us a free pass to go rogue because we assume and live under His forgiveness and goodness. No, that's not the pathway to a full life. That isn't storing up good things in our hearts. We want to avoid the hardness and harshness of horrible memories. We hear stories all of the time of people who have suffered lifetimes of pain due to things they couldn't remember. The deep and hidden things of our minds. Things that exist in our subconscious, out of the scope of our general awareness, yet still looming underneath as gaping wounds. The same can be true of positive memories that can be lost in the shuffling of confidence over the years. We can walk though life not knowing who we are.

Psalm 139:23 says, *"Search me, God, and know my heart; test me and know my anxious thoughts."* (NIV) This verse has become my anthem as an HSP. Knowing there is so much more going on under the surface, I pray God's filter of wisdom and love over *all of it.* Over who I *REALLY* am. Proverbs 2:1-5 says:

"My son, if you accept my words
and store up my commands within you,
turning your ear to wisdom
and applying your heart to understanding-
indeed, if you call out for insight
and cry aloud for understanding,
and if you look for it as for silver
and search for it as hidden treasure,
then you will understand the fear of the Lord
and find the knowledge of God."
(NIV)

That's an all-encompassing view of the relational love of God. He's given us commands, but left the choice up to us. He wants to reveal the hidden things to us, but requires us to choose to seek Him … wholeheartedly. Because everything we do flows from our heart … and into a heart truly seeking God for His will the good things and some of the hidden things will be deposited. The Voice paraphrase of this single sentence from Scripture hits sensitivity square on:

"My son, if you accept what I am telling you
and store my counsel and directives deep within you,
If you listen for Lady Wisdom, attune your ears to her,
and engage your mind to understand what she is telling you,
If you cry out to her for insight
and beg for understanding,
If you sift through the clamor of everything around you
to seek her like some precious prize,
to search for her like buried treasure;
Then you will grasp what it means to truly respect the Eternal,
and you will have discovered the knowledge of the one True God.
Proverbs 2:1-5 VOICE

In baptism, we go under the water, and come back to the surface a new person. We can experience a baptism-like occurrence in life every time we resurface from a near drowning. Every time I come back to the surface, I know Jesus on a higher personal level. When I think I have learned enough, lived enough, and loved enough to know Him, He reveals there is more. It's a squeeze of His hand this side of heaven, but an entire embrace for eternity.

Proverbs 4:23 says, *"Above all else, guard your heart, for everything you do flows from it."* (NIV) Everything. What we say, what we do, and who we are lies in our hearts. Every time I remove the stopper and let His love flow out of me He meets me in the honesty and authenticity of my faith …my life …my testimony and my witness. Looking back on choppy-channel memories, I can clearly see how not knowing I was highly sensitive affected

EVERYTHING. To be able to look back and know God is still making good of all of the pain heals the cracks in my heart and allows me to hold on in greater capacity to the good things. God doesn't repaint the walls of our mistakes and choppy-channel days to condone or erase them, He hangs posters over them, declaring who we are anyway, Who He is, and how He is good.

"Above all else, watch over your heart; diligently guard it because from a sincere and pure heart come the good and noble things of life." Proverbs 4:23 Voice.

God isn't expecting a pursuit of holiness, not perfection. Guarding our hearts means having good boundaries. Learning to listen to HSP intuition can helps me confidently construct solid God-grounded guide posts in my life. "You, a highly sensitive person, are vulnerable in ways that others are not. But that does not make you powerless. You are a delicate creature and so you must protect yourself. " (Ward)

Decide.

HSPs can decide how to love the people in their lives well, based on what they perceive. I found it interesting that we are highly susceptible to falling into relationships with narcissistic people. Narcissistic people can be hard to spot, even for highly sensitive people. Something about the way they have mastered deception scrambles our radar. They know what people want to hear, how to make others feel good, and how to say *just* the right things. (Ward) It can leave the door wide open to havoc. This is a dual power play from our enemy.

I do not believe, personally, narcissists always understand they are narcissists any more than we realize we are highly sensitive. However, we can take steps to protect ourselves. "Beware of people who seem a little to preoccupied with their appearance, their status and what people think about them." (Ward.)

The hope is always for restoration and reconciliation. God saw the good buried in His ancient people, even though they were NOT GOOD AT ALL from the outside. We have to remember this when we are tempted to judge the rotten and stinking appearances of those around us. The root of all toxicity is our propensity to lean towards the temptation and sin in a broken world. No one has an innately "good heart." We all fall short. (Romans 3:23) But through Christ, we can store up the good things. We can be good. It's HIS goodness flowing through us. We just have to pull up the stopper and let the Living Water flow.

It's not our job to fix the hearts of others, that's God's territory and their battle to fight. We are responsible for forgiving others, and accepting forgiveness from Christ. A heartfelt apology goes a long way, but it isn't powerful enough to restore what's required for reconciliation. "It's critical to know if you are an HSP, so you can seek out relationships and environments that make you shine." (Azab)

There are many positive qualities to HSP, but we are also susceptible to depression and the mental illnesses. Seek professional counseling for a proper diagnosis of mental status. I can speak only of my own experience as an HSE. When I went to my first counseling appointment, I was expecting her to echo what everyone else was saying …that I was depressed. What I discovered, instead, was HSP. This may be the same case for you, but it may not be. Don't read this book, take tests online, and assume the final answer to your mental state. Depression needs to be treated, not just understood. You are not alone. Seek professional counseling. We cannot love the people in our lives well if we are walking around with gaping wounds in our hearts. Talk to a counselor. Talk the The Counselor. Getting help is brave and courageous, wise and loving, self-care.

For those of who know they are highly sensitive, make the most of your gift. Leave some blank space on the calendar, journal feelings, express creativity, and choose to be confident. "Take advantage of your predisposition for higher empathy to strengthen relationships- to become a better co-worker and to to assure your self-worth," writes Marwa Azan, Ph. D., "Be honest about your predisposition to be an HSP, especially in close relationships. But, don't forget to highlight the positive aspects: more empathy, deep thinker, able to see things from a different perspective, appreciation of the arts and music, and other positive qualities."

We can find ourselves in the middle of choppy channels if we don't get enough rest, HSPs, mentally and physically. "Rest is the basis of activity," writes Elaine N. Aron, Ph.D. For me, this is prayer time with God, quiet hours in the morning seeking Him in His word, and walks along the water's edge at sunrise. It's getting quiet with a book while I wait in line to pick my girls up from school in the afternoon, and going to bed in time to get at least a solid five hours of sleep.

God created rest. He created for six days, and on the seventh He rested. Not because HE *needed* rest, but He built it into the very fabric of creation for our benefit. Whether we are HSPs or not, we need rest.

Unlock sensitivity. If this book puts flames to the sparks in your heart, pursue every curiosity. Ask questions, and search for answers. For those reading this seeking to honor and better understand the highly sensitive people in their lives, know this. HSPs often seem too analytical, but we offer a fresh perspective. The rich and complex inner life of an HSP can be misconstrued as too sensitive or too emotional. Avoid comments and criticism with double meanings and neutral or bland feedback. HSPs take longer to recover after criticism and can be paralyzed by negative comments, and burnout and give up because of mounting stress. "Their minds marinate in their surroundings," writes Dr. Azul, "this means they can easily get overwhelmed."

If you know an HSP, take moments to encourage, appreciate, and understand them. If we all yielded this level of compassion to each other, HSP or not, we would all be able to avoid some of the choppy channel drownings in our lives. "The sensitivity of a HSP can bring a fountain of emotions, unparalleled levels of empathy and deep level of understanding to a relationship." (Azul) We are put on this earth to look out for each other and love each other, not by our own understanding or will ...but His.

"Brothers and sisters, think of what you were when you were called. Not many of you were wise by human standards; not many were influential; not many were of noble birth. But God chose the foolish things of the world to shame the wise; God chose the week things of the world to shame the strong. God chose the lowly things of this world and the despised things -and the things that are not- to nullify the things that are, so that no one may boast before him. It is because of him that you are in Christ Jesus, who has become for us wisdom from God- that is, our righteousness, holiness, and redemption. Therefore, as it is written: 'Let the one who boasts boast in the Lord.'"

1 Corinthians 1:26-31 NIV

CHAPTER 10

SURFACE
Break-through to a Full Life.

A surge of water gushed into my ear and trickled down my face. Water balloon pieces fell out of my hair, and laughter exploded. For the next two hours, water flew from every direction. The moms raced inside to shut windows, the kids raced around in dinghies to fetch balloons and buckets of water, and the dads secured the giant sling shot.

Torrents of water flew through the air. The adults always tired of the game before the kids, and secret ambushes ensued. My stomach muscles would ache and cramp from laughing. Everyone eventually ended up in the water for a full-on splash war.

The fenders squeaked in protest to keep the fiberglass boats from crunching together while moored in the cove. Standing on the sand in the water, it seemed funny the big boats were flopping from side to side all for a few boat waves and a water fight. Leaving the safety of the sand, I swam towards the swim platform to hop out.

"Be careful," my dad reminded, "watch the pinch-points."

Pinch-points are places where the metal ladder drops off the back of the boat to hit the swim platform. When the boat rocks up and down with the waves, the ladder floats away from the platform, and then slams back down.

Pinch-points. As a highly sensitive person, it is important for me to make space to get quiet. I made my way inside the cabin to retrieve my book, and headed to the bow for some peace and quiet while the sun dried me off on that perfect summer day. When I pressed through life without taking time and taking care of myself, the ladder came down on my fingers, hard. Knowing now what I didn't back then, I'm amazed at how my instincts took over to naturally crave that time. As I crept closer to adulthood, I veered off of course, resulting in many of the near drownings we've revisited here together in our journey to unlock the gift of high sensitivity.

The title of this book came to me first, while I was talking to God in the quiet of the morning. I started to pray for *"Surface"* daily, just as I had the book before. A year later and shortly after I had discovered my high sensitivity in counseling, I knew *"Surface"* was going to be about unlocking the gift of high sensitivity.

Discovering high sensitivity was like taking a key to my own soul and unlocking a piece I hadn't been able to see clearly. God had miraculously pulled me through, despite what had not yet been revealed. I gained a new depth of understanding who I am in Christ, and chose to lean into the moments marked in my memories for a new strengthening. The happy replays *and* the hurtful highlight reels, still so palpable, remain vivid because of the wonderful way God has wired my mind.

Pinch-points. Counseling was a pinch-point for me. I was scared. I assumed something was wrong with me, and afraid I would be diagnosed with depression and anxiety. Tempted to believe those who called me "too sensitive," and afraid my fingers would get pinched, I instead discovered a piece of my soul and a new level of Peace with Christ.

God goes before me. Psalm 46:10 says, "Be still and know that I am God." (NIV) And He so faithfully whispered, "Come here …you're gonna LOVE this." Through the sun-sparkled water near the surface, a hand reached out to mine. It noticed the creases where the cracks separate the different parts of His fingers, and a beam of light went straight through the hole in His hand. I felt the water swish through my toes as I kicked to push my hand up just far enough to grab onto His.

I don't ever want to let go of the hand that pulled me to the surface.

My Savior. My Rock. My Tow-line. My Ballast. All of the capitalized words I have used to tell this story are meant to express my heart full of love for my God, and my gratitude towards my Savior. Jesus Christ. That Holy Hand. My Abba Father. My Breath. Yahweh.

Breathing Again.

Hope feels like effortless breathing restored. Sometimes, breath alone brings comfort.

I had a friend who fought for each …literal … breath. We say each breath is a gift, but she lived it. Through pain and questions that never yielded answers, she continued to breathe. We watched the fight take her strength, and Christ kick in to fight for her. Ultimately, He called her home to heaven to breathe easy.

Had I known how little time she had left, I would've dropped my agenda to be with her more. The last time I got to see my sweet warrior of a friend this side of heaven was a blur. I found myself holding onto her hand, but she was too weak to squeeze it back. No more opportunities for conversation, laughter, and seeking Jesus together. No more dinner dates just she and I and our kids. Just one last opportunity to meet her eyes and tell my friend I loved her.

Some pinch-points place us in a war with whether to go all-in with the people God places in our lives, or shy away for fear of how much it could hurt if we lose them. Pinch-point moments push us to inconvenience our own lives for the sake of another.

Shortly before she passed, our Bible Study group sat on the shore of the great lake with our Starbucks coffee, talking about everyday life and seeking Jesus through it all. Though the mountain of *ALL OF THE THINGS* she had been handed to breathe through in this life was insurmountable, her mission was to help others going through what she had gone through. She was in pain, some days barely breathing, but constantly yielding to Christ. She was strong because her Savior was her strength. She lived a life so many of us preach, teach and try to lead others to. Her life was a walking billboard for how to love the people in her life well. In times when she could have been so selfish, she chose not to be. When the pain was too much to bare, she let herself laugh with us.

Even when we lose someone we love, in Christ, we are never completely parted. The body of Christ is strung together with love, and purposefully placed. We have no control over when we get to heaven, and at times it can seem unfair and insurmountably painful that the ones we love get to go home before us. But the promise of Grace is the permanence of our eternal state: healed, whole, and together. We will live in the perfect harmony of God's love, without sickness, death, or pain.

Until then, we have hope. Hope feels like breathing easy again … even when we struggle for each consecutive breath. God makes good out of all things: illness, anxiety and depression, chronic lack of confidence, multiple mistakes, or the hidden things that haven't been revealed. Losing life is never easy. Saying good-bye is *always* crushing. Grief's process is painful. Our hearts hurt with unanswered questions. I miss my friend.

Life *isn't* fair, but God *is* good.

Hope is buoyant. Our tight circle of friends grieved the sinking loss of our young friend. I ran every mile of my first half-marathon in her honor, choking up at the start as I looked up and told her, "this one is for you." Once a runner herself, in a different set of circumstances, she might have been out there with me. Maybe when I get Home to Heaven, we'll be able to run together. I hope to leave a similar trail of strength, grace, and evidence of a life walked hand-in-hand with Jesus. When we are too worn to seek the surface, hope floats.

Walk the Dog.

One chilly Spring morning, my youngest daughter begged to sneak out and walk the dog with me. There's no possible way I can say "no" to my blue-eyed child wanting extra moments with her momma, so I waited while she bundled. Beaming as she held the dog's leash all by herself, they ran as soon as we hopped out of the car. She giggled and her puppy jumped and played alongside her. When she slowed to let me catch up, her smile stretched across her face. We walked together, laughing, talking and looking for eagles in the early morning sky.

"Lo," I said excitedly, "it's a purple sky day."

Purple was her favorite color. Her eyes got big and she dropped her jaw. We both crave quiet moments. Two highly sensitive extroverts, we sat on a bench to watch the sunrise over the great lake. Somehow, we had figured each other out long before we knew anything about high sensitivity. Motherhood is a miracle. Christ has allowed me to be the mom she and her sister need. I lean in, and He teaches me.

Motherhood strengthened my courage and confidence in Him. We call ourselves the Three Musketeers. We're the Three *Highly Sensitive* Musketeers. One introverted and two extroverted.

God goes before us.

"Sometimes I am completely perplexed by God's willingness to humor us. His mercy knows no bounds. When He wanted to lead the Magi to the Christ child, He did not lead them by a mark in the sand. He led them through a star because they were stargazers-then He went beyond anything they had ever seen. In the same way, when God wanted to lead the Ephesians to the Savior, He did not lead them through a cloudy pillar. He got their attention through supernatural phenomena, because that's where they were looking. God wants to be found. He does not will for any to miss Him, and He is so gracious to show up right where we are looking. - so He can

take us beyond anything we've ever seen." -Beth Moore, Portraits of Devotion.

Shortly after my first daughter was born, I started to blog as a way to record all the moments I feared my tired momma brain would surely forget. It grew into a reflective collection of lessons God was teaching me. When my daughters started pre-school, I signed up for a Bible Study. I voraciously took notes every Tuesday morning, craving more as I attended study after study. God was preparing, teaching, and revealing hidden things to me!

Those first Bible studies lit a spark in my heart to learn more, and when my second daughter went off to Kindergarten I poured myself into studying God's Word and writing about how He connected it so faithfully to my everyday life. I attached a Blue-tooth keyboard to my iPad, propped it up on my lap, and began working on blog entries on the waiting room floor while my daughters were in dance class. One day an editor found my blog, and I became a freelance writer. I eventually self-published a book that had been on my heart for years. God started to drop book titles into our quiet morning conversations. I love writing about everyday life within the love of Christ. One by one, I will prayerfully prepare my heart for the messages God wills me to put into words.

Grace and Peace.

"Grace and peace to you from God our Father and the Lord Jesus Christ, who gave himself for our sins to rescue us from the present evil age, according to the will of our God and Father, to whom be glory for ever and ever. Amen." Galatians 1:3-5 NIV

The beginning of Paul's letter feels akin to an anthem song in my life. Grace, peace and rescue, glory forever and ever. And lots of Amen's. God tells us many times throughout Scripture not to be afraid, but my favorite story is Jesus walking on the water. Maybe because I love and relate to the water. Many mornings, like the purple-skied one on the pier with my daughter, the water almost begs to be walked on. When a smooth layer of ice coats the surface, the melted layer on top shimmers like a piece of glass, and I envy the birds who are out there fleeting to and fro.

"Immediately Jesus made the disciples get into the boat and go on ahead of him on to the other side, while he dismissed the crowd. After he had dismissed them, he went up on a mountainside by himself to pray. Later than night, he was there alone, and the boat was already a considerable distance from land, buffeted by the waves because the wind was against it." Matthew 14:22-24

Jesus needed to get quiet. He was calm, prepared, and strong because He found a solitary place to pray for a long time. In fact, all night long. Scholars approximate the exact time to be from 3am to 6am. (NIV Study) Even when my daughter's were cute little babies crying in the middle of the night for food, *I COULD NOT* find a way to function before 4:15 am. Jesus was faithful. He knew no rest was as restorative as time with the Father. He was fully human. I'm sure he was physically tired. Jesus was no stranger to discomfort.

"Shortly before dawn Jesus went out to them, walking on the lake. When the disciples saw him walking on the lake, they were terrified. 'It's a ghost," they said, and cried in fear.' Matthew 14:25-26

They were terrified. Shocked to a state they didn't recognize Jesus. Sometimes, we can be so scared and afraid that we fail to recognize the miracle right in front of us. Or, we let fear cause us to *forget* …to get quiet.

"But Jesus immediately said to them: 'Take courage! It is I. Don't be afraid.'" Matthew 23:27 NIV

It is I. I am. The same "I am" throughout Scripture:

"I AM WHO I AM." Exodus 3:24 NIV

"...I am he. Before me no god was formed, nor will there be one after me." Isaiah 43:10 NIV

"I, even I, am he who comforts you." Isaiah 51:12 NIV

"Very truly I tell you," Jesus answered, "before Abraham was born, I am!" John 8:58 NIV

These are just a few of the "I am" moments in the Bible. The story of our Savior doesn't start in the Gospel of Matthew, but in Genesis. Peter had heard Jesus preach for some time, but what he knew was not lining up with what he saw.

"'Lord, if it's you,' Peter replied, 'tell me to come to you on the water.'"

'Come.' -Matthew 14:28-29 NIV

I'm reminded of Beth Moore's devotional entry, and how God does not hide from us. He wants to be found. He wants us to find Him. Jesus simply says, "Come." We can wrestle with our Father when we are angry or afraid. He isn't hiding. He wants us to find Him in all moments, hard and happy ...terrifying and peaceful.

"Then Peter got down out of the boat, walked on the water and came toward Jesus. But when he saw the wind, he was afraid and, beginning to sink, cried out, 'Lord, save me!'"

Immediately Jesus reached out his hand and caught him. 'You of little faith,' he said, 'why did you doubt?' Matthew 14: 29b-31 NIV

The moment right before Peter started to fear again must have been the coolest and most extraordinary of his life. Walking on the water. The surface we try so hard to reach, he was walking on. The water, and all of it's risks and soluabilties, was under his feet. But in an instant of doubt, Peter let fear cause his feet to sink below the surface of the water. Fear morphs into doubt, questions, and skepticism. Instead of faithfully facing our Savior, we start to sink. Before we know it, we're nearly drowning.

Guilt and shame are never from our Father. Forgiveness and love are His mantras, peace and understanding His banner, and compassionate care His reputation.

"Immediately."

Jesus reached out His hand *immediately* to steady Peter. He does the same for us. *Call His name.* He will pull us back to the surface. We don't have to wait, explain, or earn His trust back …all we have to do is call out to Him:

"Lord! Save me!"

And He does. And He did. And He will.

And when they climbed into the boat, the wind died down. Then those who were in the boat worshipped him, saying, 'Truly you are the Son of God.'" Matthew 14: 32-33 NIV

So often, we are not patient enough to call on our Lord, much rather trust Him to save us. We rush into panic and plans to save ourselves instead of prayer. His love for us never fails, but ours for Him does all the time. It's a mess. For we cannot love without Him. *Not truly.*

"This is love for God: to keep his commands. And his commands are not burdensome, for everyone born of God overcomes the world. This is the victory that has overcome the world, even our faith." 1 John 5:4 1 NIV

We lack patience when we forget to operate from the seat of our hearts. When God is not rightfully sitting in the seat of our hearts, we cannot faithfully pursue His purpose for our lives. When we choose our own way, we suffer consequences. Both God's commands *and* consequences stem from His love for us. Living in Christ means submitting to the power *in us* to bring honor and glory to He who created us.

Well Water.

"'Sir,' the woman said, 'you have nothing to draw with and the well is deep. Where can you get this living water? Are you greater than our father Jacob, who gave us the well and drank from it himself, as did also his sons and his livestock?'" John 4:11-12 NIV

The woman at the well could not understand how Jesus was going to draw water from it. *(which, when it was last dug in 1935, was 138 feet deep! -NIV Study)* She held a deep regard for the past, but it prevented her from seeing the great opportunity of the present. (NIV Study) When Peter walked on the water, he started to remember what he knew in the past *about* the water, and he started to sink. He missed a miraculous moment because He peered too long into the past.

This journey has been a lot about looking to the past, reframing it and embracing the lessons learned and miracles experienced along the way. But if we look to and linger in the past for too long, we'll miss the present. The woman at the well was *missing* the miracle! She was talking *to the Savior. Her* Savior!

"Everyone who drinks this water will be thirsty again, but whoever drinks the water I give them will never thirst. Indeed, the water I give them will become a spring of water welling up to eternal life." John 4:13-14 NIV

Jesus went on to tell the woman everything about herself. He knew her. Knew who she was. But she was searching for answers to what she couldn't understand with what she knew from the past. "I know that Messiah (called Christ) is coming. When he comes, he will explain everything to us," she said. (John 4:25 NIV) And to which Jesus ended their conversation with:

"I, the one speaking to you- I am he." John 4:26 NIV

Can you imagine!

In these two stories, the Living Water is talking about drawing water and walking on water.

The people in the book of Jeremiah had heard of the Messiah. They knew, like Peter and the woman at the well, who the Messiah was going to be and what He was coming to do. But they never expected Him to sit down next to them by the well or lend a hand out on the open water. The miraculous presence of Jesus Christ will never cease to stretch what we *think* we know.

Fear is not from God, but from our enemy. Courage and confidence are from God, and in a Christ-centered heart they trump fear. In Christ, we can (proverbially) walk on water without allowing fear to saturate our God-given purpose.

"'The days are coming,' declares the Lord, 'when I will fulfill the good promise I made to the people of Israel and Judah.'"
Jeremiah 33:14 NIV

The woman at the well, Peter, and we are living in the fulfillment of that promise. It took some who witnessed Him time to align their knowledge of who they thought He would be with who He was. They were expecting a military leader, a king like the ones they knew on earth, but greater. They were not expecting the Messiah to sit next to them on the well, walk out to them on the water, or seek time to pray in solitude.

"In those days and at that time
I will make a righteous Branch sprout from David's line;
he will do what is just and right in the land.
In those days Judah will be saved
and Jerusalem will live in safety.
This is the name by which it will be called:
The Lord Our Righteous Savior."
Jeremiah 33: 15-16 NIV

Miraculous moments can look different than we expect them to. Made in the image of God, we don't recognize ourselves, know our worth, or correctly estimate our purpose. But God does. He chooses to call us what who we are …Children of the Most High God.

"If you can break my covenant with the day and my covenant with
the night, so that day and night no longer come at their appointed
time, then my covenant with David my servant- and my covenant
with the Levites who are priests ministering before me- can be
broken and David will no longer have a descendant to reign on his
throne. I will make the descendants of David my servant and the
Levites who minister before me as countless as the stars in the sky
and as measureless as the sand on the seashore." Jeremiah
33:19-22 NIV

Who can alter night and day? No one. Who can count the stars in the sky to call them countless and the sand on the seashore to call it measureless? Only God. Jesus was born out of the lineage of David. The prophesies were fulfilled by the Prophecy.

Each life is one single grain of sand. God counts and cares for each one. He pursues us, individually. The Good Shepherd, He notices when we stray, and He calls for us. When we follow His voice, we find our way to the surface.

One of my favorite sermons is about an orchid and an oak tree. Orchids are super sensitive. Oak Trees are strong and sturdy. I love orchids, but I can't keep one alive. After that sermon, I tried many times to no avail. They really are super sensitive! But tall trees can tumble over, too. In a strong wind. Or simply when it's time. I love that sermon. It reminds me to rely on Jesus.

In Him, I am deeply rooted and well watered. Without Him, even the most delicate treatment isn't enough to keep me alive. Those of us who are highly sensitive are not doomed to orchid status. We actually have the potential to cultivate deep roots that retain Living Water. We all have orchid *and* oak tree days. God ultimately sees the Oak Tree in all of us.

Highly sensitive people need to get quiet like an orchid needs to be watered with ice cubes. "Recognize that you are a delicate orchid among the daisies and if you don't make your needs a priority, no one else will." (Ward) Whether we like it or not, we are an orchid in the field of daisies. That doesn't mean we can't grow rich roots and live big lives for God. By getting quiet, and leaving extra time, we can do less and accomplish more. (Aron)

HSP's, more than just limiting noise and stimulation, must quiet our thoughts. "You can develop your sense of self-awareness and intuition by spending a few moments alone each day, especially when you feel overwhelmed or upset. If you don't know what you're feeling or why, sit down somewhere quiet, close your eyes, and ask ourself, What am I feeling? Don't think, just listen. Trust your instincts. The answer will come to you, perhaps as an image or maybe a word or a feeling. And then base your actions on that trusted information, and not what someone else is telling you. They may not have your best interests at heart." (Ward)

HSPs, if we can get quiet and then align all of our answers with the Truth of God's word, we can become a deep rooted orchid. One that blooms even when flooded with an entire glass of water or set by the window on a breezy day. Yes, we've been given more than the other 80% of people in the world to process. God goes before us to make a way. Scripture tells us to take every thought captive. It is possible to quiet our minds and redirect our thoughts to align with who we are in Christ. We can unlock the gift of high sensitivity.

Take the Lead.

"If you're a highly sensitive person, trust your intuition about people. Your brain is on your side, and it's rooting for you." Solo

Maybe, like me, you never really trusted your intuition. Maybe, like me, you were overwatered, and set by the window on a breezy day. The highly sensitive person suffocated trying to live life the way the other 80% of people live. There is only one way to find out what kind of people we are, and that involves a lot of leaning in, listening, and learning.

Lean in.

"Leaning back against Jesus, he asked him, "Lord, who is it?"
John 13:25 NIV

I love reading the prose of Jesus' best earthly friend, referring to himself as "the one Jesus loved." His account of Jesus' life reflects the deep love he had for His Savior.

Leaning back against Jesus.

What a picture. John was leaning in to an epic conversation about love. "The Greek noun, agape (love), and the verb *agapao* (love), occur 31 times in chapters 13-17." (NIV Study.) The beginning of the conversation in the upper room took place at the Last Supper. The following two chapters record the journey to Gethsemane, where Jesus prayed to the point of blood-stained tears as He faced the cross for His friends. It was all about love, and John leaned in.

Lean into Love:

"A new command I give you: Love one another. As I have loved you, so you must love one another." John 13:34 NIV

"By this everyone will know that you are my disciples, if you love one another." John 13:35 NIV

"[Jesus Promises the Holy Spirit] 'If you love me, keep my commands." John 14:15 NIV

"Whoever has my commands and keeps them is the one who loves me. The one who loves me will be loved by my Father, and I too will love them and show myself to them." John 14:21 NIV

"Jesus replied, 'Anyone who loves me will obey my teaching. My Father will love them, and we will come to them and make our home with them." John 14:23 NIV

"Anyone who does not love me will not obey my teaching. These words you hear are not my own; they belong to the Father who sent me." John 14:24 NIV

"'You heard me say, 'I am going away and I am coming back to you.' If you love me, you would be glad that I am going to the Father, for the Father is greater than I." John 14:28 NIV

"but he comes so that the world may learn that I love the Father and do exactly what my Father has commanded me. 'Come now; let us leave.'" John 14:31 NIV

"'As the Father has loved me, so I have loved you. Now remain in my love." John 15:9 NIV

"If you keep my commands, you will remain in my love, just as I have kept my Father's commands and remain in his love." John 15:10 NIV

"My command is this: Love each other as I have loved you." John 15:12 NIV

John's *lean* at first glance simply means to lie back or lie down, but the Greek word for lean comes from two root words. The first, meaning *into the midst, in the midst, amidst, among, or between.* The second root means *to descend from a higher place to a lower.* (Thayer)

It was much more than a lean. Jesus was about to defeat death. John chose to get quiet, and lean on Jesus in the midst of one of the greatest moments in human history. He leaned on God. Literally!!! *Do we realize how close Christ is?*

The word *lean* doesn't show up in the book of Jeremiah in any of the English translations, but it does show up in the Voice, paraphrase. "King Zedekiah (leaning in so no one could hear this secret oath): Jeremiah, as surely as the Eternal lives and gives us life, I promise not to kill you or hand you over to those who want you dead." Jeremiah 38:6 VOICE

The NASB translates *leaning in* to *secret*, meaning *a covering shelter, hiding place, protection.* (Brown) The King swore by the Lord, but in ancient times the custom was to take solemn oaths in the name of the reigning monarch or of the speaker's deities. (NIV Study) The King had leaned in just enough to be used by God in Jeremiah's life. Did Jeremiah's life cause the King to lean in? Regardless of how, the King's heart was stirred.

When we lean in to a stirring, others lean with us. We can become an available friend to everyone, when we accept friendship from The One.

"I have called you friends, for everything that I learned from my Father I have made known to you." John 15:15 b NIV

The deep and hidden things. The secret things.

Lean in.

Listen.

The word *listen* comes up in the NIV translation of the Book of Jeremiah 57 times.

"But they did not listen or pay attention; instead, they followed the stubborn inclinations of their evil hearts. They went backward and not forward." Jeremiah 7:24 NIV

Listening means *to pay attention.* We purpose to hear when we listen. One definition says, "to wait attentively for a sound." Listen, in Jeremiah 7:24, is better translated as *to incline our ears. To stretch out, extend, spread out, pitch, turn, bend, bow* ...(Brown) Stretching our ears to listen often means to stretch out and get quiet enough to hear. It's difficult to listen if we can't clearly hear.

"We are from God, and whoever knows God listens to us; but whoever is not from God does not listen us. This is how we recognize the Spirit of truth and the spirit of falsehood." 1 John 4:6 NIV

"The Holy Spirit testifies that Jesus is the Son of God in two ways: (NIV Study)
1. The Spirit descended on Jesus at his baptism. *(NIV STUDY)*

> *"Then John gave this testimony: 'I saw the Spirit come down from heaven as a dove and remain on him. And I myself did not know him, but the one who sent me to baptize with water told me, 'The man on whom you see the Spirit come down and remain is the one who will baptize with the Holy Spirit.' I have seen and I testify that this is God's Chosen One.'" Jn 1:32-34 NIV*

2. He continues to confirm in the hearts of believers the apostolic testimony that Jesus' baptism and death verify that he is the Messiah, the Son of God. *(NIV STUDY)*

> *"As for you, the anointing you received from him remains in you, and you do not need anyone to teach you. But as his anointing teaches you about all things and as that anointing is real, not counterfeit- just as it has taught you, remain in him." 1 John 2:27 NIV*

> *"Therefore I want you to know that no one who is speaking by the Spirit of God says, 'Jesus be cursed,' and no one can say, 'Jesus is Lord,' except by the Holy Spirit." 1 Corinthians 12:3 NIV*

> *"The Spirit himself testifies with our spirit that we are God's children." Romans 8:16 NIV*

This is how God's sovereignty works, and why we sing "He reigns." In the Old Testament, God stirred the hearts of His people and those whom He used as instruments in fulfilling His will. In the New Testament, the Holy Spirit descended upon those who believed and accepted Christ's sacrifice. The Holy Spirit is our inner compass. The small, still voice in the back of our subconscious minds, active even when we are asleep. Constantly stirring and steering, He keeps us Christ-centered.

<u>Never Alone.</u>

Life is full of noise. As a highly sensitive person, I can attest to the other 80% others don't notice. It's *NOISY*. But the power of the Holy Spirit cuts through *ALL OF THE NOISE*. We can choose, in those stirring moments, to steer where He has directed us to stare. Or, we can choose not to trust our Christ-centered intuition. Much like being genetically highly sensitive, is the automatic stirring of the Spirit. In Christ, we are permanently shaken from our previous life. Re-centered and set on a new course, with a new Captain. Driven not by selfish ambition, but by Kingdom purposes. From the moment we believe and accept Christ, we are sealed. The Spirit resides *IN US*. He never leaves us alone.

We are never alone.

The very Spirit of the One True God stirs us and stays with us, by no effort of our own. Through the power of His sovereign hand, we see life through a Jesus filter. It makes all the difference. Our lives, priorities, and hearts shift.

"The Spirt of truth. The world cannot accept him, because it neither sees him or knows him. But you know him, for he lives with you and will be in you." John 14:17 NIV

The stirrings of the Holy Spirit arrive upon the birth of our salavation. Many wait on the guarantee they aren't being fooled by a nice story of a regular guy who happened to be super motivational, wise and inspiring. John didn't lean in to listen to just another man. Those surrounding were so effected by His presence they gave up everything to lean in and listen. The Bible, as a book, didn't exist for them. Not the New Testament. And certainly not as we tote it around on our phones and let it collect dust on our bookshelves. All three persons of the trinity are linked with truth. (NIV Study)

Our Savior comes alive when we open the Bible. The Holy Spirit we receive when we believe activates the content of those pages, bringing it alive and applying it to our daily life as if we are holding

His hand. The one with all the creases and cracks where the different parts of His fingers are. The hand where the beam of light shines through the hole where it was pierced, nevertheless losing no strength to grip ours.

This is listening. Throwing out the ways of the world, the chatter, and *ALL OF THE NOISE.* It's getting quiet, and allowing our hearts to hear what He stirs and speaks. The world takes no notice of the Spirit of God. (NIV Study) We seek to understand, scientifically and practically, but sometimes fail to apply the most important and miraculous notes of wisdom to all that has been revealed to us.

<u>Learn.</u>

"This is the one who came by water and blood- Jesus Christ. He did not come by water only, but by water and blood. And it is the Spirit who testifies, because the Spirit is truth." 1 John 5:6 NIV

Just a story. There were people with whom He walked among who still refused to see, accept and believe. This is our choice as humans. If Jesus knocked on our front door and sat down for coffee with us, would we still be skeptical? Would we show Him the door, say "what a nice story," and remain unchanged?

The change is *EVERYTHING.*

<u>Water It.</u>

Jesus had a sensitivity heart. Jesus got quiet. He prayed to the Father. Before He walked to the cross, His tears were stained with blood. Fully human, and fully God, He is sovereignly sensitive. We are all sensitive, some of us highly sensitive, but none of us can claim a fraction of the sensitivity of Jesus …of our great God.

God loves us perfectly. He is patient to allow us to learn to love Him in return.When we lean in, listen, and learn …we are changed day by day until we arrive home in heaven. It's a perfect process put in place by our merciful God.

Processes only work when we follow each consecutive step. Through Him, we love. By His strength, we make progress. Christ-centered lives are stories of survival. When we lean in, listen, and learn who God is, we walk confidently towards heaven, trusting He makes good of all things on the way. We breath easier when hope is our currency.

"Every individual act is determined by either the spirit of truth or the spirit of error." (NIV Cultural) It's easy to fall under the illusion we can have a piece of both worlds and live a content life. The war between worlds is *REAL*. Jesus defeated the devil on the cross, and he stomps his feet like a two-year old having a tantrum. But His stomping is deadly; he is out to kill and destroy. Everyday, we have choices to make, decisions to ponder, and voices to entertain.

Lean, listen, and learn from *the Voice*. Only then can we be sure we are operating from the spirit of truth. The devil is deceptive, quoting Scripture verbatim and framing our pain with a solution at hand. The only way we are able to decipher between the two is to live life leaning into our Savior. Through Him, the Holy Spirit allows us to listen and learn.

"Do not learn the ways of the nations or be terrified by the signs in the heavens, though the nations are terrified by them." Jeremiah 10:2 NIV

We are not to learn, teach or exercise in the ways of the world. (Brown) Living life as a highly sensitive person, I physically and mentally suffer from a lack of quiet. Spiritually, we all suffer from a lack of leaning in. For me, faith in Christ is my life. John 1:4 says, ***"In him was life, and that life was the light of all mankind."*** (NIV) *Life,* or *zoe,* meaning, *every living soul.* (Thayer)

"An absolute fullness of life, both essential and ethical, which belongs to God, and through him both the hypostatic 'logos' and to Christ in whom the 'logos' put on human nature. Life real and genuine, a life active and vigorous, devoted to God, blesses, in the portion even in this world of those who put their trust in Christ, but after the resurrection to be consummated by new accessions (among them a more perfect body), and to last for ever." (Thayer)

There is more to life.
In Life, there is more.

The root word of Zoe is Zao. "To live, breathe, be among the living. To enjoy real life. To live acting in morality and character. LIVING WATER (emphasis mine). To be fresh, strong, efficient, active, powerful." (Thayer)

LIVING WATER. Having vital power in itself and exerting the same upon the soul. (Thayer)

"Just as Moses lifted up the snake in the wilderness, so the Son of Man must be lifted up, ***that everyone who believes may have eternal life in him. <u>For God so loved</u>*** the world that he gave his one and only So that ***whoever believes in him shall not perish but have eternal life." John 3:14-16 NIV (emphasis mine.)***

<u>Surface as a verb.</u>

Surface as a verb means *to bring to the surface; cause to appear openly.* Surface is a break-through. Surface can be life changing, life-saving, and life-giving.

"Everyone who drinks this water will be thirsty again, but whoever drinks the water I give them will never thirst. Indeed, the water I give them will become in them a spring of water welling up to eternal life." John 4:13-15 NIV

Surface. Breakthrough. Breathe. Hope.

Father,

Praise You for the Surface. For Jesus, who pulls us through the surface and reconnects us to Your presence. For the Holy Spirit, and the way You stir us and lead us. We are never alone, even if we are a small percentage of the population. Whether a highly sensitive person, a Christian, or another percentage of another minority, we are all loved equally by You. We are all valued the same by our Creator. Father, the revelations of this life are never-ending. You go before us, planning for restoration and revelation. You made a way for us to feel Your hand in and on our lives, through the sacrifice of Your One and only Son on the cross.

When we look at the cross, let us not forget the Living Water that defeated death, and all of our drownings. You are bigger than all of our struggles, sufferings, and losses. Your love is in tune with the aches of our hearts. The deepest wounds. The hidden things. The secret places. You are aware of us. Father, you are close to the broken hearted.

We come to You in awe of high sensitivity, and pray for understanding and compassion towards those who are overwhelmed and overstimulated by life. Allow us to honor the gift of high sensitivity, whether we possess the genetics of it or our lives brush up against those who do. God, You place people in our lives purposefully, help us to love them well. Bless the world with compassion and empathy. Bless us to understand Love, and to be open to receive it's flow in our lives. Only then, can we truly love the people in our lives well. Only then, can we know who You say we are.

Jesus, Your hand, with the cracks and crevices where Your fingers are separated into different parts. Your hand, with light shining through the hole that pierced it on the cross. Your hand, that is so magnificently strong, we cannot break from Your grip. There is no pain we cannot endure on this side of heaven with Your hand in ours. Thank You for caring for us so deeply, personally, and completely. We love You more than anyone and anything on this earth. We will never let go. You pulled us to the surface.

Jesus, in Your Name, which is *EVERYTHING*, I pray,

Amen.

CONCLUSION

SURFACE
UNLOCKING THE GIFT OF HIGH SENSITIVITY

SERENITY

Experience All-Surpassing Joy.

"But thanks be to God, who always leads us in triumph in Christ, and manifests through us the sweet aroma of the knowledge of Him in every place." 2 Corinthians 2:14 NASB

We walked, side by side, me talking and her listening. The salt stung the cuts on my feet from their run-ins with sharp shells. I was acutely aware of the possibility of man-o-war lurking by the place the tide set down fresh shells, and on the look out for the bluish, purplish color. She loved to walk to the beach. She'd walk for miles, a couple of times a day. By the time we got down to Florida on our Spring break, she looked a different nationality all together.

The sound of the shore I had preserved in sea shells a full calendar year back in Ohio came to life with a renewed roar as the closest parts of the surf rolled over our toes …hers tanned …mine often burnt. The point came into view after we walked for a while, and I'd climb atop the choppy rock feeling like I conquered a piece of the ocean. And as we walked back, the high-rise condos would slowly become massive again.

I loved the quiet conversations on the shoreline with my Grams. I loved her laugh, and can still hear it ring fresh in my ears when I see her picture. I loved her smile, so HUGE and full of joy. I loved how she called me *Meggie,* and sang almost always. I loved how we prayed and talked about God. We talked about easy things *AND* hard things.

Her place in my life was important. She took the time to listen to me. She made time to spend with me. She invited me into her life, and taught me so much about it by the way she lived hers. I love silent leaders in life. I love my Grams.

For Grams, who'd survived and seen so much in her life, walking the beach must have felt like restoration. Why else do we do what we do? She was a big walker, even at home. And I loved every opportunity to join her. She'd listen to me talk for hours. But the walks we shared by the Florida coastline were my favorite.

Discovering high sensitivity allowed me to reach back and reframe my memories. Through this journey together, you have witnessed many of my near drownings. I've learned God is not only the God who goes before me and prepares the way, but the God of my memories. He goes before me, even in my memory, to prepare the way for me. Miraculous. The human mind is a wondrous miracle.

I lovingly call my husband the human trip-ticket. Every minute of our family vacations are planned, and relaxing on the beach to him is sitting down for twenty minutes. Sitting on the beach, on our first vacation together over a decade ago, I instinctively pulled out my book to read. My husband loomed over me, his shadow in the way of the sun and his presence in the way of my decompression. It was immediately clear we had two different definitions of the word *vacation*.

Before I knew I was a highly sensitive person, I started leaving a week early to visit with family and the silence of the beach and my book. I was protecting myself and putting up a healthy boundary before I even knew what I now know. Highly sensitive people are generally easy going and want to please others because they are highly empathetic, so we will in a way self-sacrifice our comfort for the good of the majority around us.

The walks by the Florida coastline and the trips to the cove in the summer gave me clues to the mystery that unraveled as I wrote this book and embarked on the journey of embracing high sensitivity.

"This is what the Lord says: 'When seventy years are completed for Babylon, I will come to you and fulfill my good promise to bring you back to this place. For I know the plans I have for you,' declares the Lord, 'plans to prosper you and not to harm you, plans to give you a hope and a future.'"

Seventy years after the exile of God's people, He stirred in the heart of the King of Persia to decree them home, and the journey began. (Ezra 1) It took decades for them to travel back to their homeland and rebuild what had been broken, but God fulfilled His promise, and provided for them every step of the way.

The One True God. He knows who's highly sensitive, and who's not. He's woven us together in a perfect tapestry, providing all we need and preparing the way. Every human being is unique. We are all sensitive, to some extent, and we can develop those qualities to understand and have compassion towards each other. Though only 20% of the population are highly sensitive, that is still a *LARGE* number of people. We know them. They are our neighbors, friends, family and children. We are all created with something that makes us unique. All of us are important, purposed, and loved.

Unlock the gift of high sensitivity. In your life. In another's life. In your piece of the planet. Share this book. Share the resources in the index. Knowledge is powerful, and our God will reveal the deep and hidden things in His perfect timing. But we have to lean in, listen, and learn.

"This is God's Message, the God who made the earth, made it livable and lasting, known everywhere as God: 'Call to me and I will answer you. I'll tell you marvelous and wondrous things that you could never figure out on your own.'"
Jeremiah 33:3 MSG

The Book of Consolation in Jeremiah was a promise of restoration for God's people. When God stirred the hearts of his people, seventy years later, to return to their inheritance and rebuild all that had been destroyed, I believe He called them by name. To them, a stirring, and edict from the current King (also stirred by God) to return home. A fulfilled promise they had clung to for seven decades, parting with some of their beloved before coming home. In the second book of Ezra, and in Nehemiah, is a list of people. People called home by God …who answered, "Yes."

"I will surely gather them from all the lands where I banish them in my furious anger and great wrath; I will bring them back to this place and let them life in safety. They will be my people, and I will be their God." Jeremiah 32:36-38 NIV

Someone, whether they or an ancestor, had leaned in, listened, and learned from God's words spoken to the prophet Jeremiah. So much so, their hearts had been able to hold on to God's promise through devastation, loss of all they knew and possibly everyone they loved. The promise of restoration became a reality to them as thy traveled the road back home. Every single person on the road home was counted. It's possible that a very important piece of God's promise traveled that road back home, and was included on that list. Jesus' ancestor's. The line of David. (NIV Study)

The remnant God promised would return had leaned in, listened, and learned …so they remembered. They remembered who God was, who He said they were, and His promise to them.

"They will be my people, and I will be their God." Jeremiah 32:38 NIV

My people.

Family.

Father.

They had a long road home to travel. But ever notice how the trip home after we've been away seems shorter? Even if we're ready for a vacation, and enjoy our time away, after a while we are ready to come back home. Imagine the angst of God's people in exile. They were ready to come home. God so faithfully made a way, and provided all they needed to rebuild what had been lost.

But the biggest change for those coming home, the most important change, was that of their hearts. Leaning in, listening, and learning is one thing …but the moments God executes His faithfulness in our lives are miracles. They were imperfect. We are imperfect. Yet, regardless, our names are written on God's heart, and Jesus took all of them to the cross. There is so much power in the name of Jesus. He's *our* way back Home to God.

"Rejoice that your names are written in heaven." Luke 10:20 NIV

"Yet to all who did receive him, to those who believed in his name, he gave the right to become children of God-" John 1:12 NIV

"For he chose us in him before the creation of the world to be holy and blameless in his sight. In love he predestined us for adoption to sonship through Jesus Christ, in accordance with his pleasure and will-" Ephesians 1:5 NIV

"In him we have redemption through his blood, the forgiveness of sins, in accordance with the riches God's grace." Ephesians 1:7 NIV

"Now it is God who makes both us and you stand firm in Christ. He anointed us, set his seal of ownership on us, and put his Spirit in our hearts as a deposit, guaranteeing what is to come." 2 Corinthians 1:21-22 NIV
"Come, let us bow down in worship, let us kneel before the Lord our Maker; for he is our God and we are the people of his pasture, the flock under his care.

Today, if only you would hear his voice,"

Psalm 95: 6-8 NIV

God's people sang as they left their life of slavery in Egypt behind. Now, they were singing on their way back home. How do we know? There are singers listed, labeled and counted along with those returning home. (Ezra 2) Not just regular men and woman secular singers, but also the temple singers, who in ancient customs were only men. (NIV Study) They were prepared to praise God. Singers are always singing. It's who they are. They can't NOT sing.

They had leaned in, listened, learned, remembered, and now had a reason to sing on the way home to restoration.

We have reason to sing on the way home to restoration. Lean in, listen, learn …and remember. It gives us a reason to sing. To praise the God of our memories and the God of our futures. The One True God.

High sensitivity is a life altering discovery that requires change. It gets complicated. We're misunderstood. We have to have faith in who we are, and value our lives enough to take care of them. Why should we do this? Because just like all of God's children, our names are written on His heart. We don't even tattoo our skin without great thought. Jesus took our names to the cross, and He's calling us home, hoping we will lean in, listen, learn, and remember.

Earthly life is just he prequel to the glory He has in store for those who say "Yes" and begin the journey home to Him. The ones who trust Him to provide along the way. The One who will be there through all the broken heartache this world. But also, the God who will shift our perspective to see *ALL OF THE GOOD THINGS*, too.

God goes before me. He gives me songs. He is my song. My hope. My serenity.

"But thanks be to God, who always leads us as captives in Christ's triumphal procession and uses us to spread the aroma of the knowledge of him everywhere." 2 Corinthians 2:14 NIV

When the Israelites returned to Jerusalem, they rebuilt the temple's altar before laying the foundation of the temple. They sacrificed to God for forgiveness, and to reconnect and restore their relationships with Him. Then, they laid the foundation of the temple. Their reaction is recorded in Ezra 3:8:

"No one could distinguish the sound of the shouts of joy from the sound of weeping, because the people made so much noise. And the sound was heard far away." Ezra 3:13 NIV

Home. There are still modern day refugees. People ripped from their homes and everyday lives. Unfairly and unjustly displaced. Human tragedy and suffering covers the face of the earth. Christ commands us to provide for and love them in the name of Jesus. Some of us are refugees in our own skin, towns and homes. His evidence is made manifest through our love for each other.

The Message paraphrase says *"All of the people boomed out in hurrahs, praising God as the foundation of The Temple of God was laid. As many were noisily shouting with joy, many of the older priests, Levites, and family heads who had seen the first Temple, when they saw the foundations of this Temple laid, wept loudly for joy. People couldn't distinguish the shouting from the weeping. The sound of their voices reverberated for miles around." Ezra 3:11-13 MSG*

Eugene Peterson, in his paraphrased translation of the Bible, chooses the word *reverberated*. Peterson wrote a translation of the Bible so He could meet the members of His church where they were at in the language they spoke. *Reverberated* means to reecho or resound, rebound or recoil. True to the alive and active word of God, their joy is still echoing throughout the world.

The sound of restoration was JOY. But it was two-folded joy. The younger generations celebrated the start. The older generations stood in front of what once was, and mourned the loss. We are placed purposefully, and have a great opportunity to learn from generational perspectives. Joy sustains them all.

The image of the former magnificence of the Temple inspired the passing down of God's promise for two generations after the Israelites were chased from Jerusalem. That same picture probably traveled through their minds as they made their way back home. Finally home, yet staring at the flattened state of it, brought them full circle and to their knees in joyful mourning. It's as if they were able to look back to what was, see the full scope of destruction, and finally accept and mourn what had happened. Yet their sorrowful joy did not drown out the celebratory joy of the younger generation, so eager to rebuild and be a part of God's promised restoration.

In Christ, joy can absorb sorrow and celebration simultaneously, allowing us a perspective to appreciate both and maintain peace throughout both ends of the spectrum. This is how God meets us in our drownings. In both sorrow and celebration. I've witnessed enough miracles in my memories to trust Him moving forward, and to maintain peace and joy whether I am sobbing hysterically in pain or shouting a celebration of victory. *JOY* doesn't waver. It's a constant thread woven through the tapestry of God's hand in our lives. He goes before us, is with us, and His hand is all over our past.

This side of heaven, joy is Joy. It's sustaining …through hard and happy times. It's belting out our anthems, and not just the songs we sing with our praise hands up in church. Proclaim victory over the hard things. Find Your Father in heaven. And Surface with your Savior.

Abba Father,

God Almighty. Elohim. My Peace, Hope, and Love. Life.

How can I properly string together words fitting to describe Your personal care for me? For all of us. Your love knows no bounds.

Jesus, my Savior. Living Water. Breath of Life. Prince of Peace. Best Friend. My life is forever in Your hand, safe and secure, though the trials and sufferings will continue to come.

Perseverance gives us perspective. We are able to anticipate Your saving grace in all situations, and so continue to face life daily equipped. We are strong, because You are our strength.

Keep us facing towards Home, and help us hold on to the Tow-Line when we are too weak and worn-down to see it floating aside us in the water. Our Ballast …balance us. Tie healthy knots of knowledge for us to climb on. Set our feet on the Shore-line.

I see You always and everywhere, through the filter of a Christ-centered life. Thank You.

Bless the lives of every reader of these pages, every person, highly sensitive or not. Empower the HSPs and HSEs in life to love themselves as You do, and touch lives with their gifts in Your honor.

Through the power of the Holy Spirit, may we love the people in our lives well.

We are leaning in, listening, and ready to learn.

In Jesus' Name,

Amen.

Notes

1.) Aron, Elaine N. Ph.D. "New Research on Sensory Processing Sensitivity (SPS); New research helps us better understand and support Highly Sensitive People." *Psychology Today, 07 Jun. 2018,* psychologytoday.com/us/blog/the-highly-sensitive-person/201806/new-research-sensory-processing-sensitivity-sps. Accessed 6 Feb. 2019.

2.) Aron, Elaine N. Ph.D. "Understanding the Highly Sensitive Person; Extraverted HSPs face unique challenges." *Psychology Today, 21 Jul. 2011,* psychologytoday.com/us/blog/the-highly-sensitive-person/201107/understanding-the-highly-sensitive-person. Accessed 6 Feb. 2019.

3.) Solo, Andre. "Do These Genes Help Make You a Highly Sensitive Person? Although rare, your high sensitivity may be an evolutionary advantage." *Psychology Today, Highly Sensitive Refuge*, 20 Dec. 2018, psychologytoday.com/us/blog/highly-sensitive-refuge/201812/do-these-genes-help-make-you-highly-sensitive-person. Accessed 6 Feb. 2019.

4.) Ni, Preston M.S.B.A. "24 Signs of a Highly Sensitive Person; Highly sensitive people often 'feel too much' and 'feel too deep.'" *Psychology Today, Communication Success*, 5 Nov. 2017, psychologytoday.com/us/blog/communication-success/201711/24-signs-highly-sensitive-person. Accessed 6 Feb. 2019.

5.) Azab, Marwa Ph.D. "Are You a Highly Sensitive Person? Should You Change?; A sensitive person's brain is different: Research points to some advantages." *Psychology Today, Neuroscience in Everyday Life,* 27 Jul. 2017, psychologytoday.com/us/blog/neuroscience-in-everyday-life/201707/are-you-highly-sensitive-person-should-you-change. Accessed 6 Feb. 2019.

6.) Azab, Marwa Ph.D. "What Not to Say to a Highly Sensitive Person and Why; Genes and/or certain childhoods give rise to high sensitivity." *Psychology Today, Neuroscience in Everyday Life*, 14 May 2018. psychologytoday.com/us/blog/neuroscience-in-everyday-life/201805/what-not-say-highly-sensitive-person-and-why. Accessed 6 Feb. 2019.

7.) Ward, Deborah. "The Highly Sensitive Person and the Narcissist; Protect yourself from narcissists using your own natural abilities." *Psychology Today, Sense and Sensitivity*, 16 Jan. 2012. psychologytoday.com/us/blog/sense-and-sensitivity/201201/the-highly-sensitive-person-and-the-narcissist. Accessed 6 Feb. 2019.

8.) Aron, Elaine Ph.D. "Time Magazine: 'The Power of (Shyness)' and High Sensitivity; We are not always shy or introverted, but 'Quiet' describes HSPs." *Psychology Today, The Highly Sensitive Person,* 2 Feb. 2012. psychologytoday.com/us/blog/attending-the-undervalued-self/201202/time-magazine-the-power-shyness-and-high-sensitivity. Accessed 6 Feb. 2019.

9.) Solo, Andre. "This Is Your Brain on High Sensitivity; These 4 profound brain differences make you a highly sensitive person." *Psychology Today, Highly Sensitive Refuge,* 23 Jan. 2019. psychologytoday.com/us/blog/highly-sensitive-refuge/201901/is-your-brain-high-sensitivity. Accessed 6 Feb. 2019.

10.) Smith, Shawn T. Psy.D. "The Difference Between Highly Sensitive and Hypersensitive; High sensitivity is biological. Hypersensitivity is a coping style." *Psychology Today, Ironshrink,* 10 Nov. 2014. psychologytoday.com/us/blog/ironshrink/201411/the-difference-between-highly-sensitive-and-hypersensitive. Accessed 6 Feb. 2019.

11.) Ward, Deborah. "High Sensitivity, Low Self-Esteem; 3 steps to feeling good about yourself as an HSP." *Psychology Today, Sense and Sensitivity,* 13 Nov. 2011. psychologytoday.com/us/blog/sense-

and-sensitivity/201111/high-sensitivity-low-self-esteem. Accessed 6 Feb. 2019.

12.) Aron, Elaine N. Ph.D. "The Power of Inner Silence for the Highly Sensitive; Integrating inner silence into daily life can be a powerful tool for HSPs." *Psychology Today, The Highly Sensitive Person*, 18 Jul. 2018. https://www.psychologytoday.com/us/blog/the-highly-sensitive-person/201806/the-power-inner-silence-the-highly-sensitive. Accessed 6 Feb. 2019.

13.) Aron, Elaine N. Ph.D. "Remember the Soul?; Depth therapy found to be equally or more effective than cognitive behavioral." *Psychology Today, The Highly Sensitive Person*, 14 Apr. 2010. psychologytoday.com/us/blog/attending-the-undervalued-self/201004/remember-the-soul. Accessed 6 Feb. 2019.

14.) Aron, Elaine N. Ph.D. "Time and Transitions; Slowing down and making time for the many transitions of life." *Psychology Today, The Highly Sensitive Person*, 19 Sep. 2018. psychologytoday.com/us/blog/the-highly-sensitive-person/201809/time-and-transitions. Accessed 6 Feb. 2019.

15.) Aron, Elaine N. Ph.D. "Emotional Regulation and HSPs; Emotional regulations skills can help HSP's manage overwhelming feelings." *Psychology Today, The Highly Sensitive Person*, 05 Nov. 2018. psychologytoday.com/us/blog/the-highly-sensitive-person/201811/emotional-regulation-and-hsps. Accessed 6 Feb. 2019.

16.) Solo, Andre. "4 Ways to Begin to Recover from Childhood Emotional Neglect; Childhood emotional neglect may have an outsized effect on HSPs." *Psychology Today, Highly Sensitive Refuge,* 29 Nov. 2018. psychologytoday.com/us/blog/highly-sensitive-refuge/201811/4-ways-begin-recover-childhood-emotional-neglect. Accessed 6 Feb. 2019.

17.) Aron, Elaine N. Ph.D. "Introversion, Extroversion and the Highly Sensitive Person; What does it mean to be an extroverted highly sensitive person?" *Psychology Today, The Highly Sensitive Person*, 13 May 2018. psychologytoday.com/us/blog/the-highly-sensitive-person/201805/introversion-extroversion-and-the-highly-sensitive-person. Accessed 6 Feb. 2019.

18.) The Highly Sensitive Person. Aron, Elaine N. Ph.D "Are You Highly Sensitive?" hsperson.com/test/highly-sensitive-test. Accessed Feb 2019.

19.) Highly Sensitive Refuge. highlysensitiverefuge.com Accessed Feb 2019.

20.) Aron, Elaine N. Ph.D. The Highly Sensitive Person: How to Thrive When the World Overwhelms You. Harmony Books, 2016.

21.) Cloud, Henry Dr. & Townsend, John Dr. Boundaries. Zondervan, 2017.

22.) MedicineNet. https://www.medicinenet.com/drowning/article.htm Accessed Feb 2019.

23.) THE HOLY BIBLE, NEW INTERNATIONAL VERSION®, NIV® Copyright © 1973, 1978, 1984, 2011 by Biblica, Inc.® Used by permission. All rights reserved worldwide.

24.) Scripture taken from The Voice™. Copyright © 2008 by Ecclesia Bible Society. Used by permission. All rights reserved.

25.)"Scripture taken from *The Message*. Copyright © 1993, 1994, 1995, 1996, 2000, 2001, 2002. Used by permission of NavPress Publishing Group."

26.) Scripture quotations are taken from the *Holy Bible*, New Living Translation, copyright © 1996, 2004, 2015 by Tyndale House

Foundation. Used by permission of Tyndale House Publishers, Inc., Carol Stream, Illinois 60188. All rights reserved.

27.) NIV Study Bible Notes. NIV Study Bible. Zondervan, 2011.

28.) Old Testament Hebrew Lexicon- New American Standard. Brown, Driver, Briggs, Gesenius, Lexicon, "Theological Word Book of the Old Testament."

29.) NIV Cultural Backgrounds Study Bible. Zondervan. 2016

30.) Asbury Bible Commentary. https://www.biblegateway.com/resources/asbury-bible-commentary/Book-Consolation. Accessed Feb 2019.

31.) Dictionary of Bible Themes Scripture index copyright Martin H. Manser, 2009. Accessed Feb 2019.
32.) Mounce's Complete Expository Dictionary of Old and New Testament Words, Copyright © 2006 by William D. Mounce

33.) NIV Quest Study Bible Notes. NIV Quest Study Bible, Copyright © 1994, 2003, 2011 by Zondervan.

34.) Matthew Henry's Commentary.

35.) The Powers and Perils of Intuitions. "Distortion vs. Reality." Psychology Today. 9 Jun 2016. psychologytoday.com/us/articles/200211/distortion-vs-reality. Accessed Feb 2019.

36.) Mister Steve. " Turtles." Children's Bible Ministry of Connecticut, Inc. http://www.bibleline.org/turtles.html, Accessed Feb 2019.

37. Dictionary.com Unabridged. Based on the Random House Unabridged Dictionary. Random House, Inc, 2019. dictionary.com. Accessed Feb 2019.

38.) Reynaud, Helene. "Five Essential Knots Every Diver Should Know." *Scuba Diver Life.com 2014*. scubadiverlife.com/five-essential-knots-that-every-diver-should-know/. Accessed Feb 2019.

39.) Riggio Ph.D., Ronald E. "Are You an Extravert, Introvert, or Ambivert?" *Psychology Today*, Nov 2017. psychologytoday.com/us/blog/cutting-edge-leadership/201711/are-you-extravert-introvert-or-ambivert. Accessed Feb 2019.

40.) Wagele, Elizabeth. "Are You a Helper?" Psychology Today, Jan 2016. psychologytoday.com/us/blog/the-career-within-you/201601/are-you-helper. Accessed Feb 2019.

41.) Encyclopedia of the Bible.

42.) Moore, Beth. Portraits of Devotion. B&H Publishing Group, 2014.

43.) Scripture taken from the NEW AMERICAN STANDARD BIBLE®, Copyright © 1960,1962,1963,1968,1971,1972,1973,1975,1977,1995 by The Lockman Foundation. Used by permission.

44.) NIH, National Institute of Mental Health. Suicide Rates. nimh.nih.gov/health/statistics/suicide.shtml#part_154969. Accessed Feb 2019.

45.) O'Donnell, Jayne. "More Children are Dying by Suicide. Researchers are Asking Why." USA Today, Sep 2018. usatoday.com/story/news/nation/2018/09/10/rising-child-suicide-defy-answers-prevention-month/1197113002/. Accessed Feb 2019.

46.) Aron, Elaine Ph.D. "Suicide and High Sensitivity." The Highly Sensitive Person, Feb 2016. hsperson.com/suicide-and-high-sensitivity/. Accessed Feb 2019.

47.) Gujral, Namita. "6 Decisions a Highly Sensitive Person MUST Make." Lifehack. lifehack.org/533127/6-decisions-highly-sensitive-person-must-make-part-33 Accessed Feb 2019.

48.) Mitchell, Colter. "Genetic Differential Sensitivity to Social Environments: Implications for Research." PubMed. 2013. ncbi.nlm.nih.gov/m/pubmed/23927507/ Accessed Feb 2019.

About the Author

Meg is passionate about people, and the purposeful way we've been God-placed. Author of "Friends with Everyone," she writes about everyday life within the love of Christ on her blog, Sunny&80. *https://sunnyand80.org.*

When she left the business world to be a stay-at-home mom, Sunny&80 became a way to retain the funny life-lessons God revealed through motherhood. Over time that small step of obedience led to freelance writing, leading Bible study, and serving in youth ministry. She's written two children's books, "The Hot Pink Dinosaur," and "The Purple Sparkly Unicorn."

Born and raised in a suburb of Cleveland, OH, Meg now lives in a nearby lake town with her husband, two daughters, and their Golden-doodle. Her family plays an active role in serving their local church and the surrounding community. Her hobbies are running, photography, reading, and anything outside and adventurous. Check out her daily pics on Instagram @sunnyandeighy.

"This books feels like having coffee with a friend. No matter where your relationships are, read it! It will build a foundation for friendships that will stay with you for a long time."
-5 Star Amazon Customer Review

Friends with Everyone

Available at
amazon

Made in the USA
Monee, IL
12 January 2021